Karl Barth's Christology

Religion and Reason 21

Method and Theory in the
Study and Interpretation of Religion

MOUTON PUBLISHERS · BERLIN · NEW YORK · AMSTERDAM

Karl Barth's Christology

Its Basic Alexandrian Character

By
Charles T. Waldrop

MOUTON PUBLISHERS · BERLIN · NEW YORK · AMSTERDAM

Library of Congress Cataloging in Publication Data

Waldrop, Charles T., 1938-
  Karl Barth's christology.

  (Religion and reason ; 21)
  Bibliography: p.
  Includes indexes.
  1. Jesus Christ—History of doctrines—20th century.
  2. Alexandrian school, Christian.   3. Barth, Karl,
  1886-1968. I. Title. II. Series.
  BT198.W33 1984   232   84-20701
  ISBN 90-279-3109-7

For Lyneve and Andy

Preface

This book began as a study of Barth's christological
language. In the early stages of my research, I was influenced by the emphasis among philosophers upon linguistic analysis, and my goal was to clarify and evaluate the
principles which govern Barth's uses of the term "Jesus
Christ" and its variants, such as "Jesus," "Christ," "Son
of Man," and so forth. I was particularly intrigued by
the fact that Barth assigns to "Jesus Christ" predicates
which appear startling, confusing, and even contradictory.
Following the lead of analytic philosophers, I wanted to
determine whether Barth's christological propositions are
meaningful, and if they are, what factors provide the
foundation for their meaning.

It soon became evident to me, however, that the
principles which govern Barth's christological language
are theological principles, not simply linguistic or
philosophical principles. Consequently, I found it
necessary to turn to the history of Christian theology,
especially the crucial debates about Jesus Christ. As the
final product of my research indicates, I have concluded
that the dialogue between the theologians of Alexandria
and the theologians of Antioch during the early centuries
of Christian history, when the formative creeds were being
developed, sheds considerable light upon the obscurities
present in Barth's statements about Jesus Christ. When
one becomes aware that Barth follows Alexandrian theologians in his understanding of the identity of Jesus
Christ, the divinity of Jesus Christ, and the unity of the
person of Jesus Christ, Barth's uses of "Jesus Christ" and
its variants become understandable.

At one stage of my research, I believed that Barth
was an Antiochian theologian. I was influenced by com-

mentators such as John McIntyre, who understand Barth as
though he were a representative of the Antiochian theological tradition, and I discovered that much of Barth's
christology can appear to "make sense" when it is seen
from that perspective. It was my teacher and dissertation
adviser, Dr. Gordon D. Kaufman, Professor of Theology at
Harvard University, who first raised questions in my mind
regarding the validity of that interpretation. In a pri-
vate conversation, he told me that he doubted that Barth
understands the human nature of the Logos as an individual
person, even though that human nature is described in the
Church Dogmatics as having its own personality and will.
Since those who classify Barth as an Antiochian theologian
tend to conclude that Barth identifies the human nature
which the Logos assumed in the incarnation with the individual named "Jesus," I realized that if Dr. Kaufman's
doubts were justified, the view that Barth is an
Antiochian theologian is seriously threatened. That
realization was an important turning point in my research,
for it led me both to reevaluate the idea that Barth is an
Antiochian theologian and also to give careful consideration to the possibility that Barth might stand in the
Alexandrian theological tradition. Once I began to interpret Barth from an Alexandrian perspective, I discovered
how much more sound that view is.

The last stage of the development of the subject
matter of the book had to do, again, with philosophy. I
came full circle, so to speak, in that my study began and
ended with an emphasis upon philosophical concerns.
Dr. Jacques Waardenburg, General Editor of the Mouton
series "Religion and Reason," in addition to many other
thoughtful observations, suggested that I broaden the
scope of my study beyond christology by considering the
philosophical presuppositions of Barth's theology in
comparison with the philosophical foundations of Alexandrian theology. He concluded, correctly, I believe, that
adding a discussion of this question would enhance the
quality of the book and also make it more interesting to
philosophers as well as theologians. The results of my
research and reflection on this topic to date are found
primarily in the section "Barth's Theology and the Alexandrian Theological Tradition" in the fifth chapter.
Because this issue is important and complex, and because I

realize that my examination of it is not exhaustive, I hope that my observations will stimulate others to continue the investigation.

Many people and institutions have contributed to the completion of this work, and it would not be possible to acknowledge all of them. However, I want to express my gratitude to those whose influence has been most decisive.

First, I am grateful to the members of my family, especially my parents, my wife, and my son. My mother taught me by example that religion is an important dimension of human life; without her influence I doubt that I would have chosen the study of religion as my life's work. My wife, Lyneve, is also a college professor; we have helped each other balance the demands of Ph.D. programs, teaching careers, and domestic responsibilities. She read the entire manuscript and made many valuable suggestions regarding content and style. My young son, Andy, has heard about this book almost all of his life; his growing understanding of its importance to me, and his consequent willingness to allow me quiet time have led me to admire his young maturity.

Second, many of my teachers, fellow students, and colleagues have had a significant impact on me. Dr. Dan O. Via, Jr., now of the University of Virginia, was the professor of my first religion course in college, and it was under his direction that I first experienced the satisfactions of studying religion academically. Dr. J. William Angell, Wake Forest University, was my first professor of historical and systematic theology; and Dr. Leander E. Keck, now Dean of Yale Divinity School and at one time my professor at Vanderbilt University, restimulated my interest in theology when it was at a low ebb. Dr. Gordon D. Kaufman, in addition to his insight about Barth's concept of the human nature of the Logos, presented many constructive criticisms which have enhanced the quality of this work. Also, he, Dr. Richard R. Niebuhr, and Dr. Wolfhart Pannenberg launched my teaching career by inviting me to be "Teaching Follow" in courses they taught at Harvard Divinity School, and each of them gave me valuable guidance. Others who have helped me develop my theological skills are Herbert W. Richardson, University of Toronto; George Rupp, Dean of Harvard Divinity School; Melvin Goering, Executive Director of Associated Colleges of Central Kansas; Wayne Proudfoot, Columbia University; Gene Klaaren, Wesleyan University; Marcus Hester, Wake Forest University; Robert Shellenberger, Greeley, Colorado; Ronald Vinson and Thomas F. Duncan, Atlanta, Georgia; Claude Stewart, Southeastern Baptist Theological Seminary; Tom Davis, Skidmore College; and Gerald Largo, St. Francis College.

Third, in a category by himself is Dr. Allen Hackett, now a retired churchman, who was Area Minister of the Metropolitan Boston Association, United Church of Christ, and my "superior" when I was a student-pastor.   Dr. Hackett, an expert on French Protestantism and the author of several books, took time off from a busy schedule to read my manuscript and make comments. He provided helpful suggestions and enthusiastic encouragement. He and his wife Dorothy have become honorary members of my family.

Fourth, for financial support, I want to register my appreciation to Brother Donald Sullivan, O.S.F., President, and the members of the Board of Trustees, St. Francis College, Brooklyn, New York, for providing research funds for use by faculty members. I am also grateful that the members of the Faculty Research Committee, chaired by Professor Sidney Rutar, awarded me a portion of those resources to apply toward the production costs of this volume.

Fifth, for advice regarding technical matters related to publication, I am grateful not only to the staff at Mouton, especially Asta Wonneberger, but also to Kevin Von Gonton and Francis Slade. For typing, I want to thank Sarah Braveman, Lynne Roberts, Nancy Giammarella, Elisabeth Barlow and Joe Ann Olszowy. For proofreading, I am grateful to Gerald Galgan, Jeanne-Anne Lewis, Nithya Micheletti, and Geraldine Smith.

Finally, I want to thank Professor Jacques Waardenburg, not only for his valuable advice regarding subject matter and style, but also for selecting this work for publication in the "Religion and Reason" series. I am elated that my years of study have been rewarded with this good fortune. Any mistakes of detail or judgment that remain, in spite of the efforts of my many advisers, are, of course, my own.

Saratoga Springs, New York   Charles T. Waldrop

Note on Reference

Due to the contemporary production methods used in the publication of this volume, the note numbers have been placed in square brackets on the line of type. In most instances, the bracketed number has been positioned immediately after the passage to which it refers, in the spot where a book produced by traditional printing methods would ordinarily set a small superscript. However, because of the amount of space required, it has sometimes been necessary to place a bracketed number on the line following the passage to which it refers. The notes have been numbered consecutively in each chapter, and they have been assembled in one section following the text.

Contents

Chapter 1

Introduction

The principal purpose of this book is to demonstrate that Barth's christology is predominantly Alexandrian rather than Antiochian in character. In order to achieve this goal, we shall focus upon Barth's treatment of the doctrine of the divinity of Jesus Christ, his understanding of the unity of the person of Christ, and his use of the name "Jesus Christ" and its variants. In these three areas Barth pursues a line of thought which is consistently Alexandrian.

These three issues merit attention because they have been decisive in past debates between Alexandrian and Antiochian thinkers and also because they are important topics of discussion in the contemporary assessment of Barth's theology. Consequently, concentrating upon them will enable us to portray in an efficient manner the sharp contrast between Alexandrian and Antiochian modes of thought and, at the same time, accentuate the relevance of our findings for Barthian scholarship. In addition, these boundaries will allow us to delineate crucial elements in Barth's christology while freeing us from the necessity of explicating every detail.

In order to clarify what we mean when we say that Barth's christology is Alexandrian, it is necessary to characterize Alexandrian thought and show how it differs from Antiochian. While a more detailed account of these traditional ways of doing theology will be presented later,[1] our understanding of the basic distinctions between them can be offered here.

In our judgment, it is helpful to define Antiochian and Alexandrian christologies according to how they conceive the identity of Jesus Christ. For Antiochian thought, Jesus Christ is first of all an individual human being, a concrete person. Although he has a special relation to God and performs a unique role in God's plan for all men, he nevertheless does not become something other than a man. In Alexandrian theology, on the other hand, Jesus Christ is first of all the eternal Logos and Son of God, the second "person" of the trinity who condescends to the creaturely realm and unites human nature to himself. In Antiochian theology, Jesus Christ is the man who is "also" divine, while in Alexandrian thinking Jesus Christ is the divine person who is "also" human.

Given these diverse conceptions of who Jesus Christ is, the differences between these two theologies on the three issues before us can be readily discerned. First, in Alexandrian theology the divinity of Jesus Christ is an inherent quality of his being. As the second "person" of the trinity, Jesus Christ is divine prior to and apart from his existence as a man. In contrast, in Antiochian theology Jesus Christ is divine because of his unique relation to God. Because God is present in and through Jesus Christ in his redemptive act, and since Jesus Christ participates in this act, one may say that Jesus Christ is divine. However, in the strictest sense, this divinity does not belong to Jesus Christ but to the God who is present with him. Second, according to Alexandrian thought, the unity of the one person of Jesus Christ is a unity between the fully personal divine Logos and the less-than-personal human nature of Jesus. That is, in Alexandrian thought the human nature which is related to God in the incarnation is not a complete individual person in its own right, although its human nature is complete. In opposition, according to Antiochian thinking, the personal unity of Jesus Christ is a union between two personal subjects, the divine person God in his second mode of being and the human person Jesus. Third, for Alexandrian thought the name "Jesus Christ" and its variants denote the one divine person, while in Antiochian thinking the language is more complicated. Since there are two personal beings united in one reality, "Jesus" or "Jesus of Nazareth" can be used to denote the man Jesus, and "Logos" or "Son" can be used to denote the divine person. The one reality of the union can be designated by the phrase "the incarnate Logos."

Now that the predominant features of these two modes of

christological thinking are before us, the content of our
claim about the Alexandrian character of Barth's theology
can be stated more clearly. Our view is that Barth's
doctrine of the deity of Jesus Christ is Alexandrian
because Barth conceives of the deity of Christ as the act
which constitutes his being. This conception of the
identity of Christ's divine being with his act is developed by Barth in such a way that it gives theoretical
justification for two important affirmations. The first
is that Jesus Christ's deity is fully and completely his
own deity; it is his inherent, active nature. This deity
is not simply predicated of him although it does not
strictly belong to him. The second is that the act of
being of Jesus Christ is divine because it is completely
and fully identical with the act and being of God himself.
For Barth, there is no tension between the deity of Jesus
Christ and the deity of God. The act of God is the divine
being of God, and this act is Jesus Christ. Jesus Christ
is the deity of God.[2]

Barth's understanding of the unity of Christ follows
the Alexandrian pattern, although it incorporates significant Antiochian elements. The unity of Christ is presented as a unity of the eternal Logos with the human nature
of all men. The specific human nature of the Lord is not,
for Barth, a complete person in itself, although it is, in
some sense, personal. It possesses its own will, soul,
body, personality, and even its own self-consciousness,
and it is related to the Logos in obedience and fellowship; yet it is, in the final analysis, less than a
person. The person Jesus is the Logos, and this "is"
is direct and emphatic.

Finally, Barth's christological language follows from
and is consistent with his understanding of the deity of
Christ and the unity of his person. "Jesus Christ" and
its variants are used to denote the divine subject, the
eternal Logos. While Barth uses "Jesus" and "Jesus of
Nazareth" to connote the divine Logos in his being and
action as a man, these terms do not denote a human subject
who is distinct from the divine subject. As we shall
show, a recognition of the distinction between the denota-
tion and the connotation of "Jesus Christ" and its variants clears up a lot of ambiguity in Barth's language.

In the remainder of this introduction, we wish to show,

first, that a careful analysis of the issue of whether
Barth is Alexandrian or Antiochian in his christology will
make a needed contribution to contemporary Barthian
scholarship. Concomitantly, a discussion of this topic
will offer a valuable clarification of Barth's treatment
of the divinity of Christ, the unity of his person, and
the name "Jesus Christ." We shall illustrate the need for
the analysis we propose by showing how two commentators
interpret Barth differently in respect to these questions.
Secondly, we shall indicate the method and order to be
followed in our analysis.

NEED

It may be asked, Why focus upon the problem of whether
Barth's christology is Alexandrian or Antiochian? Does
this subject merit this much consideration? The answer to
this question has several parts.

   In the first place, the question of whether Jesus
Christ should be understood in Alexandrian or Antiochian
terms is important not only because it is inherently
interesting but also because of its systematic implications. The judgment that a theologian makes with respect
to it will have a significant impact upon the way he
develops other doctrines, such as justification and
revelation. As a result, determining whether Barth's
christology is Alexandrian or Antiochian will suggest a
great deal about his theology as a whole.

   The importance of this question is evidenced by the
extensive attention that it has received in the history of
Christian thought, particularly during the era of the
Council of Chalcedon in the fifth century. Proponents of
the various positions realized that they were at odds over
matters of serious theological consequence which influenced the Christian gospel at its roots. Even today this
issue has not been resolved or become outdated.

   Secondly, in spite of the importance of this question,
no thorough investigation has been devoted to Barth's
treatment of it. Studies of Barth's christological
thought have tended to concentrate upon other significant
issues, such as the importance of the historical Jesus,
the relation of christological method to historical

thinking, christology and anthropology, christology and analogy, christology and revelation in relation to natural theology, christology and justification, christology and atonement, and christology and pneumatology.[3] Some studies have dealt with problems which are directly related to the question of whether Barth's christology is Alexandrian or Antiochian, such as the unity of the person of Christ. However, they have spent much of their energy comparing the basic thrust of Barth's position with other viewpoints, rather than going into Barth's thought in depth.[4] As a result, a careful analysis of Barth's position on this question is needed.

Thirdly, although insufficient attention has been given to Barth's stance on this question, this does not mean that the whole subject has been ignored. In fact, the attention which has been devoted to it indicates the need for further study. This is the case because there is a striking disagreement among Barth scholars as to whether Barth's christology is Alexandrian or Antiochian. Many investigators consider Barth a forthright defender of the Alexandrian way of doing christology. For example, Herbert Hartwell, Walter Guenther, and Wolfhart Pannenberg hold this view.[5] On the other hand, the influential commentators Henri Bouillard and Regin Prenter believe that Barth stands firmly in the Antiochian tradition and that his position can be accurately described as Nestorian.[6] The existence of this disparity suggests that there are elements of both traditions in Barth's theology; yet the relationship between them remains unclear.

Since there is definitely a need for an airing of this problem, it is surprising that the investigators who have explicitly dealt with it have not developed their views in more detail. Yet, they have not engaged in any significant debate with their opponents, nor have they discussed systematically either the evidence which supports their judgment or the implications which follow from it. In general, they have been content to assert their conclusion as though it were self-evident, without carefully examining the alternative. As a result, the grounds for each interpretation of Barth need to be clarified and evaluated.

Fourthly, not only is there a need for an investigation of whether Barth is Alexandrian or Antiochian, there is also a need for a study of each one of the three sub-issues which we have mentioned, the deity of Jesus Christ, the unity of the person of Christ, and the use of the name "Jesus Christ" and its variants. Although these topics are inherently interesting and important, no thorough analysis of Barth's treatment of them is available. By examining these subjects within the context of the broader question of whether Barth is Alexandrian or Antiochian, we can show how they are related to each other and to the larger issue. Showing these relationships will make a valuable contribution to Barthian scholarship because the consistency of his treatment of these subjects is not always noted. For example, Hartwell thinks that Barth's treatment of the unity of the two natures is Alexandrian; yet he thinks that Barth's language about Jesus Christ is in tension with this view.[7] We shall attempt to demonstrate that Barth's language is also Alexandrian.

As we conclude this discussion of the ways in which this study will contribute to Barthian scholarship, perhaps we should mention the rather apparent point that our findings will also shed light on studies of Barth's thought which do not directly deal with the question of whether Barth is Alexandrian or Antiochian. Once the characteristics of Antiochian and Alexandrian interpretations of Barth are made clear, it will be possible to recognize them when they appear in studies of Barth, whether or not they are labeled as such.

In the preceding pages we have made three principal points. The first is that we shall argue that Barth's christology is Alexandrian. The second is that in order to substantiate our position we shall analyze Barth's doctrine of the deity of Jesus Christ, his concept of the unity of the person of Christ, and his use of the name "Jesus Christ" and its variants. The third is that Barth's theology and the secondary scholarship about it reflect a need for this investigation. In the next section we shall clarify the second of these points and give a concrete illustration of the third by examining briefly the conflicting interpretations of Barth presented by two influential theologians, John McIntyre and Claude Welch.

McIntyre and Welch

John McIntyre interprets Barth as an Antiochian theologian, while Claude Welch sees him as standing in the
Alexandrian camp. By contrasting their views we can show
in a straightforward manner both some of the basic characteristics of these two ways of understanding Barth and
also some of the features of Barth's thinking which give
rise to these two interpretations. At the same time, the
close relationship between the deity of Christ, the unity
of the person of Christ, the use of the name "Jesus" and
its variants, and the question of whether Barth is Alexandrian or Antiochian will become apparent. In the commen-
taries of McIntyre and Welch, these issues arise directly
from the text, and a discussion of any one of them leads
inevitably to the others. This fact supports our proposal
to show Barth's Alexandrianism by concentrating on his
concept of the deity of Christ, the unity of the person of
Christ, and the use of the name "Jesus Christ."

Neither McIntyre nor Welch concentrates primarily upon
the question of whether Barth is Alexandrian or Antiochian. Welch does not mention this problem specifically,
while McIntyre argues that Barth veers closely to Nestorianism but avoids its error. Their opinions come into
explicit conflict not over Alexandrianism or Antiochianism
but in regard to Barth's concept of revelation and its
relation to the divinity of Christ. Both think that Barth
attempts to demonstrate that the event of revelation
entails the doctrine of the divinity of Jesus Christ.
McIntyre concludes that Barth fails in this derivation,
while Welch believes that Barth is successful.

The fact that Welch and McIntyre devote considerable
attention to the concept of revelation helps substantiate
our belief that whether Barth is Antiochian or Alexandrian
is not simply a minor question, with implications that are
restricted to christology in the narrow sense. On the
contrary, the findings of these interpreters indicate that
this question has direct significance for a proper understanding of Barth's treatment of revelation and also the
doctrine of the trinity. Nor should we conclude that the
relevance of this issue stops here.[8]

Although McIntyre and Welch do not self-consciously
confront one another over the issue of Barth's Antioch-

ianism or Alexandrianism, our hypothesis is that this is a primary difference between them. They understand the identity of Jesus Christ differently, and this leads to their opposite conclusions regarding the divinity of Christ, the unity of Christ, and the meaning of "Jesus Christ." For McIntyre, Jesus Christ is the human person who is the <u>form</u> of revelation and who, as such, is distinct from <u>God.</u> Jesus Christ is the man through whom God reveals himself, not the God who reveals. For Welch, on the other hand, Jesus Christ is primarily the divine agent who <u>reveals</u> himself through the form. In Welch's view, Jesus Christ is not so much the medium as the revealer, although he is also the medium as well. When this principal contrast between McIntyre and Welch is grasped, then their other differences can be clearly perceived.

We shall look first at the interpretation of Barth presented by McIntyre. Since he raises serious objections to Barth's christology, we can bring the issues into focus more quickly by considering him first. After presenting the viewpoints of both McIntyre and Welch, we shall indicate specifically how they differ on the topics of the deity of Christ, the unity of the person of Christ, and the use of the name "Jesus Christ" and its variants.

McIntyre

McIntyre states that Barth's attempt to derive the concept of the divinity of Jesus Christ from the fact of revelation is doomed to failure because the medium or form of revelation must be something or someone other than God. God is not known directly, McIntyre argues. He reveals himself through forms which are creaturely and different from God himself. The fact that God reveals himself through the life of Jesus Christ does not lead us to conclude that Jesus Christ is divine. Jesus Christ is simply the instrument or medium of God's revelation, and therefore he must be different from God. If Jesus Christ is confessed as divine, says McIntyre, this confession must be based on some firmer foundation than simply the fact that he is the form through which God reveals himself.

According to McIntyre, revelation has a triadic structure. The three components of God's revelation are "God, the reality through which God reveals himself, and our- selves as recipients of revelation." By affirming the triadic structure of revelation, McIntyre denies that revelation is "a theophany, the naked appearance of God before us."[9] God always reveals himself through some form or medium which is known directly, but which is not God. This aspect of revelation, McIntyre explains, can be designated by the symbols Non-B reveals B to C.[10]

Any notion that the medium of revelation is identical with God himself is attacked by McIntyre as "quite close to impermissible nonsense."[11] Because the medium of revelation is known directly, there would be no revelation if the subject of revelation were identical with the medium. "For ex hypothesi the medium of revelation is known directly, and if the medium and the subject of revelation are identical and thus known directly, there is no occasion for revelation."[12]

The principle of the creaturely character of the medium of revelation is upheld in the understanding of revelation found in the New Testament, McIntyre believes. In the New Testament, the medium of revelation is "the ordinary human life of the man Jesus, as it would appear to the people of his day regardless of whether they believed in him or not, his life as it would be written down by a modern scientific historian."[13]

The creaturely character of the medium of revelation is also upheld by Barth, according to McIntyre. This fact is made clear in the later volumes of the Church Dogmatics, [14] particularly 4/2, where Barth claims that the medium of revelation is the human nature of Jesus Christ.[15] In this volume, McIntyre explains, Barth explicitly affirms that God reveals himself through the human nature, through the words and actions of the man Jesus of Nazareth. The human nature is described by Barth as the "organ" of God in his revealing action to man.[16]

Although McIntyre does not say so unequivocally, it is evident that he thinks that Barth makes no conceptual distinction between the human nature which is the medium of revelation and the man Jesus of Nazareth. For McIntyre, when Barth states that the divine nature reveals itself through the human nature, this is equivalent to saying that God reveals himself through the man Jesus of

Nazareth.[17]   "Human nature" and "the man Jesus of
Nazareth" appear to McIntyre to be interchangeable terms
in Barth's theology.   For McIntyre, both these terms
denote the man Jesus as he could and can be known through
ordinary, empirical means.

This assumption of McIntyre is a crucial element in his
criticism of Barth.   Because he thinks that Barth identifies Jesus Christ with the human nature, he can conclude
that the man Jesus is not divine.   Barth clearly states
that the human nature is not divinized by its participation in revelation.[18]

McIntyre's opinion that Barth identifies the human
nature with the man Jesus is evidenced not only by the
fact that he uses these terms synonymously but also by
his belief that Barth is in danger of Nestorianism.
Barth's speaking of the human nature of revelation as the
"organ" of God, McIntyre notes, is "curiously reminiscent
of the famous sentence attributed to Nestorius, 'Mary bore
a man who was the organ of the Godhead.'"   However,
McIntyre thinks that Barth's position should not be called
Nestorian because there are not in Barth's presentation
"two complete persons present in exactly the same way at
the same time."[19]   If there were, then Barth would be
Nestorian.

Barth avoids the charge of Nestorianism, McIntyre
believes, because his stance is "rather different and much
more subtle."   Although Jesus is a person who is present
to man in "the ordinary empirical and inspectible [sic]
way," the divine person or the "divine nature is 'there'
only as it reveals itself through the human nature."   God
and his divine nature are therefore present in the human
nature "revelationally."   The two natures and the two
persons are related to each other "in terms of this quite
peculiar and unique relation of revelation."[20]   They are
not present in the same manner at the same moment.[21]

McIntyre's argument against Barth is simple and direct.
"For example, it has been argued that if it is true that
Jesus Christ reveals God, then the deity of Christ is ipso
facto demonstrated.   But such a demonstration is not by
itself valid."[22]   On the contrary, as the medium of
revelation, Jesus must be a creaturely reality, distinct
from God.

For McIntyre, there is a clear distinction between the

person Jesus Christ, who is the medium of revelation, and the person God, who reveals through revelation. God may reveal himself through any medium, such as a sunset or, more traditionally, the words of a preacher, but such an act does not make the medium divine. If the person Jesus is divine, the foundation of this divinity is not the event of revelation.[23]

Welch

In our consideration of Welch's interpretation of Barth, we shall deal with two principal points. The first has to do with the derivation of the doctrine of the trinity from revelation, and the second concerns the unity and diversity of God. These elements are related directly to the question of who Jesus Christ is.

In support of Barth, Welch argues that an analysis of the event of revelation requires the concepts of the divinity of God the Son, Jesus Christ, the divinity of God the Father, and the divinity of God the Holy Spirit. The deity of Jesus is established not in isolation but along with the doctrine of the trinity. As an element of the doctrine of the trinity, it is an immediate and analytical implication of revelation.

The event of revelation confronts us with three questions. We must ask "not only who is the self-revealing God, but also how this happens and what is the result." The answer to each of these questions is the same. We must say that "it is God who reveals himself, that he reveals himself through himself, and that he reveals himself."[24] The doctrine of the trinity is the answer to the question of whether or not there is a revelation. If there is a revelation, the doctrine of the trinity informs us who reveals, how he reveals, and what he reveals.

The manner of revelation is related closely to God's being as Son. God reveals himself by freely choosing to distinguish himself from himself. He becomes himself a second time in a second mode of existence. In his first mode of existence he is hidden from men, unavailable to them. In his second mode as Son he is revealed to man. He assumes a form and is made visible to man in that form.

His lordship is his freedom to assume a form and to be God
for man as well as God in himself.[25]

In his second mode of being, God is the same God who
also remains in a first mode of being. He is both the one
who remains hidden in himself as Father and also the one
who becomes a man and exists in the creaturely world as
the Son, Jesus Christ. This means that Jesus Christ is
not merely the means or form of revelation. He is the one
who reveals himself. "Christ reveals the Father our Lord,
but in so doing is himself our Lord and reveals himself."
[26] The work of revealing and reconciling is appropri-
ated to the Son, not to the Father or the Holy Spirit.
But since revealing and reconciling can be accomplished
only by God, we must say that the subject of this activity, the Son Jesus Christ, is "identical with God in the
full sense of the word."[27]

Although God is three, his threeness is no threat to
his oneness. Barth states that God is three modes of
existence in one divine essence. It is the one essence
which possesses subjectivity and personality; there are
not three different agents in God. God's subjectivity is
understood in analogy with human subjectivity. He is one
actor who acts in his three modes of existence. The
modern notion of personality, which denotes a "self-
conscious individuality" or a "distinct center of consciousness" is applied to the one essence of God, not to
his three modes of being.[28] God is the one true person.

This brief discussion of Welch's endorsement of Barth
indicates that Welch thinks of Jesus Christ primarily as
the Son of God, the divine subject who reveals himself.
For Welch, "Jesus Christ" denotes not merely the human,
creaturely form of revelation, but the incarnate Lord, the
one who is both God and man. This Lord reveals through
his flesh, but his flesh is not a separate person. That
Welch thinks of Jesus Christ as the incarnate Lord and not
simply as the medium of revelation is clear from the
structure of his argument.

This structure can be described as follows. First, if
God is truly known in revelation, he must be present to
man. Second, if the one who is present to man is truly
God, he must be of the same essence as the God who is the
presupposition of revelation, the whence of revelation.
The one who is known on earth must be of the same essence

as the God who remains in heaven, veiled and hidden.
Third, if the God who is known and present to man is truly
God, then he must be God in a second mode of existence,
different from his mode of existence as the whence of
revelation. Fourth, this God who is known is God the Son.
Finally, God the Son is Jesus Christ. Thus, Jesus Christ
is one essence with the Father.

The question of the form or medium of revelation is
basically irrelevant to the validity of this argument.
Therefore, it is not important for Welch to emphasize that
the medium must be some reality other than God. The
argument states that the one who is present in revelation,
and presumably in some form, must be God, if in fact God
is revealed. This God who is present is Jesus Christ,
whatever be the character of his form and the relation of
his creatureliness to his divinity.[29]

Issues

This comparison of Welch and McIntyre provides
concrete documentation that the issues of the deity of
Jesus Christ, the unity of the person of Christ, the use
of the name "Jesus Christ," and whether Barth is Alexandrian or Antiochian are inherently related to each other.
Welch and McIntyre come to different conclusions about the
validity of Barth's derivation of the idea of Christ's
divinity from the fact of revelation, and in each case
their conclusions are consistent with their understanding
of Barth's position in regard to these other issues. We
shall indicate more specifically how they interpret Barth
differently on these issues, and these differences will
indicate the problems we shall consider in our investigation.

It is clear from what has been said above that McIntyre
thinks of Jesus Christ as the purely human person who is
separate and distinct from God. He can be known by
empirical investigation as any other historical person is
known. Because he is the human form of revelation, he
must be other than God. Conversely, Welch thinks of Jesus
Christ as the one who is fully identical with the Son of
God and who, therefore, is of one essence with the Father.
He is the same personal agent as the Father, although he

exists in a different mode of being, a revealed mode
instead of a hidden mode. Jesus Christ is the God who
reveals, not merely the medium through which God reveals.
It is because of this different understanding of the
identity of Jesus Christ that we label McIntyre's interpretation Antiochian and Welch's Alexandrian.

These contrasting opinions of the identity of Christ
are paralleled by different views of the referent of the
name "Jesus Christ" and its variants. For McIntyre,
"Jesus Christ" denotes the purely human person who is
different from God. For Welch, this name usually denotes
the incarnate Lord, God in his second mode of being. For
Welch, in so far as this name denotes a person, this
person is God himself, not a human person who is united
with God. However, Welch sometimes seems to speak as
though these names can also denote the human form of
revelation, and thus it is not clear whether these names
might be used to name two persons, a man and God.[30]
Whether or not Welch does use these names to denote two
persons, it is clear that it is possible to "read" Barth's
use of "Jesus Christ" and its variants in two distinct
ways.[31] This possibility raises the question of whether
Barth uses these names to denote the divine person or the
human person. Or, perhaps, does Barth sometimes use these
names to denote the human person and sometimes the divine
person?

Given these views regarding the identity of Jesus
Christ and the referent of the name "Jesus Christ," the
difference between McIntyre and Welch on Barth's notion of
the unity of the person of Christ is clear. McIntyre
interprets the relation between the two natures of Christ
as a relation between two persons, the person God and the
human person Jesus, who is the form of revelation. This
relation should not be understood as Nestorian he thinks,
because the two persons are not present in exactly the
same way at the same time. The person Jesus is present as
are other persons, but God is present "revelationally."
On the other hand, Welch's views, which are not spelled
out in detail and are, therefore, somewhat obscure, seem
to be that the unity of Christ is constituted by the
relation between God the Son and his human nature.
Although Welch does not explicitly deny that the human
nature is a complete human person, the structure of his

argument suggests that it is other than a person in itself. As the form of revelation, the human nature is not separate from Jesus Christ; it is an aspect of his being. Jesus Christ possesses a divine and a human nature, and as this one who is both divine and human he is both the revealer and the form of revelation. Jesus Christ is the God who is in himself a person and who, in becoming man, unites to his divine person and divine nature a human nature which is not an independent person.

If this understanding of Welch is correct, it seems that Barth's doctrine is susceptible to two different interpretations in regard to the unity of Christ. Our investigation will attempt to determine which one is the more accurate.

Finally, we come to the concept of the divinity of Christ. Apparently McIntyre and Welch disagree not only about whether Barth provides a valid justification for the divinity of Christ, but also about what the concept of the divinity of Christ entails. While McIntyre does not carefully define this concept, it is clear that he thinks Barth attributes divinity to the man Jesus Christ because he is the form of revelation. This implies that he thinks that Barth defines the divinity of Christ as his capacity to reveal the Father, who is other than himself. Although McIntyre doesn't mention them, there are some statements in Barth which convey that impression.[32] On the other hand, Welch states that Jesus Christ is divine because he is of one essence with the Father and the Holy Spirit.[33] On the surface these two notions appear to be distinctly different. In the latter case, Jesus Christ is divine because he possesses the inherent quality of divinity. This notion of divinity is consistent with the idea that Jesus Christ is an agent who reveals himself through a form. In the former case, divinity is associated with a role or function rather than with an intrinsic quality. This concept of divinity would seem to be applicable to any creaturely form through which God reveals himself.

These contrasting interpretations of Barth suggest that there are diverse elements in his concept of the divinity of Christ. How these elements are related should be clarified.

METHOD AND ORDER

In this study we shall focus upon Barth's mature christology as it is found in Church Dogmatics. This major
theological work has been the principal source of both
Antiochian and Alexandrian interpreters of Barth, and
analyzing the evidence found here for both these ways of
understanding Barth is a significant undertaking in
itself. In addition, the Church Dogmatics is generally
recognized as "the clearest and most reliable guide to the
substance and development of his [Barth's] thought."[34]
While occasional references will be made to other works of
Barth, the principal purpose in such references will be to
illustrate the teachings of the Church Dogmatics, not to
provide either a synthesis of all of Barth's writing on
these issues or a survey of the historical development of
his thinking.

The principal purpose of our next chapter is to show
that a persuasive argument can be made for the claim that
Barth's christology is primarily Antiochian rather than
Alexandrian. We shall begin by discussing the characteristics of Antiochian and Alexandrian christologies, and
then we shall construct an Antiochian interpretation of
Barth's doctrine of the divinity of Jesus Christ, his
concept of the unity of the person of Christ, and his use
of the name "Jesus Christ" and its variants. This procedure will demonstrate that there is a considerable amount
of data which supports this interpretation of Barth, and
that it is not limited to just one or two of the three
issues under consideration.

In the third chapter we shall begin our response to
this serious challenge by contending that Barth's doctrines of the divinity of Jesus Christ and the unity of
his person are predominantly Alexandrian. Although there
are important Antiochian elements present, they fit within
an Alexandrian framework.

In the fourth chapter we shall carry our defense of the
Alexandrian character of Barth's theology into the area of
christological language. First, we shall consider some
relevant aspects of Barth's theory of language about
Christ, and then we shall look at the ways that he uses
"Jesus Christ" and its variants. We shall argue that the
major principles which govern Barth's language reveal its
Alexandrian nature.

In our discussion of both the Alexandrian and Antiochian interpretations of Barth, we consider the doctrines before the language. This should not be understood to mean that Barth's use of "Jesus Christ" contributes less than his doctrine to an investigation of the question of whether he is Alexandrian or Antiochian. In our judgment, there is a dialectical relationship between Barth's language and his doctrine of Christ. It does not appear possible to come to an educated conclusion about the character of Barth's doctrine without making some important assumptions about the meaning of his language. The reverse is also the case. It is not possible to analyze and understand Barth's use of "Jesus" and its variants without coming to some conclusions about his understanding of Christ. Individual statements about Jesus can be understood in different ways if they are taken in isolation from the whole configuration of Barth's thought. Thus, one cannot proceed in a linear fashion from the doctrine to the language or from the language to the doctrine. One must make a judgment, or have a flash of insight, about both at once. As a result, what we say about the doctrine of the divinity of Christ and the unity of his person in each of the two possible interpretations of Barth depends upon what we say about the way each understands Barth's language. It would have been possible to start with the language rather than the doctrine. However, because one needs to refer to the doctrines in order to explain the language, beginning with the doctrines seems to promote greater clarity than the reverse order.

In our last chapter we shall deal with the significance of Barth's Alexandrian christology. At the outset we shall show that a recognition of the Alexandrian character of this christology assists in a proper understanding of Barth's theology as a whole. Although it is not possible for us to show the implications of Barth's Alexandrianism for all his doctrines, we can indicate, for example, its relevance for his treatment of revelation. We shall also deal here with the strengths and liabilities of Barth's christology. His position possesses some of the assets which have contributed to the success of Alexandrian theology through the centuries. For example, the absolute divinity of Christ and his uniqueness are accentuated in Barth's dogmatics. On the other hand, it must be asked whether the humanity of Christ is given due emphasis. Finally, we shall make some observations regarding the question of whether Barth's entire theology, and not just his christology, should be considered Alexandrian.

Chapter 2
An Antiochian Interpretation of Barth's Christology

In this chapter our principal purpose is to construct an Antiochian interpretation of Barth's christology. While other commentators have pointed out particular aspects of Barth's thought which they think are Antiochian, no attempt has previously been made to develop these isolated observations into a systematic picture. Once a coherent presentation of an Antiochian interpretation is before us, it will be possible both to see more specifically what elements in Barth support it and also to make a judgment about its reliability.

Our hypothesis is that an Antiochian interpretation of Barth revolves around the basic assumption that Barth understands Jesus Christ as a complete human person who is distinct from the person God. Perhaps the single item of evidence which gives the most justification for this conclusion is Barth's characterization of the specimen of human nature which the eternal Logos assumed in the incarnation. According to an Antiochian understanding of Barth, Barth ascribes to this human nature a will, personality, and self-consciousness, in addition to a mind, soul, and body. Consequently, according to this interpretation, Barth means that this human nature is itself a person. How, one who holds this view might ask, could a human nature which has a will, personality, and self-consciousness be anything less than a complete individual person?

We shall begin this chapter by discussing the major differences between the Alexandrian and Antiochian schools of theological thinking. Our goal here is to augment the bare outline we presented in the introduction by filling in more of the details. At the same time, we shall indicate that our characterizations of these two theologies are grounded in the history of doctrine; they are not simply ideal constructions. Having more details of these two theologies before us will enable us to perceive more readily the Antiochian and Alexandrian elements in Barth's work. Once this foundation has been established, we shall turn to the major task of the chapter, the construction of the Antiochian theology which can be seen in Barth.

THE ALEXANDRIAN AND ANTIOCHIAN TRADITIONS

We reemphasize that our characterizations of the Alexandrian and Antiochian perspectives are offered as definitions. It is not our purpose to give a detailed account of the historical debates between thinkers of these two schools, nor shall we attempt to refute those whose judgment concerning the basic features of these schools is different from ours.[1] To do so would require an in-depth study of the involved terminology and arguments of leading representatives of each school, such as Cyril of Alexandria, who was a prominent defender of Alexandrian thought, and Theodore of Mopsuestia and Nestorius, who were proponents of the Antiochian position.   Such a procedure would take us far afield from the main object before us. Nevertheless, we believe that our characterizations are historically as well as theoretically valid, and we shall give brief documentation for them.

Our discussion of the Alexandrian and Antiochian christologies will be organized under the headings of the three principal issues we have mentioned previously. Since the question of the unity of the person of Christ has occupied the center of the stage in the classical debates between Alexandrian and Antiochian theologians, it is fitting to begin with it. Then we shall turn to the doctrine of the divinity of Jesus Christ and the use of the name "Jesus Christ."

The Unity of the Person of Jesus Christ

The way a theology conceives the unity of the person of Christ is substantially determined by the way it understands the identity of Jesus Christ. In fact, in one sense of the meaning of the concept of unity, the unity of the person of Christ is presupposed before the question of the relation of the two natures arises. In Antiochian thinking, Jesus Christ is a single, unified, human person apart from his relation to God and the divine nature. In Alexandrian thinking, Jesus Christ is the eternal Logos who already possesses his unity before he becomes related to the human nature in the incarnation. Pittenger describes these two ways of conceiving the oneness of the person Jesus Christ in these words:

> One group of Christians has tended to say that this person is God living and acting humanly. Another has tended to say that this person is the Man in whom God lives and acts. The difference between the two ways of phrasing the fact which Christians have encountered has led to almost interminable theological argument, which has been as little enlightening as it has been little edifying. Each Christian, even today, will prefer one or the other way of phrasing the fact. But at least the fact is constant. We may say that the former style is more Alexandrine or Cyrillian, the latter more Antiochene or Nestorian (or better, more like the thought of Theodore of Mopsuestia); and we may believe that there will always be some who are of the former way of thinking and some who are of the latter.[2]

The issue of the unity of the person of Christ is not, however, reducible to the question of who Jesus Christ is. It also involves the way the "two" in the God-man are united. Consistently with its view that Jesus is essentially and primarily a human person, Antiochian theology has tended to conceive the relation between the divinity and the humanity as a unity between two persons, God the Word and the man Jesus. On the other hand, in Alexandrian theology, the human reality which is related to the eternal Logos is not, in itself, fully and completely a man. It is a human nature, something other than an individual man. Of course, for the Alexandrian view, there is a man Jesus; but this man is the Word himself, the Word who became man when he united himself with human nature. In order to point out in a graphic way the contrast between these two conceptions of the unity of the person, some interpreters have used the symbol "Word-flesh" or "Person-nature" for the Alexandrian position and "Word-man" for the Antiochian.[3]

In the Alexandrian framework, because the divine Logos is already a whole person and the human nature which he assumes is not a person, it is clear that the Logos is the dominant factor in the union. The human nature is not so free and independent as to be able to act on its own. It simply follows the will of the Logos, as a man's hand follows his commands. As a result, the actions of the man Jesus, his speaking and healing, and even his sleeping and eating, are actions of God himself, the Logos, in his unity with human nature. Because God is the agent, he is able to redeem man, and it is possible to attribute salvation to Jesus Christ and to worship him. If Jesus Christ were simply a man in whom God was present, he would be unable to accomplish salvation for us, and it would be improper to worship him.[4]

For Antiochian thought, on the other hand, the man Jesus is related to God through divine "good pleasure" and his own faithful response. The man Jesus is indwelt by God the Word, and the relation between the two is one of fellowship and harmony. Through God's guidance and protection, Jesus' will was at one with God's will for him, and he was completely obedient. The relation between the two is not a mixture but a "conjunction," and it is permanent and indivisible. Nevertheless, in this unity Jesus Christ remains a man. He is capable of all the actions and feelings common to all human beings. He was hungry, he was tempted, he suffered, but he was unique in that he did not sin.[5]

Given these basic features of the two schools on this issue, it is easy to understand the criticisms they have leveled at each other. Alexandrian theology has histori-cally been accused of mitigating the significance of the humanity of Christ, and Antiochian christology has been accused of slighting his oneness. In the first case, since the agent who acts through the divine and human natures is the eternal Word of God, there is no corre-sponding, purely human agent who acts through the human nature. The human agent, critics claim, is "swallowed up" into the divine agent. In the second case since the Antiochians affirm that there are two subjects and agents in Christ, it is difficult to see how these two persons can be one person. As a result, Antiochians have been accused of professing two Sons or two Christs.[6]

One of the main reasons why the Alexandrians thought that their opponents divided Christ into two was the Antiochian insistence that there were two hypostases and two natures after the union. Since both of these terms could be understood to mean a concrete existing individual, Cyril preferred to say that there was one hypostasis and one nature after the union. This claim indicates the close relation of Cyril's thought to his predecessor Apollinarius and his successor Eutyches.[7]

The Antiochians used the term prosopon to refer to the unity of the Logos and the man Jesus Christ. This term was flexible enough to allow for the relative independence of the man and God. As Sullivan has shown, Theodore of Mopsuestia used prosopon in his scriptural exegesis to indicate the subject of whom or to whom a psalm is spoken. This subject might be an individual, a group, or even a multitude. In the same way, Jesus and God constitute one grammatical subject of whom we may say whatever pertains to each of them, although they are not one person in the sense of one specific individual.[8]

The Antiochians' response to the accusation that they were professing two Christs did not disavow that the man Jesus and the Logos were two active subjects in one prosopon. Theodore, for example, said that there were not two Sons here because the two were not members of the same class; one of the two is God by nature and the other is man by nature. The Logos is the Son by nature, and the man Jesus participates in his sonship. Because of his relation to the Logos, it is proper to say that Jesus is the Son, but it must be recognized that he is the Son only by grace, not by nature.[9]

Another basis for the Alexandrian objection that the Antiochians divided Jesus Christ into two Sons was the Antiochian use of the term "conjunction" in reference to the unity of the two natures. Nestorius was willing to use the term "union," but he preferred "conjunction" since it avoided the idea that the two natures were united as in a mixture. Although Nestorius described this conjunction as perfect, exact, and continuous,[10] it still seemed to the Alexandrians to be merely a moral union of two wills. Consequently, they argued that in the Antiochian view the union was merely an association, an external and acciden- tal union. Jesus became simply an organ or instrument through which God acted. In contrast, the Alexandrians claimed that the union was a natural reality; it was internal and permanent. To emphasize that the union was not merely artificial, Cyril stated that it was "hyposta- tic" and "natural." He preferred the analogy of the soul and body of a person, for it seemed to him to underscore the unity and preclude any suggestion of a mechanical connection.[11]

The Antiochian view of the unity of the man Jesus with the Logos understandably provided the occasion for the Alexandrians to claim that the Antiochians thought of Christ merely as an ordinary man who was indwelt by God. Consequently, the Alexandrians continued, the uniqueness of Christ is threatened. He was no different, in fact, from the saints and the prophets who were indwelt by the Spirit of God. If he were such an ordinary man, asks Cyril, how could it be said that he was the savior? Only the uncommon man, the second Adam, could conquer death and redeem man.[12]

Theodore anticipated this criticism, along with the possible charge that he was guilty of adoptionism. In response, he attempted to clarify the uniqueness of Jesus' relation to God. While God may indwell the saints and prophets, assisting them through his will and working together with them, his dwelling in Christ is unique in that it takes place "as in a Son."[13] This means that the Logos, because of his good pleasure, voluntarily united himself with Jesus from the moment of his formation in the womb. This union preceded the obedience of Jesus as a man and provided a basis for it, while in other cases, God's good pleasure and consequent indwelling accompany obedience. Thus, it is not proper to overlook the uniqueness of God's relationship to Jesus Christ, nor can it be said that the union is constituted by moral harmony. The moral harmony of the two wills is the result of the union of God with Jesus which precedes it and makes it possible. For the Antiochians, the union is not common, external, or accidental.[14]

It is clear, then, that the Antiochians and the Alexandrians conceive the unity of the person of Christ differently. The latter emphasize the oneness, while the former stress the duality. Each side attempts to deal adequately with the opposite emphasis.

The Divinity of Jesus Christ

It is apparent that Alexandrian thought emphasizes the divinity of Jesus Christ while the Antiochian stance is more concerned with his humanity. The principal problem for the Alexandrian position is how to give proper consideration to Jesus' humanity. In contrast, the major problem for the Antiochian system is how to account for Christ's divinity.

These different emphases are reflected in the grounds upon which divinity is attributed to Jesus Christ in these two schools of thought. In our view, the contrast between the two can be characterized by saying that in Alexandrian thought divinity is a "real" predicate of Jesus Christ. He is intrinsically and inherently divine, divine by nature. On the other hand, for the Antiochian view, divinity is attributed to Jesus Christ because of his relation to the Logos. Although his nature is human and not divine, the predicate of divinity is "lent" to him; it is his by association.

For Alexandrian thinking, Jesus Christ is fully identical with the Word and Son of God. He is the "second" of the trinity, and therefore he is of the same essence as the Father and the Holy Spirit. As a result, he is divine as they are divine. He becomes flesh and participates in human existence, but this involvement does not mitigate his divinity in any way. He is not changed into a creature. He simply adds human nature with all its qualities and capabilities to his divine nature, and his divine nature maintains complete control of his human nature. According to Alexandrian thought, the appearance of Jesus Christ in human form as a man is simply a second stage in his divine existence.[15]

The logic of the Antiochian view of the divinity of Jesus Christ is expressed admirably by Theodore of Mopsuestia. Theodore makes a distinction between what can be predicated of Jesus Christ "by nature" and what can be predicated of him "by relation."[16]   By nature, Jesus Christ is a man who enjoys a unique relation to God and a special place in God's plan for all men.   In this relation, he does not become divinized, nor does he become God himself.   Yet, because of God's continual presence and action in and through him, it is correct to say that he is divine.   In explanation of this basis for maintaining the divinity of Christ, Theodore often speaks of the honor which the man Jesus shares with God because the Logos dwells in him.[17]

Because of his relation to God, it is proper not only to affirm the divinity and sonship of the man Jesus, it is also correct to attribute to him those actions which can be performed only through divine power.   Jesus forgives sins, heals diseases, and he also demands worship and obedience.   He is the secondary subject of these actions, while the Logos is their direct subject.   Conversely, the actions of the man Jesus can also be predicated of the indwelling Logos.   God the Word ate, slept, talked, and suffered.   He was the subject of the actions and passions in a secondary and indirect way, because of his relation to Jesus who was their direct and immediate subject.   Of course, God is also the ultimate subject of these actions, since he established the union between himself and Jesus, making this indirect participation possible.[18]

A succinct statement of Theodore's distinction between the two types of predication is found in a discussion of the familiar question of whether Mary should be called theotokos.   He states:

> So when they ask, "Is Mary the Mother of God or the Mother of man?"--let us say "Both": the one by the nature of the thing, the other by relation (anaphorai).   For she is the mother of man by nature, since what was in the womb of Mary was a man. . . .   But she is the mother of God, since God was in the man who was born, not confined within him by nature, but in him by the disposition (schesin) of the will.   Therefore it is right for both to be said, but not in the same respect. . . .   The same answer is to be given if they ask, "Was

> God crucified or man?"--namely, "Both, but not
> in the same respect." For the latter was
> crucified inasmuch as he suffered and was
> nailed to the Tree and held by the Jews; but
> the former because he was with him for the
> reason we have given.[19]

The traditional Antiochian justification for attributing divinity to Jesus Christ is still prevalent in the
modern period. For example, W. N. Pittenger defines the
divinity of Jesus Christ as the presence and action of God
in him. "That which the divinity of Christ denotes is the
act of God the Word in him."[20] For Pittenger, this
means that God is objectively present in Christ. It is
not as though we simply learn about God through Christ, so
that God's presence in Christ is only subjective. While
God is also objectively present elsewhere, his presence in
Christ is of greater intensity than anywhere else.
Therefore, the divinity of Christ is unique.

The Use of the Name "Jesus Christ"

There are two basic differences between the Alexandrian
and Antiochian interpretations of language about Jesus
Christ. First, the Alexandrians think of the various
names and titles of Jesus Christ as denoting one single
agent, the Logos. In contrast, the Antiochians think of
these names and titles as denoting two individual persons,
as well as their unity. Second, the Alexandrians think of
the various predicates of Jesus Christ as being assigned
to one subject according to two natures. On the other
hand, the Antiochians think of the various predicates as
being assigned to two persons who are united in an inseparable manner.
    For the Alexandrian position, there is only one truly
personal subject involved in the two natures of the
God-Man, and he is God the Word. Both before and after he
unites an "impersonal" or "nonpersonal" human nature to
himself, he is one agent. He can be denoted by such terms
as "Son of God," "Word of God," "Lord," "Savior," "Jesus
Christ," "Jesus," "Jesus of Nazareth," the man Jesus," and
"Christ."

In contrast, for the Antiochian view, there is God the Word and there is also the man Jesus. Because there are two subjects of attribution and also two centers of action here, the meaning of the name "Jesus Christ" becomes quite complicated. Who is Jesus Christ? Is he God the Word, or is he the man Jesus? The traditional Antiochian response to this difficulty has been to propose careful and precise terminological distinctions. To refer to the God who is present in and with man, it is best to use "Logos" and "Word." To refer to the man who is present with God, it is best to use "Jesus," "Jesus of Nazareth," "the man Jesus," or "the human nature." To refer to the unity of the two, it is best to use "Jesus Christ," "Emmanuel," or "Christ." These terms denote the man Jesus in his special relation to God the Word and also the grammatical subject of which can be predicated the attributes of both Jesus and God the Word. Thus, when we say that Jesus Christ is fully God and fully man, we mean that the unity of the two is fully God and fully man. It would not be proper to say that God the Word in himself is fully God and fully man, just as it would not be correct to say that Jesus of Nazareth in himself is fully God and fully man.[21]

Because there are two subjects involved in the Antiochian concept of Jesus Christ, it is important to distinguish biblical statements according to which subject is intended. When the Bible says that Jesus wept, it is referring to the man Jesus. Conversely, the statements concerning Jesus Christ's divine actions, such as forgiving sins, have to do with God the Word.[22]

For Cyrillian thought, on the other hand, all the biblical statements about Jesus Christ are about one subject, not two. Consequently, in his fourth anathema, Cyril attacked the Antiochian practice of "dividing the sayings." He declared:

If anyone distributes between two persons or hypostases the terms used in the evangelical and apostolic writings, whether spoken of Christ by the saints or by him about himself, and attaches some to a man thought of separately from the Word of God, and others as befitting God to the Word of God the Father alone, let him be anathema.[23]

In spite of this opposition to the Antiochian way of interpreting language about Christ, however, the Alexandrians wanted to distinguish the two natures and also two types of statements about Christ. According to them, predicates of each of the two natures can be assigned to the one person. Some predicates belong to the Logos because of his divine nature, and others belong to him because of his human nature. Those predicates which speak of Jesus eating, growing, weeping, and so forth, do not imply that he is a separate man, subordinate to the Father. They simply tell us about the eternal Logos in his being as a man. They speak of the Logos "according to the flesh," or "humanly." The Logos does some things "divinely," through his divine nature, and some things "humanly," through his human nature.[24] Thus, Cyril of Alexandria could say that the Word did not suffer according to his divine nature, but that he did suffer according to his human nature. This is what Cyril meant when he said "He suffered without suffering."[25]

To conclude, in this section we have presented historical evidence for the hypothesis that the basic differences between the Antiochian and Alexandrian theologies have to do with the way they conceive the identity of Jesus Christ. For Antiochian thought, Jesus Christ is the rabbi from Nazareth who had a special place in God's plan for all men. For Alexandrian thought, Jesus Christ is the God who descended to earth and lived as a man.

BARTH'S CONCEPT OF THE DIVINITY OF JESUS CHRIST IN AN ANTIOCHIAN PERSPECTIVE

Turning now to our development of an Antiochian interpretation of Barth's christology, our first task is to show the evidence for classifying Barth's concept of the divinity of Jesus Christ as Antiochian. Then we shall consider those factors which support an Antiochian understanding of Barth's doctrine of the unity of the person of Christ and his use of the name "Jesus Christ" and its variants. This procedure will require the explication of important concepts and passages found in Barth's Church Dogmatics.

In an Antiochian perspective, considerable emphasis is

placed upon the rather remarkable fact that Barth affirms the divinity of the Bible and proclamation as well as the divinity of Jesus Christ. Since proclamation can occur through many creaturely media, such as the bread and wine of the Lord's supper, the water of baptism, and the words of preaching, it follows that many finite realities can be said to be divine. According to the Antiochian understanding of Barth, the grounds for affirming Christ's divinity are essentially the same as those used to establish the divinity of other creaturely media. These creatures are said to be divine because of their relation to God, not because of their inherent being. They participate in the act in which God speaks, and consequently they become God's divine Word. This concept of divinity can be designated "participatory divinity."[26]

In order to show that Barth makes this interpretation possible, we shall look first at the way he describes the divinity of Jesus Christ, the Bible, and proclamation. Then we shall discuss the following topics: the forms of revelation, indirect identity, the "is" of becoming, analytic statements, and the uniqueness of Jesus. An account of Barth's treatment of these subjects will contribute to an understanding of his concept of the divinity of Jesus Christ, since they are directly related to it. In this discussion, we shall point out the evidence for including Jesus Christ in the same category with the Bible and proclamation. In the next chapter we shall present the Alexandrian case for placing Jesus Christ in a category by himself.

The Definition of Divinity

An Antiochian interpretation of Barth is made plausible, in the first place, because of Barth's correlation of the divinity of Christ, the Bible, and proclamation with the event of revelation. Speaking specifically of the deity of Christ, Barth states, "The essence of the Divinity ascribed to Jesus is to make clear, impart, and carry out who God the Father, God in the proper sense is, and what He wills and does for man, to represent this God the Father."[27] This definition of divinity seems to imply that Jesus can be said to be divine because he reveals God the Father. Yet he is not God in the proper sense, for this God is the Father. "True and real divinity, as expressed in the predicate Kyrios, the NT already ascribes in the first instance to a completely O t h e r than Jesus."[28] Thus, it seems evident that Jesus is divine because of his relation to God in revelation, not because of his inherent nature.

Barth also states that the Bible and proclamation are divine in this sense. This conclusion is asserted most forcefully in the third and fourth chapters of the Church Dogmatics where Barth deals explicitly with these topics. For example, Barth maintains the divinity of the Bible in these words:

> As the Word of God in the sign of this pro-
> phetic-apostolic word of man Holy Scripture is
> like the unity of God and man in Jesus Christ.
> It is neither divine only nor human only. Nor
> is it a mixture of the two nor a tertium quid
> between them. But in its own way and degree
> it is very God and very man, i.e. a witness of
> revelation which itself belongs to revela-
> tion.[29]

He affirms the divinity of proclamation in this way:

> It is only from the belief that the Church's
> proclamation is really divine that the recog-
> nition of the hopelessness of its humanity
> follows, and therefore the recognition that in
> its humanity it can live only by its divinity,
> that is, by the grace of the Word of God given
> to the Church.[30]

In both these cases, divinity is attributed to creaturely forms because of the presence of God's Word revealing himself. This point will become clearer below.

According to an Antiochian interpretation, when Barth speaks of the divinity of the scriptures, proclamation, and the human Jesus, he does not mean that these creature-ly realities possess some quality that can be labeled as "divinity." Barth explicitly declares that "God is not an attribute of something else, even if this something else is the Bible."[31]. Nor does this divinity have anything to do with the creaturely excellence of scripture, proclamation, or the man Jesus. The most perfectly written and wisest thoughts in the Bible or in preaching are not, for all that, divine. Nor is the divinity of Jesus dependent upon his heroic personality or his wisdom.[32] What is important about Jesus, the Bible, and proclamation is that God speaks through them, making himself known through his Word. In these moments, they become witnesses to revelation.

Finally, when Barth affirms that the Bible, proclamation, and Jesus Christ are divine, this does not mean that their humanity is destroyed or transformed into divinity. The scriptures were written by men, and therefore they are fallible as men are. As any historical document, the Bible is limited by the fact that its writers were conditioned by their finiteness and by their historical situation. Many of their beliefs appear to us today to be false.[33] In the same way, the human words of preaching are far from perfect, even if they are modern and enlightened. They are liable to proclaim misjudgments. Nor was the man Jesus transformed into God himself, although he was sinless. He still was a finite creature, with limited knowledge and resources, subject to the same limitations as other men.[34]

There is some justification, then, for classifying Barth's concept of the divinity of Christ as Antiochian. He seems to promote a notion of participatory divinity rather than intrinsic divinity. This conclusion is given additional support by the fact that Barth clearly includes Jesus Christ among the forms of revelation. We turn next to that topic.

The Forms of Revelation

In this section we explore more thoroughly the notion of participatory divinity by examining Barth's treatment of the forms of revelation. We shall mention specifically three points. The forms are not God, they are knowable as other creaturely realities are known, and they can reveal God only through God's power and decision, not through their own power. All these points support an Antiochian interpretation in that they show that these forms are not inherently divine. When we come to the next section on the idea of indirect identity, then we shall see more clearly the basis for predicating divinity to these forms. Throughout this discussion, we shall point out that Barth includes Jesus Christ among the many possible forms of revelation.

As we shall see in our treatment of these subjects, Barth sometimes speaks as though the human nature of Christ is the form of revelation, while at other times he implies that it is the man Jesus who is the form. In the Antiochian interpretation, this manner of speaking indicates that Barth conceives of the human nature of the Logos in a concrete sense, as an individual human being. Since Barth also states that the human nature of the Logos has its own personality, will, and self-consciousness, this conclusion seems plausible.[35] If it is correct, Barth follows a pattern that has been prevalent among Antiochian theologians since Theodore of Mopsuestia.[36] According to this pattern, whatever Barth says about the human nature of the Logos applies to the man Jesus; the human nature of the Logos and the man Jesus are one and the same reality.[37]

Barth argues that God is not known directly but through creaturely forms which are not in themselves divine. In his presentation of this point, Barth often lists Jesus or the human nature of Jesus among the creaturely forms through which God reveals himself. For example, Barth states:

> We hasten to add that also there is no Word of God without a physical event. We are reminded of that by the homogeneity of preaching and sacrament. We are reminded of that by the verbal nature of Holy Scripture. We are reminded of that finally and most highly of all by the corporeality of the man Jesus Christ.[38]

The fact that Barth often mentions the man Jesus along with the Bible, preaching and the creaturely elements of the sacraments should not be interpreted to mean that God reveals himself only through these forms. The prominent forms of the Old Testament are the words of the prophets, Moses, the angel of the Lord, the name "Yahweh," and Yahweh's attributes. In addition, "God may speak to us through Russian communism or a flute concerto, a blossoming shrub or a dead dog. We shall do well to listen to Him if He really does so."[39]

While it is clear that Barth includes the man Jesus among the many forms through which God has manifested himself, it must also be said that he is unique among them. God's revelation through Jesus is "incomparably more direct, unambiguous, palpable"[40] than his revelation through other forms. Barth makes this assertion in a comparison of the name "Yahweh" and the man Jesus. The name "Yahweh" is the form which stands out above other forms in the Old Testament.[41] Yet, in spite of the fact that this name in inherently related to Yahweh himself, it is still merely a linquistic and therefore an intellectual and theoretical phenomenon. In the New Testament, the form which stands out is Jesus. He takes the place of the name "Yahweh," and his "contingent, somatic, human existence" is "so much more direct" that other forms appear to be mere "shadows" in relation to it.[42]

According to an Antiochian interpretation, Barth's explanation of the uniqueness of Jesus in relation to the name "Yahweh" does not emphasize that Jesus is a divine reality or that he is more than a man. Jesus is more direct than "Yahweh" because he is a man with a physical existence. Consequently, Barth's views do not conflict with the Antiochian belief that Jesus is a person distinct from God.

The way the creaturely forms are known indicates that they are not transformed into divine realities by the revelatory presence of God. When God assumes a form, the creatureliness of the form is not distinguished in a way which makes it unambiguously clear that God has assumed it. The Bible, preaching, and Jesus do not differ from other words, events, and persons in a way that prevents them from being interpreted simply as ordinary phenomena. Barth states:

> When God speaks to man, this happening is
> never so marked off from the rest of what
> happens that it might not promptly be also in-

terpreted as a part of this other happening.
The Church in fact is also a sociological
entity with definite historical and structural
features. Preaching in fact is also an
address. Sacrament in fact is also a symbol
in compromising proximity to all other possible symbols. The Bible in fact is also the
document for the history of the religion of a
tribe in Nearer Asia and of its Hellenistic
offshoot. Jesus Christ in fact is also the
Rabbi of Nazareth, historically so difficult
to get information about, and when it is got,
one whose activity is so easily a little
commonplace alongside more than one other
founder of a religion and even alongside many
later representatives of His own "religion."
[43]

Because the forms of revelation are not marked off in some
obvious way as an event of God's speaking, a neutral
observer apprehends only the form and does not interpret
it as a form of revelation. He sees the Bible as only a
human, historical document, not as a book chosen by God to
witness to his revelation. Nor does he understand Jesus
as other than a first-century religious visionary. Barth
affirms:

What the neutral observer of these events
might apprehend or may have apprehended of
these events was the form of the revelation,
not regarded by him as such and, moreover, not
to be regarded by him as such, some sort of
happening unrolling itself in the human
sphere, having all the possibilities of
interpretation appropriate to this sphere, but
in no case revelation as such. . . . Thousands
may have seen and heard the Rabbi of Nazareth.
But this historical element was not revelation.[44]

Finally, even though God reveals himself through a
form, this does not mean that the form has the power to
reveal God. God is hidden in his unveiledness. He

remains free to reveal or not to reveal himself in the form which he assumes. His revelation of himself is always the result of a fresh decision on his part to make himself known. "It i s n o t t h e f o r m that reveals, speaks, comforts, works, helps, b u t G o d i n t h e f o r m." [45]

This limitation of the power of the form applies even to the human nature of Christ. The man Jesus has only creaturely power, and he has no way of evoking God's decision to reveal himself. Barth makes this clear in his discussion of God's freedom in relation to Jesus Christ. He states that Jesus was the revelation of God because of "the power and continuity of the divine action in this form and not in the continuity of this form as such." In the New Testament, revelation "is clearly not in itself or directly ascribed to His [Jesus'] existence as such." It is a "constantly recurring new thing, that becomes real from God's side in definite circumstances."[46]

Nevertheless, the form of revelation is not superfluous, nor can the content of revelation be separated from the form. This is a general condition which applies to the principal revelation through Christ. Barth states that the content of the revelation of the Father is

> completely limited and tied down by its impartation in the Person of the revealer, Jesus of Nazareth. Its content cannot be abstracted from this form. There is here no question of any possibility of distinguishing content and form, and regarding the content as divine and necessary, the form as human and accidental; the former as the essence, the latter as the historical appearance of revelation.[47]

These observations about the way Barth characterizes the forms of revelation imply that the forms are creaturely realities which have their own nature and qualities, apart from their participation in revelation. They exist in relative independence, although God from time to time chooses to reveal himself through them. Since the man Jesus, who is eminent among these forms, can be recognized as an itinerant rabbi even by neutral observers, he seems to be a complete person in himself. When God speaks through him, he is recognized as the Word of God. The fact that the forms become the Word of God is the point to which we turn now.

Indirect Identity

Not only are the forms of revelation inseparable from God, who is the content of revelation, they are also, in a sense, identical with God himself. Therefore, it is proper to say that they are divine. The identity of a form with God, however, comes into existence only through God's decision. To point out this limitation, Barth states that the identity is indirect.

Barth uses the concept of indirect identity primarily in relation to the Bible, proclamation, and the humanity of Jesus. However, he also indicates that it applies both to the relation between Yahweh and the angel of Yahweh and also the relation between Yahweh and his name. The angel of Yahweh and the name "Yahweh" are forms through which Yahweh reveals himself. In the moment of revelation, these forms become indirectly identical with God. Speaking of the angel of Yahweh, Barth explains:

> The "angel of the Lord" in [the] OT is obviously identical with the Lord Himself a n d not identical. It is quite impossible that the non-identity too should not become and remain visible.[48]

Because there is a difference as well as an identity here, it must be said that the identity is indirect.[49] In reference to "Yahweh," Barth explains that this name is "a separate being," yet it is "identical with Him [Yahweh] in a way not to be explained." A consequent of this identity is that predicates of Yahweh may be applied to the name "Yahweh."[50]

Barth's clearest discussion of the indirect identity of the Bible and proclamation with the Word of God is found in the paragraph entitled "The Word of God in its Threefold Form."[51] In the following passage, he correlates the concept of indirect identity with that of becoming,

stating that because the Bible and proclamation become
God's Word, their identity with the Word is indirect.

> From the standpoint of the comprehensive
> concept of the Word of God we must say that
> here, in God's revelation, God's Word is
> identical with God Himself. Among the three
> forms of the Word of God that can be said
> unconditionally and with strictest propriety
> only of revelation, not with the same unre-
> servedness and directness of Holy Scripture
> and Church proclamation as well. For if the
> same may and must also be said of them, it
> must at all events be added that their identi-
> ty with God is an indirect one. Without
> wishing to deny or even merely to limit their
> character as God's Word, we must think of the
> fact that here the Word of God is mediated,
> through the human persons of the prophets and
> apostles, who received and handed it on, and
> again through the human persons of their
> expositors and proclaimers; that Holy Scrip-
> ture and proclamation must always be
> b e c o m i n g the Word of God in order to be
> it.[52]

Barth is also explicit about the fact that the concept
of an indirect identity applies to the relation between
God and the humanity of Christ. In making this point,
Barth compares the relation between God the Word and the
humanity of Christ to the relation between the divinity
and humanity of the Bible and proclamation. For example,
Barth states:

> Again it is quite impossible that there should
> be a direct identity between the human word of
> Holy Scripture and the Word of God, and
> therefore between the creaturely reality in
> itself and as such and the reality of God the
> Creator. It is impossible that there should
> have been a transmutation of the one into the
> other or an admixture of the one with the
> other. This is not the case even in the

> person of Christ where the identity between
> God and man, in all the originality and
> indissolubility in which it confronts us, is
> an assumed identity, one specially willed,
> created and effected by God, and to that
> extent indirect, i.e., resting neither in the
> essence of God nor in that of man, but in a
> decision and act of God to man. When we
> necessarily allow for inherent differences, it
> is exactly the same with the unity of the
> divine and human word in Holy Scriptures.[53]

In this passage, Barth denies that the identity of God
and man in Christ is an identity of essence. The divinity
attributed to Jesus and the Bible is not based on their
natures but on their relation to God, a relation established by God's decision.

Although Barth does not, so far as we have been able to
determine, state in so many words that the man Jesus of
Nazareth is indirectly identical with the Word of God,
those who interpret Barth as an Antiochian theologian can
assume with reason that such a statement is possible for
Barth. Since Barth claims that the human nature of the
Logos is indirectly identical with God, and since, according to the Antiochian interpretation, Barth understands
the human nature of the Logos in a concrete sense, as an
individual person, it follows that the man Jesus is
indirectly identical with God. From an Antiochian point
of view, Barth appears to mean that Jesus only becomes the
Word of God when God decides to speak through him. In
himself, Jesus is not divine; he is only an ordinary,
first-century rabbi who can be said to be divine only
because God establishes an indirect identity with him in
the moment of revelation.

The "Is" of Becoming

The concept of indirect identity implies that the "is" in
the statements "The Bible is the Word of God," "Proclamation is the Word of God," and "Jesus of Nazareth is the
Word of God" means "becomes." According to the Antiochian
interpretation, Barth accepts this implication and ac-

knowledges it in several ways. In reference to the Bible, he states, "The Bible therefore b e c o m e s God's Word in this event, and it is to its b e i n g in this b e-c o m i n g that the tiny word 'is' relates, in the statement that the Bible is God's Word."[54]

When Barth phrases this conclusion with respect to the human words of preaching, he compares the use of "is" here with that found in the doctrine of the two natures of Christ. In this way he indicates that preaching is the Word of God in much the same way that the man Jesus is the Word of God. Barth states:

> In and for all that it is in itself, it [human language] can only serve the actual Word of God. And that divine self-Word does not cease to be itself because it lets itself be served by human language. But because it permits this service on its part, It is itself this human language, and because this human language serves It, It is itself the divine self-word.
>
> For the proper explanation of this "is," reference would have to be made thus early to the Christological "doctrine of the two natures."[55]

Again, those who accept an Antiochian interpretation of Barth would have to admit that Barth does not explicitly say that the "is" in "Jesus of Nazareth is the Word of God" is an "is" of becoming. Nevertheless, what he says seems to lead directly to that conclusion. Since Barth includes the human nature of Jesus Christ in the list of these forms which become divine because of their function rather than their essence, it follows that the same can be said of the man Jesus himself.

If it is true that statements such as "Jesus of Nazareth is the Word of God" affirm an indirect identity, the question remains as to whether the claim that Jesus of Nazareth is the Son of God is also an indirect identity. According to an Antiochian interpretation, Barth understands the identity of Jesus of Nazareth with the Son of God as an indirect identity. An evidence for this conclusion is that Barth clearly identifies the Son of God and

the Word of God.[56] Consequently, Barth often makes
statements such as the following: "God's Son or God's
Word is identical with a man, with this man, whose name is
Jesus of Nazareth."[57] It seems not to matter to Barth
whether he speaks of an identity between Jesus Christ and
the Word or between Jesus Christ and the Son. Both can be
understood as affirming an indirect identity, based upon
the "is" of becoming.[58]
    Another evidence that the identity of Jesus Christ with
God is indirect can be found in Barth's claim that certain
crucial statements of this identity are analytic. Barth's
account of analytic statements can be used to support the
Antiochian interpretation because included among them is
the statement that the Bible is the Word of God.

Analytic Statements

Barth maintains that the statements which affirm an
identity between Jesus Christ and God are analytic.
Speaking of the New Testament witnesses, Barth declares:
"On their lips the statement 'Jesus is God's Son' is
entirely a self-authenticating statement as much as its
counterpart: the Word became flesh. On their lips both
of these are analytic, not synthetic statements."[59]
    Barth's claim that these statements are analytic might
be seen by some readers as a threat to the Antiochian view
that they express an indirect identity. This is the case
because predicates of analytic statements are often
understood to affirm the essence of the subject. In fact,
Barth seems to accept this definition when he states that
certain statements "were not understood analytically, as
if the subject were in essence what the predicate states
concerning it."[60] If "Jesus Christ is God's Son" states
that Jesus Christ is in essence the Son of God, this would
imply that the divinity of Jesus Christ is his by nature,
not just by relation. Consequently, the "is" would appear
to affirm a direct, permanent identity, not an indirect
identity of becoming.
    However, this threat to the Antiochian view is overcome
by the fact that Barth also describes the identification
of the Bible with the Word of God as analytic. He says:

> We have to admit to ourselves and to all who
> ask us about this question that the statement
> that the Bible is the Word of God is an
> analytical statement, a statement which is
> grounded only in its repetition, description,
> and interpretation, and not in its derivation
> from any major propositions. It must either
> be understood as grounded in itself and
> preceding all other statements or it cannot be
> understood at all.[61]

This quote implies that the operative element in
Barth's understanding of analytic statements is that they
are self-authenticating. In any case, the fact that Barth
groups the identification of Jesus and the eternal Son in
the same class with the identification of the Bible and
the Word implies that the identity involved is indirect
and that, therefore, the "is" means "becomes." It is
clear that Barth does not mean that the Bible is in
essence the Word of God. He emphasizes the humanity of
the Bible too much for that interpretation to be given
serious consideration.

Uniqueness of Jesus

While we have already mentioned one respect in which Jesus
of Nazareth differs from other media of revelation, in
that he is more direct and unambigious since he is a
man,[62] it is appropriate for us to consider here some of
the other aspects of his uniqueness. It is important to
show that an Antiochian interpretation of Barth does not
entail the claim that Barth understands Jesus to be like
other creaturely media in all respects.
    Although Barth does not devote a single section to a
thorough discussion of the uniqueness of Jesus as a form
of revelation, he makes several observations with regard
to this topic. Perhaps the principal difference between
Jesus and other forms of revelation is that the revelation
through Jesus is the original revelation. It is the
revelation, and all other revelatory events are witnesses
to it. This point is made clear in Barth's discussion of
"The Word of God in its Threefold Form."[63]   Revelation

through the Bible and proclamation are dependent on this original revelation, which is ontologically prior.

Secondly, Barth says that the revelation through the human nature of Jesus happened only once, while the revelations through the Bible and proclamation require repetition. This means that the original revelation of God through the life he lived on earth is past. It is complete and finished in a way that the Bible and proclamation are not, for they continue to exist in their natural form in the present. God does not have to assume human nature and act in a human way again, for he has spoken in a decisive way in the original revelation.

Thirdly, the original revelation does not depend on faith. It exists apart from faith, while God's speaking through the Bible and proclamation must be successful in stimulating a response of faith in order to be described as God's Word and therefore divine. Both the second and third distinctions are expressed by Barth in these words:

> The Bible is not Word of God on earth in the same way as Jesus Christ, very God and very man, is that Word in heaven. The being of Jesus Christ as the Word of God even in His humanity requires neither promise nor faith. The act in which He becomes the Word of God in His humanity requires neither repetition nor confirmation.[64]

This third difference between Jesus and the other forms of revelation has to do with his being "in heaven." It is closely related to the fact that the human nature of Jesus is exalted in a way that the Bible and proclamation are not. The human nature of Jesus was exalted into a new fellowship with God, becoming obedient and sinless. Therefore, he is a perfect instrument for God. In this exaltation, Jesus in his human nature has the power to convey God's revelation by his presence. On the other hand, we can read the words of the Bible without hearing God's Word. Barth states:

> It is also that if we are serious about the true humanity of the Bible, we obviously cannot attribute to the Bible as such the

> capacity--and in this it is distinguished, as
> we have seen, from the exalted and glorified
> humanity of Jesus Christ--in such a way to
> reveal God to us that by its very presence, by
> the fact that we can read it, it gives us a
> hearty faith in the Word of God spoken in
> it.[65]

It is possible to understand these distinctions of
Jesus and his relation to God without abandoning the
Antiochian position. According to this interpretation,
none of these unique features of Jesus threatens his being
as a complete human person. He is ontologically prior to
all other media through God's election of him from the
beginning. [66] It is also clear that God does not need
to recreate the life of Jesus on earth or establish a
similar relation with another person. His presence in
Jesus accomplished his purpose and does not need to be
repeated. For the Antiochian view, the other two points,
that Jesus is the Word of God independently of faith and
that his humanity has the power to reveal God, have to do
with Jesus' exaltation. Since his exaltation is the
result of God's act, it is clear that the power of the
human nature is lent to it by God's grace. In the final
analysis, this power does not belong to him as such.

While Barth has more to say about the uniqueness of
Jesus, we have mentioned the principal factors which arise
in his discussion of Jesus as a form of revelation. We
shall later take note of the concept of the incarnation
and the light it throws upon this topic.[67]

In conclusion, it must be admitted that a rather
persuasive case has been presented for the Antiochian view
that Barth conceives of the divinity of Christ as a
divinity of participation rather than a divinity of
essence. Barth's close association of Jesus with the
Bible and the creaturely phenomenon of proclamation
throughout his development of the notions of the finite
character of the forms of revelation and their indirect
identity with God's Word suggests that Jesus is simply a
man who occupies a special role in God's plan.

According to an Antiochian interpretation of Barth, it
is God's presence and action in Jesus and other creaturely
forms which are, strictly speaking, divine. However,

since these forms actually do convey God's message in the moment of revelation, they become a part of that message. The content cannot be separated from these forms. Further, since God's message or Word is identical with God Himself, these forms must also become, in some sense, identical with God. Because of this identity, the attribution of divinity to these forms is allowable. However, it must be clearly recognized that this divinity does not belong to them as such. In themselves, the forms have no divine power.

BARTH'S CONCEPT OF THE UNITY OF THE PERSON OF JESUS CHRIST IN AN ANTIOCHIAN PERSPECTIVE

Having discussed the Antiochian view of Barth's concept of the divinity of Christ, we turn now to the unity of his person. Since Barth identifies Christ with his history, his act, and his work, the concept of his unity covers considerable territory.[68] Our purpose here is not to investigate thoroughly all the dimensions of this subject but to focus upon those which are particularly relevant for an Antiochian interpretation. Because this topic has been and still is an important area of debate between Antiochian and Alexandrian ways of thinking, many aspects of it are pertinent for the question before us. In the Antiochian view, Barth's treatment of these aspects is intended to safeguard the independence of the man Jesus as a person distinct from God.

   It is appropriate to begin with Barth's handling of the question of whether the eternal Son exists apart from his unity with human nature. Then we shall consider Barth's treatment of the incarnation. In this respect, the concepts of anhypostasis and enhypostasis are particularly significant, since they pertain to the nature of the existence of the human nature in its relation to the existence of the Logos. Next, as we deal with Barth's doctrine of the two natures, we shall follow his order by looking first at the relation between God and the human nature, second at the characteristics of the resulting unity of the two natures, and third at the accompanying coordination of the divine and human aspects of the one work of Christ. Finally, we shall discuss briefly the significance of Barth's claim that Jesus Christ is a history.

The Logos Asarkos

Since Antiochian theology emphasizes the distinction between Jesus and God, the Antiochian interpretation of Barth tends to minimize the implications of his rejection of the logos asarkos. It argues that Barth's affirmation of the logos ensarkos means that all the activities of the Logos are determined by his intention to become man. Therefore, the Logos with whom dogmatics deals is not without form and content.[69]

Since Barth accepts the concept of the logos ensarkos, this raises the question of the preexistence of the flesh. If there is no Logos without the flesh, it follows that the flesh exists, in some sense, throughout eternity, even prior to the incarnation. Barth accepts this implication, stating "But the man Jesus already was even before He was."[70] Does Barth mean that the man Jesus exists in a real sense, as a concrete being, before his temporal life as a man? In order to safeguard the importance of Jesus' life as a man in time, one who follows an Antiochian interpretation of Barth may turn to the concept of God's intention. According to this view, Barth means that the man Jesus exists in God's plan before that plan is executed in time. Since God decides in his eternity for Jesus to exist as a man and to play a significant role in the salvation of all men, it follows that Jesus exists in the mode of God's intention. However, this does not mean that he exists as a concrete being. This Antiochian interpretation of Barth can be supported by many specific texts in the Church Dogmatics.[71]

While arguing that the Logos does not exist and cannot be known apart from his unity with the flesh, Barth affirms the logos asarkos in a very limited, theoretical sense. He admits that the concept is necessary for theological reflection.[72] Although the logos asarkos is an abstraction, it safeguards the idea of the freedom of God. The Logos chose to become man; however, since he might have chosen otherwise, his flesh is not his by necessity but through his free choice. By nature, the

Logos is divine.[73] According to the Antiochian view, the concept of the logos asarkos, even in the restricted form affirmed by Barth, denies that the man Jesus is a mere aspect of God's being. Therefore, the concept of the logos asarkos grants to Jesus a relative degree of independence.

Despite Barth's admission of a limited value for the logos asarkos as an abstraction, his major concern is to point out the defects of the concept. Because the logos asarkos is an abstraction, Barth explains, it has no form and content; it is an empty concept. Therefore, even when we are considering the eternal Word of God who precedes the activity of God in time and who participates in all God's work, it is "pointless" and "impermissible" to refer to the logos asarkos. The Logos became man, and it is this act and the decision which is presupposed by this act which give him form and content. If we attempt to go behind this act and decision to a logos asarkos, Barth argues, then we are tempted to invent all sorts of content for him. That would make us guilty of worshipping an image of God which we have created for ourselves. It is hard to see how such an attempt to bypass the form and content which the Word has in the incarnation could be considered real faith and obedience. Furthermore, it would lead to the question of whether the logos asarkos might not reveal himself through other media than the man Jesus.[74]

In the eyes of an interpreter who sees Barth as an Antiochian, these explanations of the weaknesses of the idea of the logos asarkos do not imply that the man Jesus already exists in God before his incarnation in such a way that his existence in time is merely a revelation of what has already happened in God. According to an Antiochian interpretation, Barth's reliance upon the concept of the decision of God indicates that Jesus is present in the mode of intention.[75] The decision of the Logos gives him content and form even before this event is actualized in time.[76] Since he is the one who is to become incarnate, it is proper to say that he is fully God and fully man from eternity.[77] Further, in the Antiochian view, Barth uses other means to maintain a distinction between Jesus' life in time and his being in eternity. Those who accept an Antiochian understanding can point out that

Barth states that Jesus' life is limited in time, just as
that of other creatures.[78]   Such a statement is
difficult to make consistent with the claim that Jesus'
primary existence is located in heaven with God prior to
his incarnation, a claim which implies that his time is
unlimited.   Consequently, those who follow an Antiochian
interpretation of Barth tend to conclude that Barth
rejects the idea of Jesus' being with God eternally.[79]
    Other means of maintaining the distinction between
Jesus' existence in time and the existence of the Logos
include the claim that Jesus is "not eternal as God
is"[80] and the belief that Jesus' incarnation is a new
actualization in history.[81]   If Jesus' eternity is
different from God's, and if his entrance into history is
a really new event in time, then his being in eternity
does not obscure the reality of his human existence as a
man.
    According to Kehm, moreover, we must not restrict
Jesus' preexistence to his being in God's intention.   His
preexistence has two other forms.   In the first place, he
was prefigured in the history of the people of Israel.
This does not mean that Israel performed the deeds that
Jesus was to perform, but the convenant which was fulfilled and revealed in Jesus was operative in the relation
between God and Israel.   In the second place, Jesus'
history was prefigured in the structure of creation.
Because Jesus was the object of the divine will, creation
was structured for the sake of the election of Jesus.[82]
In none of these modes, however, is the significance of
Jesus' existence in history undermined.
    Finally, in the attempt to show that Jesus' being with
God prior to the incarnation does not undercut his relatively independent life as a human person in time, those
who defend the Antiochian position might argue that the
preexistence of Jesus should be contrasted with his
existence after the resurrection.   In the former existence, Jesus does not exist as an actual being in God,
while in the latter he does.   The resurrection is not
merely a reinstatement of Jesus' eternal mode of being, it
is the beginning of a new state.   Jesus Christ now exists
in the mode of God.[83]

The Incarnation

Although Barth's development of the doctrine of the incarnation involves concepts such as theotokos, anhypostasis, and enhypostasis,[84] which have traditionally been used to defend the Alexandrian viewpoint, there is considerable evidence for the claim that even here Barth stands within the Antiochian framework. Both the overall structure and also the details of his doctrine contain important Antiochian elements. In order to present a statement of Barth's doctrine of the incarnation which captures the pattern of his thinking and accentuates the features which support an Antiochian interpretation, we shall focus upon five points. First, we shall note Barth's emphasis upon the fact that the incarnation is an act of God himself in his second mode of being. Next, it is important to consider Barth's characterization of this act as an assumption. The third point has to do with the reality which is assumed in this act. Fourth, the concepts of anhypostasis and enhypostasis, which play a crucial role in Barth's doctrine of the incarnation and which offer grounds for debate between interpreters of Alexandrian and Antiochian persuasion, demand attention. Finally, we shall investigate Barth's claim that the subject who acts through the human nature is God himself.

The Act of God the Word

Barth is noted for his emphasis upon the freedom, transcendence, and sovereignty of God. This theme expresses itself in Barth's treatment of this doctrine in the claim that the incarnation is the act of God alone. If God had not taken the initiative, making himself an object of man's knowledge, there is no way we could know him through our own powers of discovery. Nor is there any way that we could reconcile ourselves with God. Our knowledge of God, reconciliation, and redemption depend upon the fact that God becomes incarnate.

God's act in the incarnation is free. It stems from his will, yet it is not arbitrary, a mere whim. It executes the decision that God made in his inner being in eternity, and all other acts of God and men have their purpose and reality in it. God is not coerced by anything outside himself nor by any inner need to express himself in this way. His being lacks nothing, for he enjoys love and fellowship in himself. This act is the outward expression of his loving and graceful nature.[85]

In order to safeguard the divine character of this act, Barth is quite specific that there is a radical dissimilarity between the incarnation and the creation. The former is not simply the continuation of the latter. Jesus Christ as a man is not the result of the powers and possibilities of the created order. Jesus' life in history, his human existence, requires a new and special act of God, distinct from the creative act which brought the rest of the created order into being.[86]

Because it is necessary to affirm that the incarnation is the act of God alone, it is also important to indicate how this act is related to God's inner threeness. Barth explains that all three "persons" of the trinity are involved in this act, each one in his own way. Through the principle of appropriations we affirm that it is the Word or Son of God, and not the Father or the Holy Spirit, who assumes human nature and becomes a man.[87]

These points are consistent with an Antiochian theology, for they emphasize the grace of God and the distinction between God and man. We have mentioned that Antiochian thought is characterized by an emphasis upon God's "good pleasure." This term indicates that it is through God's voluntary act that he became united to man in a special way in the incarnation. The union with Jesus precedes his birth in time; it is not merely the result of Jesus' obedience. Consequently, the incarnation stems from God's love and grace; it is not an act of man.[88]

Becoming and Assuming

Alexandrian theology has tended to emphasize the scriptural proclamation that the Word became flesh. Antiochian thought, while arguing that it is the Word who acted in the incarnation, has tended to interpret that becoming as an "assuming." In that way, it avoided the implication that the Word was transformed into something other than himself when he became man.[89] Barth's interpretation follows this line. He emphasizes this "becoming," but he explains that it really is an "assuming." The concept of this assumption by God the Word plays a crucial role in his theology.[90]

The verb "becoming," Barth explains, designates a miraculous act. How can the Word become something different from himself without surrendering his divinity? The claim that the eternal Word of God has become flesh is startling and incomprehensible, for it declares that the eternal God exists in the same way that creatures exist. "He the eternal Subject now exists--a stumbling-block to all Jewish ears and foolishness to all Greek ears--just as anything else or anyone else exists."[91] Since becoming is a process usually ascribed to creatures rather than God, it is in tension with the concept of the Word and cannot be systematically coordinated with it.

Barth explains that the act of becoming is initiated by the Son or Word of God; it is not something which happens to him. However, the term "becoming" seems to imply passivity and dependency, and it is normally applied to realities which come into being through some power other than themselves. As a result, we must be quite clear about its meaning in this instance. "In the sense of the concept familiar to us, we can therefore assert 'becoming' only of the human being, in order by that very means to give expression to the inconceivable becoming of the divine Word." Barth appears to mean that "becoming" applies strictly to the human nature, and then secondarily to the Word because of his relation to the human nature. There is "no becoming which as such can be the becoming of the Word."[92]

A closer and more exact characterization of this act, insofar as it is the act of the eternal Son, can be given by the terms "assuming," "adopting," "incorporating," or "taking up." Barth states:

> Accordingly we have to give a closer explana-
> tion of the act peculiar to this miracle, the
> incarnation of the Word. As the Word of God
> becomes flesh He assumes or adopts or incor-
> porates human being into unity with His divine
> being, so that this human being, as it comes
> into being, becomes as a human being the being
> of the Word of God.[93]

These alternative terms indicate that the Word or Son is
in control of this action, and there is precedent for them
in the scriptures and traditions of the church.[94]

Another advantage of the paraphrase "the Word assumed
flesh" is that it guards against the misinterpretation
that the incarnation is such a uniting of divine and human
being that it produces a third kind of being. In the
incarnation Jesus Christ is not a third being, rather he
is the mediator between God and man in such a way that he
is both God and man.[95]

In conclusion of this discussion of becoming and
assuming, we should point out that Barth's position seems
to imply a theory of predication similar to that of
Theodore's. "Becoming" does not apply to the Word but to
the human nature. However, since the Bible uses this term
in reference to the Word, this usage implies that all
predicates which belong to the human nature can also be
applied to the Word, although they do not apply to him in
the strict sense. While Barth does not work out a detailed theory here, it is possible to conclude that he
means that "becoming" applies directly to the human nature
but indirectly and by relation to the eternal Word who is
united to the human nature.

What Is Assumed

When Barth comes to this topic, he attacks the terminology
favored by Theodore of Mopsuestia, who spoke of the Word
assuming a man.[96] To say that the Word assumed flesh,
Barth declares, does not mean that the Word assumed a
particular man. The word "flesh" should not be understood
to mean a man, but humanity or human nature, "that which
makes a man man as opposed to God, angel, or animal."[97]
If we were to suppose that God assumed an already existing
man, this would lead to erroneous conclusions. In the
first place, it would make one an adoptionist, suggesting
the Pelagian overtones of that position.[98] Secondly, it
would imply either that God was transformed into a man,
surrendering his own existence and ceasing to be God, or
that the Son of God was no longer existing as one but as a
duality, maintaining his own existence alongside the
existence of this individual man.[99]

What existed over against God and what was assumed by God, Barth explains, was the possibility of being a man, the potentiality of human existence. Concretely, the potentiality over against God the Word in this particular case was

> the one specific possibility of the first son of Mary. The Word appropriated this possibil-ity to Himself as His own, and He realized it as such when He became Jesus. In so doing He did not cease to be what He was before, but He became what He was not before, a man, this man.[100]

This explanation of what was assumed guards against the errors mentioned above. God does not merely approve of some man and adopt him into a special relation, nor does he change himself into a man. In the union, he is not divided into two; in fact the man which the Word became does not exist outside of his union with God. Barth states:

> As the Son of God made His own this one specific possibility of human essence and existence and made it a reality, this Man came into being, and He, the Son of God, became this Man. This Man was thus never a reality by Himself, and therefore, since the Son of God became this man, He is not another being in Jesus Christ alongside of the Son of God.[101]

The creaturely reality assumed by God into unity with himself was not merely the possibility of the man Jesus but also the human nature and essence of all men; "it is not merely one man, but the humanum of all men, which is posited and exalted as such to unity with God."[102] Because the human nature of all men is involved, this act has universal significance.

Finally, Barth turns to the question of whether the human nature that was assumed is sinless or sinful. He chooses the latter alternative, concluding that the Son of God "though without sin . . . was made to be sin."[103]

In his discussion of the ramifications of this choice, Barth makes a point which Antiochian interpreters consider to be quite significant because it suggests that the human nature of the Logos is a person. Barth states that the human nature has its own will, distinct from the will of God. If we did not maintain the existence of this human will, Barth thinks, then we would not be able to guarantee that Jesus was truly a man like us and therefore tempted, although he did not sin.

> It was in this wrestling, in which He was in solidarity with us to the uttermost, that there was done that which is not done by us, the will of God. . . . From this may be seen how right was the attitude of those who in the so-called monothelite controversy of the 7th century upheld and eventually led to victory the doctrine that along with the true human nature of the God-Man there must likewise not be denied His true, human will, different from the will of God although never independent of it.[104]

If one thinks of the will as the constitutive element of the self, it would seem to follow that the assumed human nature is a true, individual self, although it is also the human nature of all men. Austin Farrer, for example, argues that the will is the basic characteristic of a self because it provides continuity of the self through time.[105] Groff believes that the will is the "finite substance" which is the human subject or self, and he interprets Barth accordingly.[106]

In the next section on Barth's concepts of anhypostasis and enhypostasis, we shall encounter more information which supports the idea that the human nature is a person. We shall also explain how Barth's claim that the Word assumes a possibility of a man rather than a man fits into an Antiochian framework. Those who defend an Antiochian interpretation of Barth can reasonably conclude that although the human nature is not a man before the act of assumption, it becomes a man in that act.

Anhypostasis and Enhypostasis

There are three major topics in Barth's analysis of anhypostasis and enhypostasis which bear directly upon the question of whether Barth is Alexandrian or Antiochian. They concern the concept of existence, the personality of the human nature, and the uniqueness of Jesus' existence in comparison with the existence of other creatures. We shall present Barth's position with respect to these issues, and then we shall indicate how that position can be interpreted from an Antiochian perspective.

Barth turns to the concepts of anhypostasis and enhypostasis to defend his argument that the human nature which God assumed exists neither prior to nor apart from its assumption by God. According to Barth, anhypostasis states that the human nature has no independent existence, while enhypostasis states that the human nature has its existence in and through the existence of the eternal Son. Thus, these two ideas are integrally related to one another, and both are necessarily implied by a proper understanding of the act of the incarnation. Barth states:

> But from the utter uniqueness of this unity follows the statement, that God and Man are so related in Jesus Christ, that He exists as Man so far and only so far as He exists as God, i.e. in the mode of existence of the eternal Word of God. What we thereby express is a doctrine unanimously sponsored by early theology in its entirety, that of the anhypostasis and enhypostasis of the human nature of Christ. Anhypostasis asserts the negative. Since in virtue of the egeneto, i.e., in virtue of the assumptio, Christ's human nature has its existence--the ancients said, its subsistence--in the existence of God, meaning in the mode of being (hypostasis, 'person') of the Word, it does not possess it in and for itself, in abstracto. Apart from the divine mode of being whose existence it acquires it has none of its own; i.e., apart from its concrete existence in God in the event of the

unio, it has no existence of its own, it is anhypostatos.   Enhypostasis   asserts   the positive.   In virtue of the egeneto, i.e., in virtue of the assumptio, the human nature acquires   existence   (subsistence)   in   the existence of God, meaning in the mode of being (hypostasis, 'person') of the Word.   This divine mode of being gives it existence in the event of the unio, and in this way it has a concrete   existence   of   its   own,   it   is enhypostatos. . . . The aim of the doctrine, erected into dogma at the Second Council of Constantinople in 553 (Anath. de tribus cap., can. 5, Denz. No. 217), was to guard against the idea of a double existence of Christ as Logos and as Man, an idea inevitably bound to lead either to Docetism or to Ebionitism. We have seen earlier that what the eternal Word made His own, giving it thereby His own existence, was not a man, but man's nature, man's being, and so not a second existence but a second possibility of existence, to wit, that of a man. [107]

Concerning the relation of the two concepts to the personality of the human nature, Barth reports that some opponents of anhypostasis believe that this concept denies that the man Jesus is a real person with his own personality. Such an interpretation is based on a misunderstanding of the terms impersonalitas and individualitas; Barth explains:

In recent times the doctrine of the anhypostasis and enhypostasis of Christ's human nature has occasionally been combated by the primitive argument, that if the human nature of Christ is without personality of its own, it is all up with the true humanity of Christ and the Docetism of early Christology holds the field. In other words we moderns should be aware that personality really does belong to true human being. This argument is primitive because it rests simply upon a misunderstand-

ing of the Latin term impersonalitas used
occasionally for anhypostasis. But what
Christ's human nature lacks according to the
early doctrine is not what we call personality. This the early writers called individualitas, and they never taught that Christ's
human nature lacked this, but rather that this
qualification actually belonged to true human
being. Personalitas was their name for what
we call existence or being. Their negative
position asserted that Christ's flesh in
itself has no existence, and this was asserted
in the interests of their positive position
that Christ's flesh has its existence through
the Word and in the Word, who is God Himself
acting as Revealer and Reconciler.[108]

Thus, the personalitas denied by the ancients referred to
existence or being; personality, which they called
individualitas, was not denied to the human nature.
 Finally, the concepts of anhypostasis and enhypostasis
are especially significant because they specify the
uniqueness of the existence of the man Jesus and his human
nature. Because Jesus is not independent of God's existence in the manner of other creaturely beings and because
he has his existence only in the existence of God, Jesus
Christ is identical with God in a way that distinguishes
him from all other beings.
 There is a unity of God with all creation, because God
is present in it and because it has its existence through
God. However, created being has its own existence which
is different from God's existence. There is also a unity
of God with the human words of preaching, the elements of
the sacraments, and the hearts of believers. They are
inseparably bound to God, but they also have their own
existence and, therefore, are not identical with God.[109]
 There are several reasons why Barth's development of
the concepts of anhypostasis and enhypostasis seem to
support an Antiochian interpretation. In the first place,
since Barth attributes a personality, in addition to a
will, to the human nature, it is clear that the human
nature is personal, at least in a limited sense. Further,
when we examine what Barth means by personality, and when

we discover that he correlates this concept with self-consciousness and person, the impression that he conceives the human nature as a concrete individual receives reinforcement.

When he discusses the doctrine of the trinity in the first part-volume of the Church Dogmatics, Barth states that the modern notion of personality differs from the ancient concept in that it adds the attribute of self-consciousness.[110] Similarly, in response to a question regarding the doctrines of appropriations and perichoresis in Karl Barth's Table Talk, he equates the modern notion of personality with "centre of consciousness."[111] Consequently, when Barth asserts above that the human element of the incarnation has what "we moderns" call personality and what the ancients called individualitas, he clearly means that it has its own self-consciousness.

The question now arises as to whether Barth thinks that self-consciousness is the essential characteristic of a person. He does not answer this question directly, but he often speaks as though personality and person were identical concepts. For example, in his principal elaboration of the doctrine of the trinity, Barth argues that God is one person and one personality. Understood in their modern sense, these concepts apply to God's essence rather than his threeness. Used in this way, they emphasize that God is a single willer and doer, one "I." If they were used in reference to the three in God, Barth explains, they would suggest there are three self-consciousnesses in God. The resulting doctrine would be open to the charge of tritheism. Throughout this argument, Barth uses the terms "personality" and "person" interchangeably, and he gives no indication that they have different meanings.[112]

Whether or not Barth consistently defines a person as a being with a self-consciousness, some Antiochian theologians accept such a definition.[113] As a result, they are inclined to conclude that Barth's characterization of the human nature of the incarnation is consistent with their theological emphasis upon the distinction of the person Jesus from the person God.[114]

Therefore, if the human nature which God assumes is a person, why doesn't Barth call it "a man"? The answer to this question lies in the fact that Barth ties the concepts of anhypostasis and enhypostasis to the idea of existence. Consequently, these concepts deal directly with the exact moment in which God the Word comes to exist in time, the beginning of his life as a man. They are used to explain the character of that instant in which the human nature passes from a state of possibility into a state of existence. This use of anhypostasis and enhypostasis contrasts with their traditional function of describing the relation between the divine nature and the human nature during the life time of Jesus, between his birth and his death as a man.[115]

The fact that Barth uses anhypostasis and enhypostasis in this way gives considerable credence to an Antiochian interpretation. In such an understanding, Barth uses the concept of human nature rather than man because it does not imply that there was some individual, a man, who was in existence prior to the act of assuming. If he existed prior to this moment, he would have an independent existence, and thus the concept of enhypostasis would not apply. However, according to an Antiochian interpretation, Barth apparently means that once the human nature of Christ passed from a state of possibility to a state of existence, it became a complete human person who finds his fulfillment in his unique relation to God the Word.

As a result, Barth's denial that there was a man existing prior to the act of assumption poses no threat to an Antiochian theology, although it contradicts Theodore's usual manner of speaking. Antiochians are not necessarily adoptionists, and therefore polemics against adoptionism do not come to grips with the heart of Antiochian thought.[116] Antiochian theology at its best affirms that Jesus comes into being and accomplishes his mission through God's grace. He does not earn or merit his unique relation to God; this is chosen for him by God.

Nor do Antiochians claim that God transformed himself into a man. They argue that the Logos is still the Logos, unchanged in his nature, even though he is united to the man Jesus. Thus, the errors that Barth hopes to avoid by arguing that the Logos assumed flesh or human nature, and not a man, are errors that the Antiochians also wish to preclude.

In an Antiochian view, then, Barth's denial that the Logos assumed a man has rather limited import. It is understood to apply strictly to the moment in which the Word is incarnated. Barth does not deny, according to this interpretation, that after this initial moment there was a man named Jesus who was related to God. Although the human nature involved was not a complete person before the act of assuming, it was after this event.

The question upon which the Antiochian and Alexandrian interpreters of Barth divide is this: in the affirmation that the Word of God existed as a man in time, does "a man" refer primarily to God the Word or does it refer primarily to the human nature which is united with the Word? Those who see Barth as an Antiochian theologian choose the latter alternative; they understand "a man" as a reference to the human nature after the initial instant of the incarnation. Those who understand Barth as an Alexandrian theologian interpret the "a man" as a reference to the Logos who, after the moment of assumption, possesses a human nature.

The Antiochian view of what Barth means by "a man" seems to be given support by Barth's treatment of the concept of becoming. We have noted that Barth indicates that "becoming" is misleading when it is applied to the Word. Since this term suggests that whatever "becomes" is subject to circumstances beyond its control, it applies directly to the human nature and indirectly to God the Word. When we speak strictly of the act of the Word, the term "assumes" is more appropriate.

If the predicate "becomes" applies, strictly speaking, to the human nature, it would seem to follow that the same principle operates with respect to the predicate "a man." The term "a man" also implies that the reality designated by it is subject to circumstances beyond its control, and that would apparently not be true of the Logos, at least not in the strictest sense. The Logos places himself under the conditions which determine men, of course, but he does not relinquish his control over these conditions. Thus, it appears that he can be said to be a man and subject to these conditions because of his relation to Jesus.

Further, if we say that it is the human nature which, in the correct sense, "becomes," the question arises: what does the human nature become? The Antiochian interpretation of Barth provides a ready answer: a man. In the act of incarnation, the human nature of the Logos, that is, the particular possibility of the man Jesus, became what it was not before; it became the man Jesus. This particular specimen of human nature passed from a state of possibility into a state of existence.

Those who accept an Antiochian interpretation of Barth, then, understand the affirmation that the Word of God is a man in a secondary and derived sense. The Word of God can be said to be a man only because of his relation to the man Jesus. By nature he is divine, not human. This conclusion is consistent with the view that the identity of the Word with Jesus is an indirect identity, based upon the Word's act of assuming.

The Antiochian interpretation of Barth's treatment of the anhypostasis and enhypostasis is also supported by Barth's statement that humans become persons not in themselves but through their relation to God.

> Man is not a person, but he becomes one on the basis that he is loved by God and can love God in return. Man finds what a person is when he finds it in the person of God and his own being as a person in the gift of fellowship afforded him by God in person. He is then (in his own way as creature) a person wholly and exclusively in the fellowship of Him who (in His way as creator) is it in Himself.[117]

If one applies this to the incarnation, it seems to imply that the human nature which God assumed could become a person through its fellowship with God.

Given this perspective, some passages which seem to be directly opposed to Antiochian thought, because they deny that the human nature of Jesus is a person, can be interpreted in a way that makes them consistent with Antiochian beliefs. For example, when Barth states that "humanity, without being or having itself a person, is caught up into fellowship with the personality of God,"[118] an Antiochian can interpret this pronouncement as meaning that the human nature of Jesus is not a person in isolation or in separation from God the Word. But in its relation to the Word, the human nature of Jesus is understood to become a person who is distinct from the person of the Word himself.

Similarly, when Barth denies that there are two beings "side by side" or "alongside" each other in Christ,[119] those who accept an Antiochian view of Barth focus upon the "side by side" and the "alongside" rather than the "two." They believe that Barth is denying that there is a mechanical or external relation between Jesus and God; they do not conclude that Barth is denying that the man Jesus is a person over against God. Consequently, they can agree with what they think Barth means.

Although those who follow an Antiochian interpretation of Barth conclude that the human nature becomes a person who is distinct from the person of God, they do not assume that this person exists apart from or outside the existence of God. As a man, Jesus can be understood to exist within the existence of God the Word. This is the import of the concept of enhypostasis. What is crucial for the Antiochian interpretation of Barth is that it is a person, a man, who exists in the existence of God, not simply a human nature which is not fully individualized.

But how can those who interpret Barth as an Antiochian theologian give credence to Barth's claim that the man Jesus has no independent existence? For these interpreters, Barth's denial of Jesus' independent existence means that the man Jesus was brought into being by God's creative act and that he existed in a unique and intimate relation to God himself. He did not exist outside, or independently of, the guiding power and influence of God himself. He was obedient to God in a unique degree, and through his service to God he accomplished a special mission. In his role as a revealer and reconciler he occupies a place in God's plan that is unique. Yet, in this relationship, the man Jesus enjoyed freedom and responsibility as did other men.

According to an Antiochian interpretation, Barth's claim that Jesus has no independent existence should be understood in a relativistic sense, to indicate that the difference between Jesus' relation to God and the relation of other creatures to God is a matter of degree. Jesus is less independent from God, and more closely bound to him, than any other creatures, although this does not make him an aspect of God's being. He is still a man who is inseparably bound to God. But since it is also proper to say that the human words of the Bible and the creaturely

phenomena of proclamation are inseparably bound to God,
some means must be found to specify the unique degree to
which Jesus is united with God. The concepts of anhypostasis and enhypostasis serve this purpose.
    In the Antiochian interpretation of Barth, God's
existence includes the man Jesus in such a way that this
relation can not be fully understood and which is, therefore, a mystery. The concepts of anhypostasis and enhypostasis point to this mystery. They affirm that Jesus'
relation to God is unique, but they do not specify exactly
how this uniqueness is to be understood. In the final
analysis, God's presence in Jesus and his relation to
Jesus differ only in degree, not in kind, from his presence in, and his relation to, other creatures.[120]
    A question arises regarding the boundaries of the
concepts anhypostasis and enhypostasis. Although it is
clear from what we have said above that Barth's emphasis
upon the idea of existence demands that these two concepts
have direct implications for the instant in which God
enters the creaturely realm, it is not so clear that the
significance of these concepts is limited to this moment.
Because Barth emphasizes the act of God and because this
act can have duration in time, it seems unwise to restrict
the incarnation to one moment. If anhypostasis and
enhypostasis apply to the beginning of God's existence as
a man in time, should they not also apply to the whole of
God's existence as a man in time, that is, to the time of
Jesus's life? It is our view that Pannenberg fails to
take account of Barth's actualism when he limits the
significance of anhypostasis and enhypostasis, in Barth's
theology, to the entrance of God into time.[121] It seems
more reasonable to apply them as well to the mode of the
relation between God and the human nature in the one life
of Jesus Christ.
    If the notions of anhypostasis and enhypostasis are
intended by Barth to apply to the mode of the relation of
the human nature to God, would that pose a serious obsta-
cle to an Antiochian interpretation of Barth? We have
seen that the application of these concepts to the beginning of Jesus Christ's existence as a man can be explained
reasonably by those who classify Barth as Antiochian.
Such interpreters can agree that there was no man in
existence before the event of the incarnation but still

conclude that after the initial moment a particular man came into being and was established by God's grace in a special relation with God. If the notions of anhypostasis and enhypostasis apply to every moment of the life of Jesus as a man, would it follow that in every moment God the Word assumes a human nature? And if so, would it also follow that the human nature itself cannot become a man?

It is our view that the application of the concepts of anhypostasis and enhypostasis to the whole life of Jesus Christ as a man does not pose an insurmountable problem for an Antiochian interpretation of Barth. While it might appear that a renewed assumption of the human nature, instead of a man, in every moment would not allow any "time" for the human nature to become a man, actually it would allow as much "time" for the human nature to become a man as it allows for the Word to become a man. And Barth is quite clear that a man does come into being in this event. Thus, one who accepts an Antiochian interpretation can apply the concepts of anhypostasis and enhypostasis to the whole life of Jesus Christ, understanding them as affirming that in each moment two things happen: first, the Word assumes a human nature, which is to say that the Word assumes the possibility of a man, and, second, the human nature which he assumes becomes a man.

Whether anhypostasis and enhypostasis are limited to the initial moment of Jesus Christ's existence as a man or whether they apply to every moment in his life, the Antiochian interpretation of Barth does not appear to be undermined. There may be elements of occasionalism in Barth, but this occasionalism allows the continual positing of the man Jesus who has a special relation to God the Word.[122]

In conclusion, it is clear that the concepts of anhypostasis and enhypostasis are not restricted to Alexandrian theology. They can be used to substantiate key points in an Antiochian position.[123] This is also true of Barth's treatment of the claim that God is the subject who acts through the man Jesus. To show how this is the case, we need to consider Barth's position on this topic.

God Is Subject

Barth affirms that God is the subject of the qualities and actions of the man Jesus. This point is not simply a restatement of the fact that God initiates the incarnation by assuming flesh. It states that God also completes this work by existing in and acting through the human nature of Jesus. He is the dominant and decisive agent of the union. Barth's amplification of this idea consists of several steps.

Because God the Word assumes human nature and becomes identical with a particular man, it can be said that God exists as anything and everything else exists. He is visible just as other earthly forms are visible.[124] In fact, it is God's existence in an earthly form which gives reality to the human being and action involved.

> Thus the reality of Jesus Christ is that God Himself in person is actively present in the flesh. God Himself in person is the Subject of a real human being and acting. And just because God is the Subject of it, this being and acting are real. They are a genuinely and truly human being and acting.[125]

The beginning of the existence of the Son of God as a man was his birth from Mary. Because God is the subject of this event, it is proper to say that Mary is the Mother of God.

> He whom Mary bore was not something else, some second thing, in addition to His being God's Son. . . . In this case human being has an existence identical with the existence of the eternal Son of God.[126]

Because God himself is the subject who acts in and through the creaturely form, and because his existence is identical with Jesus' existence, the predicates which are attributable to men in general are also attributable to God. God has a human soul and body, and he is subject to the same limitations of temporality and environmental factors which impinge on the lives of ordinary men. Barth states:

> God's revelation to us takes place in such a
> way that everything ascribable to man, his
> creaturely existence as an individually unique
> unity of body and soul in the time between
> birth and death, can now be predicated of
> God's eternal Son as well.[127]

The fact that the qualities of human nature can now be
predicated of God himself is startling and confusing to a
mind characterized by ordinary thinking. We normally
think that the qualities of the divine nature distinguish
God from all reality which is not God, and that the
qualities which belong to men in general distinguish them
from God. Since these two sets of qualities are radically
different, it is difficult to conceive how they could be
said to belong to one subject. Barth admits this conceptual problem.

> It is apparent at once that divine and human
> essence cannot be united as the essence of one
> and the same subject. Offense at the state-
> ment that Jesus Christ is the One who is of
> divine and human essence, in whom the two are
> united, is quite unavoidable.[128]

Nevertheless, the reality of Jesus Christ demands this
statement. It is made not as a general statement about
what may happen or about a unity which exists everywhere
and at all times. Rather, the affirmation that Jesus
Christ is both human and divine is an affirmation about
this particular subject and what took place and still
takes place in him.[129]

Because this statement can and must be made about this
one subject, our willingness to make it is evidence
that we are using reason correctly. Since reason should
conform to its object, only a reason which is committed to
certain general presuppositions, such as the view that
divine and human essence cannot be united under any
circumstances, will fail to acknowledge the reality of
this particular object.[130]

Not only are the qualities of human nature in general
predicable of God because of his identity with the man
Jesus, the actions of Jesus are also attributable to him.

When Jesus called his disciples, preached, walked, and
ate, God was the agent. Further, the experiences of Jesus
were also the experiences of God. Barth says:

> God Himself is in the world, earthly,
> conceivable and visible, as He is this man.
> We have to do with God Himself as we have to
> do with this man. God Himself speaks when
> this man speaks in human speech. God Himself
> acts and suffers when this man acts and
> suffers as a man. God Himself triumphs when
> this One triumphs as a man.[131]

The fact that the eternal God himself existed in a
human form which was characterized by man's fallen condition does not mean that God actually sinned. In Barth's
understanding, the sinlessness of Jesus Christ is directly
dependent upon the identity of Jesus Christ with God
himself. Because God is the subject who acts in Jesus, it
is inconceivable that he could sin. Barth declares:

> This Man would not be God's revelation to us,
> God's reconciliation with us, if He were not,
> as true Man, the true, unchangeable, perfect
> God Himself. . . . In it (our human being) God
> Himself is the Subject. How can God sin, deny
> Himself to Himself, be against Himself as God
> . . .?[132]

Through the presence of God in this human form, the
human form which is common to all sinful people is made
into a sinless human form.[133]
Because the subject who acts here is God himself, it
cannot even be said that he was seriously tempted. Jesus
Christ was bound to win in the struggle with temptation,
because he is identical with God. Thus, even though we do
not deny a distinct human will to the human nature which
God assumed, there is an unavoidable contradiction between
the claim that Jesus Christ is identical with God and the
claim that "a true man had a serious struggle" with
temptation. We cannot provide "a systematic connexion"
between these claims, but only acknowledge them.[134]
Because God is the subject who acts in and through

the human nature which he assumed, we must also affirm
that he maintains all his divine powers in this state. To
do otherwise is to negate God's deity. This means,
according to Barth, that we must deny the views of the
so-called "kenotic" theology, according to which God the
Son surrendered his majesty when he became a man. Nor
should we accept the view that in the incarnation the
eternal Son suspended the use of his divine powers although he continued to possess them. On the contrary, we
should affirm that Jesus Christ, as the Son of God,
continues to possess and use his divine powers in his
incarnation, although he does so invisibly and in a way
that is not directly apparent. By attributing these
powers to Jesus Christ we undergird his unique relation
with God.[135]

Finally, because God is the subject who acts through
Jesus, the event of Christ is of universal significance.
Barth states:

> The human speaking and acting and suffering
> and triumphing of this one man directly
> concerns us all, and His history is our
> history of salvation which changes the whole
> human situation, just because God Himself is
> its human subject in His Son, just because God
> Himself has assumed and made His own our human
> nature and kind in His Son, just because God
> Himself came into this world in His Son, and
> as one of us "a guest this world of ours He
> trod."[136]

One who follows an Antiochian exegesis of Barth must
admit that Barth's development of the idea that God is the
subject of the actions and qualities of Jesus Christ
contains nothing that specifically requires an Antiochian
interpretation rather than an Alexandrian one. Barth does
not say explicitly, for example, that God is the direct
subject of the divine actions and the indirect subject of
the human actions of Jesus Christ. On the other hand,
since Barth does not specifically reject this Antiochian
theory, it is possible to interpret his elaboration of
this topic along Antiochian lines.

In this way of understanding Barth, the claim that God

exists now in a way that he had not existed before is permissible. This new form of existence is God's because of his unique participation in the existence of the man Jesus. Similarly, the Logos possesses ordinary human qualities and performs all the actions attributed to Jesus in the New Testament, but he does so indirectly rather than directly. It is also proper to say that the Logos was born of Mary, and that Mary is the Mother of God, but, again, these statements are possible because of the unique relation of the Logos with Jesus.

One who defends an Antiochian interpretation can also accept Barth's assessment of the limitations of human reason with respect to the claim that God is the subject of Jesus' actions. It seems inconceivable that God could be so intimately and uniquely related to this man that he experiences what this man experiences. The precise relation between God and this man remains beyond our power to comprehend. That the Word united with Jesus could not sin is clear, but how Jesus could be tempted and yet protected from sin remains a mystery. Jesus was guided and directed by the Word in such a way that he accomplished God's purpose; yet he did not become a mere automaton nor did he achieve his sinlessness through human power alone, in a Pelagian sense.

Finally, the Antiochian interpretation is not seriously threatened by Barth's belief that the incarnate Son exercises his divine power, although he refrains from its visible use. According to the Antiochian perspective, Barth attributes this power directly to God, but only indirectly to the man Jesus who is united with him.

With these remarks about Barth's understanding of God as the subject who brings the man Jesus into existence and acts through his humanity, we conclude our discussion of the incarnation itself. Now we turn more specifically to the question of how the unity of God with the human nature in the one person of Jesus Christ is conceived by Barth and interpreted in an Antiochian manner.

God the Word and the Human Nature

According to Barth, one must make a clear distinction between the union of God with the human nature and the union of the divine nature with the human nature. The union of God with human nature, the unio hypostatica, is different from the union of the two natures, the communio naturarum, in at least two ways. First, the unio hypostatica has to do with "the direct unity of the existence of the Son of God with the man Jesus of Nazareth."[137] That is, the unio hypostatica concerns the concept of existence, while the communio naturarum deals with the concept of nature or essence. Second, the unio hypostatica has to do with the foundation of the communio naturarum. Because "it was not the divine nature, the divinitas, but the Word which became flesh," it follows that the unio hypostatica precedes and establishes the communio naturarum. Therefore, one should consider first "the union of the Logos with the human nature" and then the communio naturarum which is included in it.[138]

Barth emphasizes that the union of the existence of God with his human nature is sui generis. Consequently, it cannot be understood on the basis of some other kind of union. To show that this is the case, Barth compares it with other unions, including the soul and body and husband and wife. In each instance, Barth explains how these other unions differ in crucial respects from that between God and the human nature he assumes in the incarnation.[139]

Those who defend an Antiochian interpretation of Barth can appreciate the central thrust of Barth's discussion. Antiochian theologians too consider it necessary to confess that the unio hypostatica is unique. Further, Antiochian theologians may take special interest in Barth's recognition that the Word has no need of human nature and that his uniting himself with the human nature is an act of love and grace. In this way, the unity established is different from the relation between the soul and body. The body is indispensable to the soul while the human nature is not indispensable for God. In addition, the eternal Son of God gives the human nature existence, while the soul does not give existence to the body.[140]

The Antiochian interpretation of Barth does not appear to be seriously threatened by Barth's assessment of the analogies of the unio hypostatica which Antiochian theologians have often preferred.[141] Barth emphasizes that

the union of God with the human nature is different from
the union of two human persons, such as friend and friend
or husband and wife. The oneness of mind between two
persons, Barth explains, rests upon mutual agreement or
the power of attraction, while the union of God with the
human nature in Christ rests upon the one-sided action of
God in condescending to man. Another difference, Barth
states, is that the two human persons involved in such
unions are self-existent, while the human nature of Jesus
does not exist independently from God.[142] According to
an Antiochian interpretation, Barth's analysis of the
limitations of this analogy does not imply that Jesus is
other than a human person, nor does it render the analogy
valueless. Barth's emphasis upon the limitations of all
analogies does not lead directly to the conclusion that no
analogies should be used.

Barth's treatment of another analogy, the relation
between God and the creaturely elements involved in the
sacraments, also lends itself to an Antiochian interpretation. One who defends an Antiochian view can note that
Barth admits that the sacramental union, or unio sacramentalis, is conceived by the older dogmatics in a way which
makes it remarkably similar to that between God and the
human nature of Jesus. Barth preserves the uniqueness of
the latter by denying that there is any sacramental unity
apart from Jesus Christ. There is only one unio sacramentalis, Barth declares, and that is the unio hypostatica.
It cannot be admitted that the union of God and the human
nature in the incarnation is analogous to that between God
and the creaturely elements of the sacraments. This
admission, Barth explains, would lead to the conclusion
that the church must be understood as the prolongation of
the incarnation. Since this doctrine of the church must
be rejected, so also must this analogy.[143]

According to an Antiochian interpretation, however,
the relative value of the analogy of the unio sacramentalis which is allowed by Barth should not be overlooked.
Since Barth often groups the man Jesus in the same category with the Bible and the creaturely realities involved
in proclamation, and since Barth affirms that the sacraments are forms of proclamation, it follows that there can
be an indirect identity of God with the bread and wine of
the Eucharist just as there can be an indirect identity of

God with Jesus. In the Antiochian view, Barth does not rule out the relative value of the analogy of the unio sacramentalis by his argument regarding its logical consequences. An Antiochian theology does not have to hold that this unity can be established at will by the church, and it can indicate the uniqueness of Jesus among the sacraments by referring to Barth's claim that Jesus has no independent existence while the sacramental phenomena do.

The Union of the Two Natures

The Antiochian interpretation of Barth receives considerable support from the way Barth develops the concept of the union of the two natures in Christ. Barth historicizes and actualizes this concept, emphasizing both the integrity of each nature and also their fellowship with each other in a historical process. The two natures seem to be understood as independent and personal in such a way that they are two persons, God and Jesus, united in fellowship through historical time. In order to show that this is the case, we need to look more carefully at Barth's explication of this doctrine.

In explaining his innovative interpretation of the union of the two natures, Barth states that he uses the traditional concepts of the unio hypostatica and the communio naturarum "as concentrically related terms to describe one and the same ongoing process." This process is Jesus Christ, who is the history in which God became man and man is exalted. As this history, Jesus Christ includes in himself all men and all history, and he continues to exist now as he has in the past.[144]

In this history, the two natures participate in each other. Because the Son of God became man, all the elements which are common to human beings are involved in the life of the Son. Therefore, the human essence participates in the divine essence. Conversely, the elements of the divine essence participate in the Son's life as a man. Therefore, they participate also in the human essence. [145]

When Barth explains the content of this participation, however, the basic thrust of his thought becomes

clear. The human nature is exalted into fellowship with
God. The mutual participation of the divine and human
essence is the fellowship of God and man.[146] This
fellowship is characterized more precisely by Barth in
three steps.

Impartation

The first of these steps is the mutual impartation of the
two essences. In this impartation, Barth explains, there
is a giving and a receiving. The divine essence gives or
imparts itself to the human essence, and the human essence
receives the divine essence. Conversely, the human
essence imparts itself to the divine essence, and the
divine essence receives the human. This relationship of
openness to each other is the fellowship of God and man in
history.[147]
    This mutual impartation of the two natures also means
that the qualities and actions of both natures can be
predicated of the one Son, Jesus Christ. The impartation
does not involve two Sons side by side.[148] Nor do the
qualities of either nature become the properties of the
other. If we assign divine qualities to the human nature,
so that the human nature is said to be, for example,
omnipotent, then we compromise both the humanity and the
deity of Christ. The two natures are imparted to one
another in the one Christ, but they maintain their separate identities.[149]

Address

The second step in Barth's detailed characterization of
the fellowship and mutual participation concerns the
address of God to man. An elaboration of this address
requires the concepts of confrontation and determination,
for Barth states that Jesus Christ is the history in which
the two natures confront one another and are determined to
one another through God's address.[150]
    The address is initiated by God, not by man. Through
his grace, God condescends to man and confronts him. In
this act, God determines to humiliate himself.[151] As a

result, the divine nature is determined to the human essence, and the human essence is determined by the divine essence. To say that the divine nature is determined to the human nature is to say that the human nature is not without God's grace. God cares for man. God's attention is focused upon man, and man is not alone. To say that the human essence is determined by God's divine grace is to say that no other force or power controls and determines it. In the confrontation, the human nature is determined exclusively by the divine. God makes the human nature his own.[152]

The mutual determination of the two natures has four results. The first is that the human essence is exalted to a state of harmony with the will of God. By God's grace, the human nature is granted the freedom to obey God and become sinless.[153] When this occurs, the human nature is not changed or divinized. Sinning is not a necessary constituent of humanity, but a contradiction of it. The human nature which is freed to obey God is "our true human essence."[154]

A second result of the exclusive determination of the human essence by the divine is that it becomes a participant in the inner life of the trinity and in the outward works of the Father and Holy Spirit. As man, however, the Son of Man does not make the trinity into a quartet. The human essence participates in God's inner life, but it does not do so as a fourth mode of being.[155]

A third result of this mutual determination is that the human essence becomes the instrument of the eternal Son in his mediational act of revealing God to man and reconciling man to God. Because of its determination it receives the power and authority to render a faithful service to God. Through grace the human nature is an effective witness.[156]

This does not mean, however, that the human nature possesses the power that belongs to God himself. Barth places two restrictions upon that which the human essence receives when God makes it suitable as his medium of revelation. The first is that the human essence receives the power to attest God and witness to him only in the event of revelation. This power is not something which the human nature appropriates and makes its own.[157] The second restriction is that although the human essence

receives divine power, authority, and universality, it
does not receive the divine omnipotence nor does it become
divine. "And it does not follow from this . . .that
omnipotence and therefore divinity accrue to the human
essence of this man as such."[158]
    A fourth result of the mutual determination is that
the human nature is exalted to a dignity and majesty which
is possessed by the eternal Son. As the human essence of
the Son, it shares the precedence of God over the created
order.[159]

Actualization

The final step in Barth's analysis of the fellowship and
mutual participation of the two natures concerns the
concept of actualization. According to Barth, the two
natures achieve a new actualization in their union.
Although the divine essence was actual previously, in this
union it becomes the divine essence as it is determined by
this act.[160] Similarly, although many other human
individuals bear human essence, and it cannot be said that
the human essence is actualized only in Christ, there is a
new actualization in that the human essence is now exalted
to fellowship with God. The human essence is determined
by the divine essence and directed to the divine essence.
[161]
    In this common actualization, each of the essences
achieves a realization which is fitting for its own
inherent being. In the one Jesus Christ, the divine
essence "rules and reveals and gives" while the human
essence "serves and attests and mediates." The two
essences work together harmoniously in relation to each
other, but each performs distinct functions. Barth
states:

> The divine and the human work together. But
> even in their common working they are not
> interchangeable. The divine is still above
> and the human below. Their relationship is
> one of genuine action.[162]

The distinction of the two essences can be specified

clearly through the concept of obedience. There are two wills involved in the one Jesus Christ, the divine and the human. The divine will commands and the human will obeys those commands.[163]

Now that the basic features of Barth's concept of the union of the two natures are before us, it is not difficult to see why some interpreters have considered him to be an Antiochian theologian. His analysis of this union is, at the same time, an analysis of God's relationship with men throughout the entire span of history. Jesus seems to be one among many, united with God in harmony because of his unique obedience. We wish to point out four principal characteristics of Barth's doctrine which support an Antiochian interpretation.

First, Barth carefully safeguards the differences between the two natures. Neither of them is transformed into the other, nor are they blended in such a way that their inherent distinctions are impaired. In this way, Barth allies himself with the traditional Antiochian opposition to any confusion or mixture of the two natures. At the same time, he makes it possible for the two natures to be understood as two distinct persons, God and Jesus.

Second, the way Barth historicizes the relation of the two natures grants to each of them a degree of independence which we might expect to occur in relations between persons. The contrast between Barth and older theologies on this point can be illustrated briefly by recalling Barth's rejection of the metaphor that the two natures are united as two planks glued together.[164] According to this metaphor, the two essences are externally compressed together in one visible form. By rejecting this figure, Barth appears to separate the two natures from each other, making them more distant from one another and giving each of them greater independence. This is not to say that God is not present in and through the human nature, for God is present everywhere, and he is present here in a unique way. Nor is it to deny that the two natures are related directly to one another. Yet, with the rejection of the analogy of the two planks and its replacement by a historical relation, the two natures stand apart from each other so that they can confront each other.

Third, the relationship between the two natures is

active rather than static. It is an event, not a state,
and therefore it is continually changing in significant
ways.[165] In every moment, each nature actively responds
to the other; the divine nature commands, and the human
nature responds in obedience. This is not to say, however, that the relation can cease or that it is in any
sense contingent upon external factors which might affect
it. Although the relation is dynamic, it has been firmly
established. This conception seems to require the kind of
independence between the two participants, and the kind of
freedom on the part of each of them, that we find in
persons.

Fourth, the way that Barth conceives the relation
between the two natures as a relationship of confrontation
and fellowship seems to support the Antiochian perspective. The notion of fellowship seems to require at least
two personal realities to communicate with each other.
Further, the way Barth develops this concept, with its
emphasis upon the two natures mutually interpenetrating
one another, determining one another, and actualizing one
another, lends itself to a personal interpretation. They
are related in a way which might be described as an
"I-Thou," a true meeting of persons.[166]

The Coordination of the Work

Since the unity of the person of Christ in Barth's theology involves the unity of his saving work, it is important
to see whether his coordination of the divine and human
aspects of this work can be interpreted in an Antiochian
sense. The evidence for such an interpretation is found
in the way Barth correlates the divine and human elements
with Christ's two states, humiliation and exaltation, and
his three offices, priest, king, and prophet. Barth
distinguishes the two natures, the two states, and the
offices of priest and king in such a way that there appear
to be two agents involved, God and Jesus. To show how
this is the case, we shall observe Barth's account more
closely.

In the fourth volume of the Church Dogmatics, Barth
discusses God's act of reconciliation. He begins with the
first moment in that act, God's humiliation, his conde-

scension toward creaturely reality. God, in his mode of being as Son, became a man; the Lord became a servant. By participating in creaturely life and accepting man's place on the cross, the eternal Son performed his role as priest. As a priest for man, the eternal Son overcame sin and accomplished the justification of all men before God.

In his condescension to man, the Son of God became the judge who allowed himself to be judged. In the place of sinners, the Son took the judgement upon himself that is due them. He became the rejected one. By performing this action, he exercised his true judgment in pronouncing us righteous.[167] In this act, God the Son fulfilled and revealed God's justice and love.[168]

The humiliation and condescension of the Son of God can be described in various ways. For example, it is discussed in scripture in financial terms, as the payment for sins, or in military concepts as the victory of God over sin. It can also be described in the language of the ritual of the Old Testament. The Son of God is the priest who intercedes for man. He offers a sacrifice on behalf of his people, but the sacrificial victim is himself rather than an animal. The act of sacrifice is his death on the cross, and this act, as the sacrifice of old, is a judgment upon men for their sins. The offering of this priest is perfect, and it is accepted by God as satisfaction for man's sins.[169]

The one reconciling act of God in Jesus Christ has a second dimension, the exaltation of human essence. By condescending to man, God at that moment exalts human nature into fellowship with himself. In this exaltation the Son of Man overcomes the sin of sloth and performs his kingly office. He rules his people and the cosmos, establishing their sanctification.

In his office as king, the Son of Man was present to other men in a royal manner. He could not fail to be seen and heard; he was among men in an inescapable way. He demanded decision from men, and he made a decision concerning them. He was with men in a way that cannot be forgotten or revoked. Although he has been present in this manner in the past, this does not mean that he is no longer present. As the living Lord, he is still present to men in the same way that he has been present in the past.[170]

As the royal man, Jesus' existence is analogous to
God's existence and work. Like God, he is held in low
esteem, and he ignored the important and wealthy people of
his day in favor of the lowly, weak, and poor. He calls
into question all man's institutions and beliefs, and he
does so without opposing man but by standing with
him.[171] In his kingly being, the words and accomplish-
ments of Jesus are united in one work, one life-act. This
life-act is itself the being of Jesus Christ.[172]
Finally, the kingly work of the Son of Man is sanctifying
because it is performed in complete obedience to God's
will.[173]

These two dimensions of the one act of God are
associated with the divine and the human natures respectively. It is through his divinity that the eternal Son
becomes man. This act reveals that his divinity is of
such a kind that it can become a participant in humanity.[174] This means, for Barth, that it is the eternal
Son of God who becomes a man, not the Son of Man. On the
other hand, it is the human nature and not the divine
nature which is exalted into fellowship with God. This
means that it is the Son of Man, who is exalted, not the
Son of God.[175]

The prophetic work of Jesus Christ is the fact that
this twofold act of his, his humiliation and his exaltation, makes itself known as such. Christ's prophetic work
is not simply his preaching as a man. It is not limited
to his human words in the first century, as is often the
case in older christologies which assign Jesus' prophetic
office to his preaching, his priestly office to his death,
and his kingly office to his resurrection and continuing
lordship.[176] For Barth, the prophetic work is the
self-declaration of the total act of Jesus Christ. In its
downward and upward movements, this one act proclaims
itself today as it has in the past.

In an Antiochian interpretation, the way Barth
restricts the humiliation and priestly function of Jesus
Christ to his divine nature, and the exaltation and kingly
function to the human nature, indicates that there are two
independent agents cooperating in one work. The divine
nature apparently does not participate in the exaltation,
and the human nature evidently does not participate in the
humiliation. If this is what Barth means, it is hard to

avoid the conclusion that reconciliation is exclusively a divine work. It is not the God-man who reconciles; it is God who reconciles and man who is reconciled.

Similarly, the prophetic office of Christ, in an Antiochian view, does not bind the two natures together in one person. Although both natures participate in the prophetic office, they do so as two separate movements in one event. The oneness is that of a single event, not a single agent. As a result, there appear to be two distinct agents cooperating in one work. God is the priest who is humiliated, and Jesus is the exalted, kingly man.[177]

Jesus Christ as a History

In his development of the concept of the unity of Christ, Barth depicts Christ as the history and the act of God. Christ is not simply the man who is related to God in the event of reconciliation; he is the event of reconciliation itself. How can an Antiochian interpretation, which emphasizes that Jesus Christ is primarily a human person, incorporate this aspect of Barth's thought in a convincing manner?

We have noted earlier that the ancient Antiochians, notably Nestorius and Theodore of Mopsuestia, used the term prosopon to designate both the unity of the Logos and the man Jesus and also each one as individuals. Barth's characterization of Jesus Christ as a history, an act, and an event can serve much the same purpose. If Jesus Christ is the history in which both God and the man Jesus are participants, it is proper to say that Jesus Christ is fully God and fully man. This history is both God and man in the sense that it includes the two personal realities.

Does this mean that this history is really a third kind of reality, neither God nor man? And, is the name "Jesus Christ" simply placed upon a phenomenon which is not really a person in any real sense? Consequently, does this interpretation of Barth turn him into an Arian? One who accepts an Antiochian interpretation can answer "No" to all these questions, basing this negative response on Barth's claim that a person is his act. Since Jesus Christ is his act and not simply a being behind an act, he is the act, and therefore the event, in which both God and man are present. He is this act and event without ceasing to be a person.

One who defends an Antiochian interpretation can make this claim intelligible by arguing that a person should not be defined strictly in terms of an ego or self who exists apart from his acts, his relationship with other humans, and his environment. If one thinks of a person as identical with his life, then his being includes his interrelations with his fellows. Insofar as a person is his life, he is an event and a history.

When this concept is applied to Jesus, it is possible to understand him as an event. This is not to say that a mere happening is given the name "Jesus Christ." It is to say that the being of the human subject Jesus includes his history as well as the agent who acts in that history. Further, it is possible to say that Jesus Christ is divine in the sense that God is also present in this event. God is present guiding and directing the man Jesus. However, insofar as Jesus is an agent who is presupposed by his actions, he is not a divine agent but a human agent. This Jesus is, however, an abstraction from the event which he is.[178]

BARTH'S USE OF THE NAME "JESUS CHRIST" IN AN ANTIOCHIAN PERSPECTIVE

In keeping with traditional Antiochian terminology, those who interpret Barth as a representative of this position believe that he uses different terms to distinguish the two persons, God and Jesus. Such terms as "Jesus," "Jesus of Nazareth," "the man Jesus," and "Son of Man" are understood to denote the individual human being who is related to God in the incarnation. Sometimes, "human nature" or "humanity" also seem to be used by Barth to denote this man. "Son of God," "Word of God," and "Logos" are thought to denote the agent God. "Christ" and "Jesus Christ" are somewhat more ambiguous, denoting the man Jesus and his history, the event in which he is related to his fellows and to God.[179] This event can be understood in both a narrow and a broad sense; it is the instant in which God speaks through Jesus to particular recipients,[180] and it is also the entire span of history, which is, in a sense, included in Jesus' history because of God's unique presence there.

One principal factor which supports an Antiochian interpretation of Barth's language is that he often seems to substitute those names which appear to denote a human person for the human nature which God assumed in the incarnation. While Barth does not say explicitly that the human nature is named "Jesus" or "Jesus of Nazareth," the apparent substitution suggests that Barth thinks of the human nature in a concrete sense, as a complete individual.

This apparent substitution occurs primarily in two different contexts, revelation and reconciliation. In our discussion of these topics earlier in this chapter, we encountered this substitution, but we did not draw attention to it as such. Here we shall give examples, relying upon the earlier discussion for clarification.

As we have seen, Barth groups the man Jesus and the human nature of Christ among the creaturely forms of revelation. He seems to equate the two when he speaks of them in parallel constructions, apparently substituting the one for the other. For example, Barth says:

> We may at once conclude from the fact that such attempts at secularisation are n o t undertaken in the NT, that in it, too, the humanitas Christi comes under the reservation of God's holiness, i.e. that the power and continuity in which the man Jesus of Nazareth, according to the testimony of the evangelists and apostles, was in fact the revealed word, consisted here also in the power and continuity of the divine action in this form and not in the continuity of this form as such.[181]

In this quote, it appears that the form of revelation can be described either as the humanity of Christ or the man Jesus. If so, it seems that Jesus is a human person, and not a divine one.

Another example of an apparent use of "Jesus" to denote the human nature as though this human nature were a person in itself is found in Barth's discussion of the two

types of christological statements. Barth mentions these
two types in the context of an explanation of the mysteriousness of revelation. In order to understand his point,
we need to say a word about the mystery.

Barth states that in revelation the form veils the
content in such a way that we can know either the creaturely form or the divine content, but not both, at any
given moment. "But if one moment the one becomes true for
us in experience and thought, we must the next moment have
faith in the other which does not become discernible by
us."[182]

To illustrate the one-sidedness and mysteriousness of
revelation, Barth turns to the two types of christological
statements. These two types are of such a different
character that there is no systematic connection between
them. Both of them speak of the humanity and the divinity
of Christ, but, says Barth, they do so with "such variety
in the direction of interest and emphasis" that it is
reasonable to assume that they are antithetical to each
other.

> It is impossible to listen to the two state-
> ments at the same time, Jesus of Nazareth is
> G o d ' s   S o n, and God's Son is J e s u s
> o f   N a z a r e t h. Here we listen to
> either the one or the other, or we listen to
> nothing at all.[183]

The point we wish to emphasize is that "Jesus of
Nazareth" in the two types of statements might be understood to denote the human nature and its personality. If
so, then Barth apparently personalizes the human nature,
conceiving it as a person distinct from the person God.
This interpretation is based upon the fact that Barth
indicates that both statements are about the humanity and
the divinity of Jesus Christ. Further, the statements are
illustrations of Barth's claim that we can know or perceive only the form or the content of revelation at any
given moment. The appearance of these sentences in this
context implies that the term "God's Son" denotes the
content of revelation, and "Jesus of Nazareth" denotes the
form.

If this is the way Barth intends for these terms to be

understood, then the Antiochian interpretation of the two
types of christological statements is complementary
with its view of Barth's concept of indirect identity.   If
the "is" in the christological statements means "becomes,"
then it seems clear that "God the Son" denotes the divine
person and "Jesus of Nazareth" denotes a human person.
     Turning now from revelation to reconciliation, we
note that Barth's language implies that there are two
agents involved in the reconciling event.   Barth explains
that it is the divine nature which is humilated and the
human nature which is exalted.   The divine nature is not
exalted, nor is the human nature humiliated.   In explanation of these distinct roles, Barth states that it is the
Son of God who is humiliated and the Son of Man who is
exalted.   For example, "The atonement as it took place in
Jesus Christ is the one inclusive event of this going out
of the Son of God and coming in of the Son of Man."[184]
It is possible to conclude from this manner of speaking
that Barth is substituting "Son of Man" for "human nature"," and that he means, therefore, that the human
nature is itself a concrete person with his own name.
     Because of the reconciling act of God in the incar-
nation, a unity has been established between God and men,
and also between the divine nature and the human nature.
In discussing this unity, Barth appears to substitute
"Jesus," "Jesus of Nazareth," and "Son of Man" for the
human nature, and "God" and "Son of God" for the divine
nature.   To illustrate this flexibility in Barth's language, we offer two examples.   In the first Barth talks of
the unity of the human nature with the Son of God.

> What happens to the familiar cosmic reality
> now that the human nature in Christ is adopted
> and taken up into unity with the Son of God,
> is substantially a restoration and confir-
> mation of its original connexion with
> God.[185]

     In the second example, Barth talks of a unity of the
Son of God with the man Jesus.   He says:

> The Son of God in His unity with the Israelite
> Jesus exists in direct and unlimited soli-

darity with the representatively and man-
ifestly sinful humanity of Israel.[186]

In this second example, Barth seems to be talking of
two persons who are united. There are two names involved
here, and the implication is that two persons are related
in some direct way. In ordinary language we would not
speak of one person being united with himself by using two
different names to refer to that one person.

Once those who understand Barth as Antiochian have
concluded that Barth uses these names to denote two
persons, they employ that conclusion as a key for understanding Barth's christological language. According to an
Antiochian interpretation, when Barth speaks of "Jesus" or
"Jesus of Nazareth" having human qualities and performing
human actions, it is reasonable to conclude that Barth is
speaking of the human person. On the other hand, when
Barth ascribes divine predicates to "Jesus" or "Jesus of
Nazareth," it is reasonable to conclude that these predicates apply directly to the divine person but indirectly
to Jesus because of his relation to God.

CONCLUSION

In the first section of this chapter we discussed the
basic features of Antiochian and Alexandrian christologies. We introduced evidence to support our hypothesis
that the different ways these two schools of thought
approach the doctrine of the divinity of Jesus Christ, the
unity of the person of Christ, and the meaning of the name
"Jesus Christ" are directly related to the way they
conceive the identity of Jesus Christ. For Antiochian
thought, Jesus Christ is a human person distinct from God.
Therefore, he can be said to be divine only because of his
relation to God, not his essence. The unity of Jesus with
God is a fellowship of a divine person with a human
person, established by God's grace. The name "Jesus"
denotes a human person, not a divine one. For Alexandrian
thought, on the other hand, Jesus Christ is directly
identical with the eternal Son of God. He is divine by
nature, and in his second stage of existence he unites to
himself a human nature which is other than a complete

person.   "Jesus" and its variants denote this divine
person, not a human one.

In the rest of the chapter we have constructed an
Antiochian interpretation of Barth's treatment of the
divinity of Jesus Christ, the unity of his person, and the
meaning of the name "Jesus Christ."   The way Barth groups
the man Jesus among the creaturely forms of revelation
suggests that he is a complete human individual who
becomes identical with God's Word when God speaks through
him.   His divinity appears to belong to him because of his
participation in the revelatory event.   Similarly, when
Barth explains God's assumption of the human nature in the
incarnation, he grants to the human nature a will, personality, and self-consciousness.   As a result, although the
human nature is not an existing person before the incarnation, it seems to become one in this event.   Further,
the way Barth historicizes the resulting relation between
the Word and the human nature indicates that the human
nature is a subject capable of responding to the Word in
faith, obedience, and fellowship.   The impression that
there are two persons involved in this union is reinforced
by the way Barth correlates the divine nature with the
humiliation and priestly office of the Son of God and the
human nature with the exaltation and kingly office of the
Son of Man.   Finally, Barth seems to use "Jesus" and its
variants to denote the human nature of the Logos, implying
that he is a person who is relatively independent from the
person God.

Chapter 3
Barth's Alexandrian Christological Doctrine

In spite of the formidable data which support an Antiochian interpretation of Barth, it is our view that his
position is basically Alexandrian. The structure of
Barth's doctrine of the divinity of Jesus Christ, his
concept of the unity of the person, and also his language
about Christ support this conclusion. In this chapter we
shall present evidence for an Alexandrian interpretation
of Barth's development of the first two of the three
topics mentioned. Our analysis of his christological
language will be found in the fourth chapter.

Our principal thesis in this chapter is that Barth
conceives of Jesus Christ as directly identical with God.
Both in God's inner-trinitarian life, and also in his
existence as a man in time, Jesus Christ is the person God
and the act of God. In order to show that Barth understands Christ in this way, we must examine his claim that
Jesus Christ is the act of God.

In the first section of the chapter we shall show that
Jesus Christ is the act of God and therefore the essence
of God. The phrase "essential divinity" in the title of
this section indicates that Jesus Christ is divine by
nature, not by relation. Divinity is predicated of him
because it belongs to him, not simply because God is
present in and with him. In Barth's analysis, the act of
Jesus Christ is his essence and also his divinity. This
act is fully divine because it is the trinitarian act
which constitutes God's being. Although Jesus Christ is
divine, there is no opposition between this claim and
belief in one God. The divinity of Jesus Christ is
directly identical with the divinity of God.

In the second section of this chapter we shall turn to
the unity of the Son of God with the human nature which he

assumes. Here we shall argue that Jesus Christ is directly identical with God because his existence is the existence of God and because he is the divine subject who acts
through his human nature. Although the human nature is
the subject of human actions and qualities, there is
insufficient evidence to conclude that it is a complete
human person. The bearer of the human nature is God, not
a man who is a person distinct from God.

THE ESSENTIAL DIVINITY OF JESUS CHRIST

We shall begin our discussion of Barth's concept of the
essential divinity of Jesus Christ by showing that Barth
identifies Jesus Christ with God's act. Then we shall
consider his claim that Jesus Christ is the act which is
the essence of God, not simply one of many acts of God.
Barth's grounds for making this affirmation are found in
the event of revelation. An analysis of this event leads
to a concept of the trinity, and this doctrine affirms
that Jesus Christ is both the act of God and the essence
of God. The divinity of Christ is the essence which he
shares with the Father and the Holy Spirit. The fact of
Christ's essential divinity will be reinforced, and its
nature clarified, by a discussion of Barth's identification of God's act with his being. This equation leads to
a consideration of God's act of positing himself and
loving himself in Jesus Christ. Next, we shall turn to
Barth's claim that the one act of God has two dimensions,
an inner and an outer, and that these dimensions are two
moments in the divinity of Jesus Christ. Finally, we
shall show that Jesus Christ is the person God.

Jesus Christ as the Act of God

Since the concept of the essential divinity of Jesus
Christ is dependent upon the claim that Jesus Christ is
the act of God, it is important to show that Barth explicitly emphasizes this identity. Particularly important
statements of this relation are found in Barth's development of the doctrines of reconciliation and revelation,
and therefore we turn to them.

Barth declares that Jesus Christ is the history of reconciliation in which God condescends to man and exalts man to himself.

> In every theological context in which we must name the name of Jesus Christ--and there is none in which we do not have to name it at the decisive point--it is this history which is meant according to our assumption: the act of God in which the Son of God becomes identical with the man Jesus of Nazareth, and therefore unites human essence with His divine essence, and therefore exalts the human into fellowship with the divine; the act of God in which He humbles Himself to exalt man. The Subject Jesus Christ is this history.[1]

This history of reconciliation is also the event in which God reveals himself to man. Reconciliation, revelation, and Jesus Christ are identical. "Revelation in fact does not differ from the Person of Jesus Christ, and again does not differ from the reconciliation which took place in Him."[2]

Barth's identification of Jesus Christ with God's act does not mean merely that Jesus Christ is dependent upon God as other creatures. It means that Jesus Christ is divine in his essence and therefore he is God himself. To show that this is what Barth means, and to indicate his grounds for affirming it, we shall discuss his development of the relation of revelation to the concept of the trinity.

Revelation and the Trinity

Our purpose here is to show that Barth understands Jesus Christ as the act which is God's second mode of being and that he bases this claim upon revelation. Because Jesus Christ is the second of the trinity, he is of the same essence as the Father and the Holy Spirit. His divinity is absolutely his own determination, just as the Father's divinity is his own.

Since Barth identifies Jesus Christ with revelation,

his insistence that Christian theology must begin with revelation means that it must begin with Jesus Christ. In addition, because Jesus Christ is also of the same divine essence as the Father and the Holy Spirit, to begin with revelation is to begin with the divinity of Jesus Christ. [3] When we begin here, we are led to a doctrine of the trinity.

If God is truly known in revelation, Barth argues, then the God who is known there is the triune God. This is true because an analysis of the event of revelation attested in the Bible leads immediately to a doctrine of the trinity.[4] The event of revelation has a threefold structure. This trinitarian arrangement is implied in the fact that the event of revelation confronts us with three questions. In order to understand this event, we must ask who reveals himself, how he reveals himself, and what is the result of this revealing. The answer to all three questions is the same. It is God who reveals himself. He reveals himself through himself, and therefore the event of revelation is himself. Finally, the result is the revealedness of God himself. He is the one who is revealed.[5]

According to scripture, Barth points out, that through which God reveals himself is Jesus Christ. He is the event of revelation, the act of God, and therefore God himself. The scripture acknowledges that Jesus Christ is God in his second mode of being when it attributes to him the title "Lord."[6] If we interpret this assessment of Christ in ways which deny that he is fully divine, then we jeopardize our knowledge of God. Unless this act of revelation is God himself, it is not God that we know but someone or something less than God.[7]

According to Barth, if Jesus Christ is truly God, then God must maintain distinctions in himself, and Jesus Christ must be God's second mode of being. This conclusion follows from the fact that Jesus Christ points beyond himself to the Father, the one to whom he prays and to whom he is obedient.[8] As the Father, God remains free and hidden even in his revelation. In his self-unveiling, God becomes an object of human thought and speech. But this presence before men is the result of his decision. It presupposes his ability to assume a form, to become God himself a second time, in a second way, distinct from his hiddenness.[9]

Barth states that the formal characteristics of the event of revelation indicate the way God is related to himself in his inner being. Just as in the event of revelation there is the origin of revelation, revelation itself, and the result of revelation, so also in God there is an origin and two issues from that origin.[10] The distinctions of the event of revelation are grounded in the essence of God.[11] God can become the Son known to us because he is already the Son in himself.[12] He can become the one we know as the Father of Jesus because he is already the Father in himself.[13]

In order to state how God can be three and yet still one, Barth prefers to use the concept "essence" (Wesen) for God's oneness and the concept "way of being" (Seinsweise) for each of the three in God.[14] God is God in three modes of being, Father, Son, and Holy Spirit. But these are not three personalities or three gods.[15] The three are of one essence, and that means that they are the same identical essence.[16] The divinity of Jesus Christ is that he shares in the one essence of God, an essence which is shared also by the Father and the Holy Spirit.[17]

Because Jesus Christ is divine in this sense, he is different from all other men. Barth explains that the divinity of Jesus Christ is

> that which Jesus Christ has in common with the Father and the Holy Spirit as the Son of God, that which distinguishes His being and its nature from the being and nature of man, and of all other reality distinct from God, with an absolute (and infinitely qualitative) distinction.[18]

Thus, when Barth states that Christ's divinity is his revelation of the Father,[19] this does not mean simply that Jesus Christ is a human medium who is said to be divine because he mediates the knowledge of God. Rather, it means that Jesus Christ is the revelation of God as the act which is God's second mode of being. Even in himself, in the inner-trinitarian life, prior to the existence of the creature, Jesus Christ is the act of God by which God knows and loves himself.[20] He can reveal God because he is God, not simply because he is a creature who has a special relation to God.

For Barth, then, the event of revelation in Christ indicates that Jesus Christ is the second mode of God's triune being and that he is, therefore, identical with God himself. "Jesus Christ, the Son of God, is God Himself, as God his Father is God Himself."[21]   Many questions remain, however. The doctrine of the trinity functions to identify God, but it tells us little about his nature.[22] Can Barth give more complete information about the nature of the God who is three? What do the three modes of God participate "in"? What is God's essence? Barth's answer to these questions gives support to the conclusion that Jesus Christ is fully and absolutely divine. He states that the essence of God is his act.

God's Act as His Being

Barth defines God's essence as his act. He states:

> To its very deepest depths God's Godhead consists in the fact that it is an event--not any event, not events in general, but the event of His action, in which we have a share in God's revelation.[23]

This identification is inherently related to the concept of the divinity of Jesus Christ. Because Jesus Christ is the act of God, and because God is his act, it follows immediately that Jesus Christ is the essence of God. Further, since God's essence is his deity,[24] it follows that the deity of God is also the deity of Jesus Christ.

While this equation of Jesus Christ, as the act of God, with the essence of God follows a coherent pattern of thought on the abstract level, it has the appearance of emptiness. What does it mean to say that God's act is his being, and how is the claim to be understood? Our purpose here is to show that the identity of God's act with God's being is directly related to God's act in his inner-trinitarian life. Barth states: "This essence of God which is seen in His revealed name is His being and therefore His act as Father, Son and Holy Spirit."[25]   Since the trini-

tarian act of God is also God's act in Jesus Christ, it
becomes clear why Jesus Christ is the essence of God. The
nature of God's act is, at the same time, the nature of
Jesus Christ.[26]

In himself, in his inner being, God acts in a particular way. The act which is his being is not merely
activity in general. God performs one "specific act with
a definite content";[27] yet it has different dimensions
and can be described in various ways. This act is the act
in which God knows and loves himself. It is the act in
which he repeats himself, in which he posits himself a
second time.

The act which is God has a trinitarian structure.[28]
The way in which the three in God constitute the structure
of this act probably can best be presented through the
concept of original relations.[29] There is in God an
origin of his act, the act itself, and the relation of the
origin to the act. Barth states:

> This threeness consists in the fact that in
> the essence or act in which God is God there
> is first a pure origin and then two different
> issues, the first of which is to be attributed
> solely to the origin, the second, different in
> kind, to the origin and likewise to the first
> issue.[30]

The Son of God, Jesus Christ, is the act of God, the
first product of God which is at the same time fully
identical with God. It is not possible, Barth explains,
to conceive how Jesus Christ can be the act of God and
also the essence of God. "We, too, cannot say how an
essence can be at once its own producer and in a twofold
sense its own product." Yet the revelation attested in
the Bible requires this statement.[31]

Although Barth conceives of Jesus Christ both as the
act of God and also as the Son who is posited and loved in
this act, it should not be supposed that he means that
there are two "Sons" in God. Jesus Christ is the Son who
is loved because he is the act of loving itself.

Some confusion is created because Barth applies the
concept of act both to God in his second mode of being and
also to God as a whole. That is, since God is defined as

act, and since the structure of this act is threefold, the concept of act designates one of the three elements in the structure and also the whole which the structure establishes. This fact is related to the inconceivability of God's triune character, yet it also attests the importance of the concept of Jesus Christ as the act of God. As the act of God, Jesus Christ contributes to the structure of God's being because he is the "whole."[32]

The affirmation that God's act is his being, then, is rooted in the doctrine of the trinity. The content of this act needs to be explored in more detail. As we specify this content, we also specify the nature of Jesus Christ, for this act is his being.

In the first place, says Barth, the act which is God is his act of revelation. It is the act in which God knows himself and in which he allows men to participate in that knowledge. If God had not revealed himself in Jesus Christ, we could not know him, but because he has, our knowledge is certain.[33]

Secondly, the act which constitutes God's being is the act which makes him alive. At the core of his being God is active. That means that we have "to resist the threatened absorption of the doctrine of God into a doctrine of being."[34] His life is the act by which he knows and loves himself as Father, Son, and Holy Spirit; it is his act in Christ.

Thirdly, the act which is God's being is completely self-motivated and self-moved. God is not determined by something outside himself. His being is simply his decision to be what he is. "The fact that God's being is event, the event of God's act, necessarily . . . means that it is His own conscious, willed and executed decision." In this respect, God is absolutely unique. "No other being is absolutely its own, conscious, willed and executed decision."[35] All other beings are determined by external factors. This decision is identical with Jesus Christ. [36]

Fourthly, God's act is also his love. Barth indicates that it is proper to say "God is love," for love is not merely a quality of God, it is his essence. However, this claim can easily be misunderstood. To say that God is love is to say that God loves.

That He is God--the Godhead of God--consists
in the fact that He loves, and it is the
expression of His loving that He seeks and
creates fellowship with us. It is correct and
important in this connexion to say emphatical-
ly, His loving, i.e., His act as that of the
One who loves.[37]

In himself, because he is triune, God has love and
fellowship. His positing himself a second time is the act
in which he loves himself, and it is also the act in which
this loving flows outward to men in revelation. In all
its dimensions this one act is Jesus Christ.

As and before God seeks and creates fellowship
with us, He wills and completes this fellowship in Himself. In Himself He does not will
to exist for Himself, to exist alone. On the
contrary, He is Father, Son and Holy Spirit
and therefore alive in His unique being with
and for and in another. The unbroken unity of
His being, knowledge and will is at the same
time an act of deliberation, decision and
intercourse. He does not exist in solitude
but in fellowship. Therefore what He seeks
and creates between Himself and us is in fact
nothing else but what He wills and completes
and therefore is in Himself.[38]

Finally, God's act is free. This does not mean merely
that God is free in relation to the reality which is other
than himself. He has a positive freedom in himself in the
fact that he is grounded in his own being and is determined by himself alone.[39] This freedom consists in the
act of loving in his inner-trinitarian life. "We have
seen that the freedom of God, as His freedom in Himself,
His primary absoluteness, has its truth and reality in the
inner Trinitarian life of the Father with the Son by the
Holy Spirit."[40]
This freedom that God has in himself is the basis of
God's freedom in relation to the world. His freedom in
the world, his secondary absoluteness, is the natural
expression of his inner freedom. Because Jesus Christ is

the inner-trinitarian act, he is also this outward expression of the same act. Barth states:

> Before all worlds, in His Son He has otherness
> in Himself from eternity to eternity. But
> because this is so, the creation and preserva-
> tion of the world, and relationship and
> fellowship with it, realized as they are in
> perfect freedom, without compulsion or neces-
> sity, do not signify an alien or contradictory
> expression of God's being, but a natural, the
> natural expression of it ad extra. The world
> is, because and as the Son of God is.[41]

As a result, it is clear that the "freedom of God . . .
consists in His Son Jesus Christ."[42]
    In this discussion of God's act, we have encountered an
important distinction between God's act in himself, ad
intra, and his act outside himself, ad extra, in relation
to the world. It is necessary, Barth argues, to make this
distinction in order to preserve the freedom and sovereignty of God. If we made no distinction between God's
act ad intra and ad extra, we would turn his act ad extra
into a necessary attribute of God. We would make the
world and man indispensable for God.[43] The inner act of
God as Father, Son and Holy Spirit provides the ground and
the possibility for God to act ad extra, but it does not
require that act ad extra.[44]
    In conclusion, we have shown that Barth's identifica-
tion of God's act with his essence is grounded in God's
trinitarian being. The act which is God's essence is his
positing himself in his Son, Jesus Christ. Since there is
one act involved here, and it is the act of Jesus Christ,
it is clear what Barth means when he says that Jesus
Christ is divine. Jesus Christ is the act and the essence
of God. His deity is God's deity, and therefore it too
determines itself, loves freely, and reveals itself to
men. It is also a deity which acts both inwardly and
outwardly. To these two dimensions we must give more
attention.

The Two Moments in the Divinity of Jesus Christ

The identification of the divinity of Jesus Christ with the divinity of God applies to Jesus Christ's life in time as well as to his being in the inner-trinitarian life of God. To make this point clear, Barth describes God's act ad intra and his act ad extra as two moments in the one act which constitutes God's being. Since Jesus Christ's existence as a man is the second moment of this one divine act, his existence is also the existence of God.

Barth discusses the two moments of the divinity of Jesus Christ in his treatment of the concept of reconciliation. In explaining the humiliation of God the Son, Barth encounters the problem of the obedience of Jesus Christ. Christ's obedience constitutes a puzzle because it raises the question of how one who is already assumed to be God can also be obedient.

This question becomes even more poignant when the implications of that obedience are spelled out. Jesus Christ, as the eternal Son of God, was obedient even to the extent of becoming the particular Jewish man who suffered and died on the cross as a man rejected by God.

> He, the electing eternal God, willed Himself to be rejected and therefore perishing man. That is something which never happened in all the dreadful things attested in the Old Testament concerning the wrath of God and the plight of man.[45]

In this obedience of Jesus we learn what the deity of Christ is. His deity is not primarily the possession of supreme attributes; it is his willingness to humble himself and become a man. "That God as God is able and willing and ready to condescend, to humble Himself in this way is the mystery of the 'deity of Christ'--although frequently it is not recognized in this concreteness."[46]

This humiliation of Jesus Christ, and therefore his deity, has two moments. The first of these is the obedience of the eternal Son in the inner life of God. The second moment is the Son's becoming a man, his "self-humiliation, His way into the far country, fulfilled in His death on the cross." The first moment "is a matter of the mystery of the inner being of God as the being of the Son in relation to the Father." The second moment "is a matter of the mystery of His deity in His work ad extra, in His presence in the world."[47]

Barth first discusses the second moment of the deity of Christ. In it, Barth affirms, the eternal Son of God freely assumes human nature, and he does so without suffering any change or setting up a contradiction in God. The mystery of the deity of Christ is that he is able to become man without causing a conflict between God's essence and his work as reconciler in the world. Although Jesus Christ places himself in the sinful condition of man, accepting as his own the contradiction of man before God, he does not join in man's opposition toward God. "He makes His own the being of man in contradiction against Him, but He does not make common cause with it." The deity of Jesus Christ allows him to act "as Lord over this contradiction even as He subjects Himself to it."[48]

For Barth, what God reveals in the second moment of the divinity of Christ corresponds to his divine nature. From his revelation it is clear that God can be absolute and relative, infinite and finite, exalted and humiliated, transcendent and immanent, eternal and temporal.[49]

God's becoming man can be understood as the exercise of his divine perfections. His dwelling in the creaturely realm is the exercise of his omnipresence. His assuming the form of weakness and impotence is the application of his omnipotence. He is able to become temporal without ceasing to be eternal. His righteousness is seen in his identifying himself with the unrighteous. God's being both in the form of God and also in the form of a servant is what we honor and worship as the deity of Christ. This we do without concluding that there is a division in God himself.[50]

At this point, Barth turns from the second moment in Christ's deity to the "first and inner moment of the mystery of the deity of Christ" which is presupposed by the second.[51] When we look at the obedience of Jesus Christ as a man, we infer that it must be grounded in God himself. If the humility and obedience of Jesus Christ as a man are not simply accidental, then God must be obedient to himself in the inner-trinitarian life. His act ad intra provides the foundation for his act ad extra. Barth states:

If, then, God is in Christ, if what the man
Jesus does is God's own work, this aspect of
the self-emptying and self-humbling of Jesus
Christ as an act of obedience cannot be alien
to God. But in this case we have to see here
the other and inner side of the mystery of the
divine nature of Christ and therefore of the
nature of the one true God--that He Himself is
also able and free to render obedience.[52]

How can it be said that there is in God an obedience?
"Obedience implies an above and a below, a <u>prius</u> and a
<u>posterius</u>, a superior and a junior and subordinate."[53]
Does not the claim that there is an eternal obedience in
God's inner life compromise the unity of the divine being?
Does it not imply that there are two divine beings, "the
first and commanding properly divine, the second and
obeying only divine in an improper sense?"[54]
  Because of the difficulties involved, many Christians
have concluded that it is wiser to refrain from stating
that there is a commanding and an obeying in God's inner
act. Barth opposes such conclusions because he thinks
that they deny that the true God has a real part in
atonement. In order to guarantee that it is really God
who acts in reconciliation, justifying and sanctifying
man, we must affirm, Barth declares, that the obedience of
Jesus as a man is the continuation and reflection of God's
obedience to himself as Son to Father.
  Because of this necessity, we have to affirm that there
is a real above and below, first and second, superiority
and subordination in God himself. The divine unity does
not preclude this diversity but consists in it. Both,
Barth argues, are maintained by a proper understanding of
the trinity. The Father is the one who commands and the
Son is the one who obeys, but both are the same God. They
are one because they participate in the one act which
constitutes God's being.[55]
  Not only is the obedience of the man Jesus as such
grounded in the eternal obedience of the Son to the
Father. The relationship between the Father and the Son
in eternity is identical with the relationship between God
and one of his creatures.

In the work of the reconciliation of the world
with God the inward divine relationship
between the One who rules and commands in
majesty and the One who obeys in humility is
identical with the very different relationship
between God and one of His creatures, a man.

This identity is possible because God, as Son, has become
that creature. In his existence as the man Jesus, he is
obedient to himself in time as he is in eternity. "God
goes into the far country for this to happen. He becomes
what He had not previously been." In becoming an obedient
man, God not only reflects his inner being and represents
it in the relation between Creator and creature, he now
causes his inner being to take outward form. This outward
action is simply a continuation of "the history in which
He is God."[56]
     This fact, that God's inner dialectic of obeying and
being obeyed takes outward form, distinguishes the outward
act of God in Jesus Christ from his previous acts.
Before, his inner life was merely represented and reflected. Now, it takes outward form.

It is the free grace of the atonement that He
now not only reflects His inner being as God
as He did in creation, that He not only
represents it in a likeness as He did in the
relationship of Creator and creature, but that
He causes it to take outward form in itself
and as such.[57]

     In his development of the concept of the two moments of
the divinity of Christ, Barth is careful to avoid the
suggestion that the one who obeys in eternity is God the
Son while the one who obeys in time is a human person
called Jesus who is distinct from the person of God the
Son. The one who obeys both in eternity and in time is
the one Jesus Christ. When he becomes a man, he continues
the obedience which he practices in eternity. There is
one person, one obedience, and one divinity involved here.
Barth states:

He is as man, as the man who is obedient in

humility, Jesus of Nazareth, what He is as God
(and what He can be also as man because He is
it as God in this mode of divine being). That
is the true deity of Jesus Christ, obedient in
humility, in its unity and equality, its
homoousia, with the deity of the One who sent
Him and to whom he is obedient. . . . Jesus
Christ is the Son of God who became man, who
as such is One with God the Father, equal to
Him in deity, by the Holy Spirit, in whom the
Father affirms and loves Him and He the
Father, in a mutual fellowship.[58]

In conclusion, this discussion of Barth's understanding
of the two moments in the deity of Jesus Christ makes it
clear that the deity of Christ is at the same time the
deity of God. Barth states: "The deity of Christ is the
one unaltered because unalterable deity of God."[59] The
second moment of Jesus Christ's act, his existence as a
man in the creaturely realm, is just as divine as its
first moment, his participation in God's inner-trinitarian
love and fellowship. This means that his act and existence as a man are identical with the act and existence of
God.

Jesus Christ as the Person God

Jesus Christ is divine not only as the act and the essence
of God, he is also divine as the person God. In Barth's
thought, Jesus Christ is not merely a human individual who
becomes a complete person in fellowship with God through
grace. Nor is he said to be the divine person because he
becomes identical with the Word of God in revelation, as
is true for the Bible and proclamation. He is the person
God in the strictest sense of the word "is."

The claim that Jesus Christ is the person God is
grounded in Barth's correlation of the concept of person
with the doctrine of the trinity. God is one person in
his trinitarian act of being. Because Jesus Christ is the
second of the three which constitute this one person, it
follows that he is identical with this person. To demonstrate more clearly that this is Barth's view, we shall

begin with Barth's affirmation that God is a person.
When we consider Barth's account of God's being as a
person, we encounter again his correlation of act and
being. Barth defines a person as one whose being is in
act. This means, Barth explains, that a person is one who
determines himself fully through his decision to be what
he is. Since God is the only reality who fulfills this
condition, only he is truly a person. In determining
himself, God is the one person who is three. Barth
states:

> Now, if the being of a person is a being in
> act, and if, in the strict and proper sense,
> being in act can be ascribed only to God, then
> it follows that by the concept of the being of
> a person, in the strict and proper sense, we
> can understand only the being of God. Being
> in its own, conscious, willed and executed
> decision, and therefore personal being, is the
> being of God in the nature of the Father and
> the Son and the Holy Spirit. . . . The real
> person is not man but God. It is not God who
> is a person by extension, but we.[60]

When Barth states that God is a person, he means that
God is an agent. To make this clear, he describes God as
"a knowing, willing, acting I,"[61] and as "a single,
unique Willer and Doer."[62] The fact that "God's being
is absolutely His act" does not mean either that God is
act and not an agent or that he is an agent apart from his
act.[63] He is the agent who is identical with his act in
an incomprehensible manner.[64]

Because Barth assigns the concept of person to God's
one essence rather than to his three modes of being, it is
clear that Jesus Christ, insofar as he is a person, is the
person God. He is this person just as are the Father and
the Holy Spirit.[65] Barth accepts this implication.
Using the phrase "the One" to denote God, he states:

> The One, the person, whom we really know as a
> human person, is the person of Jesus Christ,
> and even this is in fact the person of God the
> Son, in which humanity, without being or

having itself a person, is caught up into
fellowship with the personality of God. This
one man is therefore the being of God making
itself known to us as the One who loves.[66]

Even more explicitly, Barth asserts that "the eternal God"
not only foresees "the divine-human person of Jesus
Christ," he "actually is this person."[67]
    Although we usually speak of Jesus Christ as the one
who reconciles, the Father as the creator, and the Holy
Spirit as the redeemer, this does not imply that the three
are different agents. The one God performs all the divine
works ad extra, and the three modes of God's being participate in each of his works. The doctrine of appropriations functions to guarantee that God is one agent, while
drawing attention to his inner distinctions. It indicates
that some actions are more appropriate to one or another
of the three "persons," but it denies that any action is
performed exclusively by one of the three.[68]
    The identification of Jesus Christ with the person God
is reinforced and reflected in Barth's claim that Jesus
Christ's person is his work. This equation is inherently
related to that between God's act and being. As we have
seen, Jesus Christ is the act and the essence of God.
Consequently, if the act and the essence of God are
identical, it follows that Jesus Christ's act and essence
are also identical. In addition, since Barth states that
only God's act is fully his essence, the affirmation that
Jesus Christ's person is his work implies that he is God.
    Barth's equation of Christ's person and work applies to
the life of Jesus as a man. For example, Barth says, "But
His being as a man is the whole of His action, suffering
and achievement. His being as man is His work."[69]
However, this equation is not limited to Jesus Christ's
existence as a man in time; it applies as well to Jesus
Christ's participation in the act of God. For example,
Barth states, "But His being as God and man and God-man
consists in the completed act of the reconciliation of man
with God."[70] More clearly, Barth explains that the work
of Jesus Christ occurs in God's inner-trinitarian life.

But the point which concerns us here is that
according to the Fourth Gospel it is not

> merely the eternal but the incarnate Logos and
> therefore the man Jesus who is included in
> this circle. He did not give up His eternal
> divinity when He concealed it to become
> man.... It is only as He is a mode of the
> divine being, and therefore a moment in the
> circle of the inner life of God, that He can
> be in the Father and the Father in Him; that
> He and the Father can be one; that the work of
> the Father assigned to Him can also be His own
> work and the work performed by Him can be also
> the Father's work; that He like the Father can
> have life in Himself, that He can love the
> Father with the same love with which the
> Father loves Him; that He can glorify the
> Father and the Father glorify Him. Undoubt-
> edly all these things describe the inner
> relations of the Godhead.[71]

Since the work which is the person of Christ is also
the act and work of God, it follows that Jesus Christ and
God are one person. As God, Christ determines himself
through his decision, and he fulfills himself in
spontaneous self-realization. At the same time, he
reconciles man to himself.

In conclusion, this consideration of the concept of
essential divinity has made it clear that Jesus Christ is
identical with the act, the essence, and the person of
God. Because Jesus Christ shares in the essence of God,
his divinity is his own. He is God himself, both in God's
inner-trinitarian life and also in his act ad extra, his
existence as a man. The directness of the identity of
Christ's deity with the deity of God can be substantiated
further by mentioning three points which are implied in
the preceding discussion.

First, Barth states that Jesus Christ is "by nature"
God. "It is He, Jesus, who is in the beginning with God.
It is He who by nature is God." Similarly, Jesus Christ is
"intrinsically divine." As the Word of God, divinity is
ascribed to him in "the strictest and most proper sense,"
because he "participated absolutely in the divine mode of
being, in the divine being itself."[72] These statements
threaten the Antiochian view that Jesus Christ is divine
by relation rather than by nature.

Secondly, the divinity of Christ does not depend upon God's decision to speak through him at a particular moment, as is the case with respect to the Bible and proclamation. Barth states:

> Of course, the fact that Jesus Christ is the Son of God does not rest on the election. What does rest on it is the fact that as such he became man, that as such (to use the Johannine concept) He is 'sent,' that as such He is the bearer of the divine name of the Father in the world.[73]

He does not become the Son of God or the Word of God; he is the Word of God in the beginning, before all time.

Thirdly, Barth states that the "is" which is used to identify Jesus Christ with God is understood in the strictest sense. It is not simply an "is" of becoming, as is the case in the statement that the Bible is the Word of God. Barth explains:

> The phrase "the one" Lord unites Jesus Christ immediately to the Father, of whom the confession in the first article had said emphatically, He is o n e God. If there can be no rivalry between the two concepts "God" and "Lord," if they refer to the one Being, to the one Being in the way in which statements about creation and reconciliation refer to the one operation of this one Being, then by means of this stipulation the decisive statement is already made, that Jesus Christ is himself this Being, not His legate or plenipotentiary merely, but identical with Him. Therefore because he is the one Lord, because in this strictest sense he is t h e Lord, his lordship for us in his revelation has no beginning and no end, it breaks over us with the unheard-of and incomparable fall of eternal truth and reality itself, it cannot be realized or inferred from any standpoint whatsoever, knowledge of it begins with the acknowledgment of it.[74]

These three points undermine the Antiochian interpretation of Barth. Further, because Antiochian thought
regarding the divinity of Christ begins with the assumption that Jesus is a human person who becomes divine in
revelation, it appears that it moves in a direction which
is almost exactly opposite that of Barth. Barth begins
with the concept of Jesus Christ as the act of revelation
which constitutes God's being. He stresses that Jesus
Christ is the divine being who is "also" human. This
emphasis continues in his development of the concept of
the unity of the person of Christ, to which we now turn.

THE UNITY OF THE PERSON OF JESUS CHRIST

Following the pattern used in the second chapter, we shall
begin our discussion of an Alexandrian interpretation of
Barth's doctrine of the unity of the person of Christ with
a consideration of the logos ensarkos. Then we shall deal
with his concept of incarnation. Under this category,
five principal topics demand attention: the incarnation
as an act of God, becoming and assuming, what is assumed,
the concepts of anhypostasis and enhypostasis, and God as
the subject of human activity. Next we shall turn to the
relation of God the Word to the human nature, the resulting union of the two natures, and the correlation of the
two aspects of the work of Christ. Throughout this
discussion, we shall argue that Barth understands Jesus
Christ, even in his existence as a man, as directly
identical with God. He is united with a human nature
which is less than a complete, human person.

The Logos Ensarkos

According to an Alexandrian interpretation, Barth's
development of the concept of the logos ensarkos emphasizes Jesus Christ's divine being. As both God and man,
Jesus Christ participates in the inner life of God, prior
to his incarnation in time, because he is the decision of
God. Since God's decision is the act which constitutes
his being, the equation of Jesus Christ with the decision
of God stresses his divinity.

Barth makes this point most explicitly in his discussion of the doctrine of election. He denies that Jesus Christ is with God prior to creation simply in God's intention, in the same way that other creatures are with him. He is with God as his decision.

> Jesus Christ was in the beginning with God. He was so not merely in the sense that in view of God's eternal knowing and willing all things may be said to have been in the beginning with God, in His plan and decree. . . . He was also in the beginning with God as "the first born of every creature" (Col. 1:15), Himself the plan and decree of God, Himself the divine decision with respect to all creation and its history whose content is already determined. [75]

Because Jesus Christ is the eternal decision of God, he is completely identical with the person God. He is not merely one who is elected; he is the agent who elects. Drawing on Augustine for support against Thomas Aquinas, Barth states:

> Thomas, and many others after him, spoke of the election of Jesus Christ only in this second and passive sense, and with reference only to the man Jesus. Augustine, too, had spoken of it in this way, and we ourselves must do the same. But Augustine--and in this we must at once follow him--also looked upwards to the place where the incarnation, the reality of the divine-human person of Jesus Christ before the foundation of the world and all other reality, is identical with the eternal purpose of the good-pleasure of God, and where the eternal purpose of the good-pleasure of God which precedes all created reality is identical with the reality of the divine-human person of Jesus Christ. He looked upwards to the place where the eternal God not only foresees and foreordains this person, but where He Himself, as the

presupposition of its revelation in time, actually is this person.[76]

It is clear, then, that Barth's analysis of this concept emphasizes Jesus Christ's unity with God rather than his distinction from God. In this respect, it threatens the Antiochian concern to safeguard the integrity of Jesus as a complete, historical person.

The Incarnation

The Act of God the Word

The Alexandrian view is in substantial agreement with the Antiochian on this topic, in spite of the latter's understanding of Barth's concept of the logos ensarkos. Barth clearly affirms that the event of the incarnation depends ultimately upon the free grace of God, not creaturely power. The original decision of God to become man involves his human nature, so that he cannot be said to be without it. Therefore, when God enters creaturely existence, he does so with his human nature. Nevertheless, his humanity is dependent upon his divinity, and it cannot, in itself, initiate the incarnation or reconcile man to God. God is the agent of the incarnation, both in his original decision and also in his execution of that decision.

Becoming and Assuming

Those who accept an Antiochian interpretation of Barth, as we saw, may reasonably conclude that Barth applies the concept of becoming directly to the human nature, which becomes a man, and indirectly to the divine Word. On the basis of this conclusion, these interpreters may also reasonably infer that, for Barth, creaturely predicates apply to the divine Word by relation and that divine qualities are ascribed to the man Jesus by relation. However, this linguistic principle is not explicitly affirmed by Barth, and assuming that this is his intention is unwarranted.

According to an Alexandrian interpretation of Barth, the two verbs "become" and "assume" may be viewed as complementary and mutually corrective, each applying directly to the divine Word. The Word does not become a man in the sense that He is forced into a passive role by external factors, as is the case with human becoming. Nor does he become identical with a man who was already in existence. "Assume" indicates that the divine person is in full control of this act. Yet, "become" also suggests the continuity of the agency, a point which is important for an Alexandrian interpretation. The one who existed in the inner being of God and who is God himself now becomes a participant in human existence. This is a new determination for him, but he is not transformed into something or someone else by it. It is a new stage of his existence, as when we speak of a person becoming an adult. The fact that Barth continues to use "becomes" when speaking of this act of the Word suggests its value.[77] It is not completely replaced by "assumes." Understood correctly, it is a useful term when used directly of the Word himself and not simply because of his relation to the human nature.

What Is Assumed

In an Antiochian interpretation of Barth, considerable emphasis is placed upon the fact that Barth ascribes a personality and a will to the human nature which the Word assumes in the incarnation. According to the Antiochian view, if this human nature has a personality and a will it must be a person. On the other hand, in order to defend an Alexandrian interpretation, one may argue that Barth makes a distinction between a person and personality in this context. The human nature of Christ, according to the Alexandrian view, has its own personality or individuality, but it is not, in itself, a person.

One fact which makes this conclusion plausible is that there is a precedent for it. Brunner in The Mediator makes a radical distinction between the human personality of Jesus and his divine person. For Brunner, the personality of Jesus is available for ordinary knowledge, but the divine person is known only in faith.[78] While

Barth does not refer specifically to Brunner in his discussion of this point, the fact that such a distinction is possible among "neo-orthodox" theologians indicates that one cannot conclude without argument that Barth identifies the two concepts of person and personality.

More importantly, there is a passage in Karl Barth's Table Talk which distinguishes person from personality. Because this text is not without ambiguity, it is best to record it here and then discuss it further.

> S: What is the relation of the doctrines of Perichoresis and Appropriations to the human nature of Christ?
> B: What do you mean by "human nature"? Jesus Christ is a "Person" of the Trinity, but this does not mean that he has a "personality" in the modern sense of a "center of consciousness." His personality is that of Son of God.
> S: But if human nature lacks personality, is it really human nature?
> B: Individuality is necessary to human nature, but not Person. A person exists in human nature. Of course Christ had a "center of consciousness." Personality means just this or that man. It can only be applied to the existence of a particular man. His thisness or thatness is his personality. If the old Christological doctrine denied personality to Christ, it meant to deny that there was a man as such and then the Word became that man. No, this man never existed except as Son of God--from the beginning. God chose one possibility of humanity out of a mass of possibilities and realized its existence in the Son of God. Humanity means the nature or essence of man. Personality means the existence of a man. The Father and the Holy Spirit are also concerned in the incarnation (Periochoresis), but not so that you can speak of the "incarnate Father," etc. We might use the illustration of three men: two of them help the other put on a coat, but only this one wears it.[79]

The first response by Barth might be interpreted to mean that the human nature of Jesus Christ has no personality and thus no center of consciousness in itself. This understanding is possible because the questioner focuses upon the human nature and Barth begins his answer with this same subject. If this interpretation were correct, we would have here a radical denial of the Antiochian view. The human nature has no personality and thus, apparently, is not a person in its own right.

The student seems to understand Barth in this way. Only one concept of personality has appeared so far, and it is the concept of center of consciousness. Thus, when the student says "But if the human nature lacks personality, is it really human nature?" he appears to conclude that Barth intends to say that the human nature lacks a self-consciousness.

Our conclusion is that Barth, in the first response in the quotation, is speaking of the trinity. What he means is that Jesus Christ is one of the three in the trinity, but he does not have a separate center of consciousness. There is only one personality in the trinity, and therefore one center of consciousness, which is shared equally by the three modes of being. This point would be clearer if Barth had added that the personality of Jesus Christ is the personality of the Father and Holy Spirit as well as that of the eternal Son.

In his second response, Barth appears to utilize traditional rather than modern terminology with respect to the concept of personality. As we have seen, Barth explains that the ancients used the term individualitas to designate what moderns mean by "personality," namely, self-consciousness.[80] Consequently, when he states that individuality but not person is necessary for the human nature, he clearly means that the human nature has its personality in the sense of self-consciousness, although it is not a person. To be a person, Barth continues, one must exist.

There are two important distinctions in this argument. One is between ancient and modern concepts of personality, and the second is between essence and existence. The concept of person and a corresponding concept of personality are inextricably connected to the concept of existence. On the other hand, although the essence of man

does not exist as a person, it includes individuality and,
therefore, personality in the limited sense of self-
consciousness.[81]

In spite of its ambiguities, this passage clarifies
those in the Church Dogmatics where Barth reports that the
ancients sometimes used the term impersonalitas for the
human nature but that they did not mean by it what moderns
do. Here the denial that the human nature is a person and
the affirmation that it has its own self-consciousness
appear side by side, indicating that Barth does make a
distinction between the concept of person and one meaning
of the concept of personality. This distinction undermines the belief that the human nature of Christ must be a
person because it has personality.

This denial that the human nature is a person also
effectively opposes the view that the human nature is a
person because it has its own will. For Barth, the
crucial element in the concept of a person seems to be
existence rather than personality or will. This leads us
again to the doctrines of anhypostasis and enhypostasis,
which deal with the existence of the human nature.
Although the human nature may not be a person in its
essence, the question still remains whether in the incarnation, when the human nature comes into existence, it
becomes a person over against the person of the Son of
God.

Anhypostasis and *Enhypostasis*

Barth's treatment of these concepts indicates that he
thinks that the human nature of Christ is not a person
either before or after the initial moment of the incarnation. We shall mention three points which support this
Alexandrian interpretation of Barth, and two of them are
found in the following important passage.

> We can and must, indeed, speak of a presence,
> even of a personal presence of God in all
> created being, and to that extent of a unity
> also of God with all created being. But then
> this created being has an independent exis-
> tence (selbstaendige Existenz) in relation to

God. It is real only in virtue of creation
and preservation, through God, and to that
extent only in unity with God. But it is real
in this unity, not as though it were itself
God, but in such a way that, being in God, it
is different from God, in such a way that
through God it possesses an existence of its
own different from the existence of God. It
is the same with God's gracious presence in
the word preached and in the sacrament (so far
as by that is meant the outward creaturely
sign of word and elements), and with God's
gracious presence in the hearts of those
chosen and called by faith. Unity with God in
the former case means that man's speech, that
water, bread and wine, are real not only
through God, but as inseparably bound to God,
and similarly in the latter case, that believing man may live not only through God but
inseparably bound to God. But unity with God
cannot mean in the former case that man's
speech, that water, bread and wine, or in the
latter case that believing man, is identical
with God. What is proclaimed by the unity of
God and man in Jesus Christ is as follows.
This man Jesus Christ is identical with God
because the Word became flesh in the sense
just explained. Therefore He does not only
live through God and with God. He is Himself
God. Nor is He autonomous and self-existent.
His reality, existence and being is wholly and
absolutely that of God Himself, the God who
acts in His Word. His manhood is only the
predicate of His Godhead, or better and more
concretely, it is only the predicate, assumed
in inconceivable condescension, of the Word
acting upon us, the Word who is the Lord.[82]

First, this quote states that human persons are related
to God differently from the way the human nature of Christ
is related to him. All created beings, including human
persons, exist independently from God. Although they are
brought into existence by God, their existence is differ-

ent from his. Yet, the human nature of Christ, even after
it comes into existence, has no independent existence.
Its existence is identical with God's existence.[83]
Since the human nature of Christ does not have an independent existence as persons do, it is presumptuous to assume
that it is, in itself, a person distinct from God.[84]

Second, this passage describes the identity between
Jesus Christ and God in such a way that it is difficult to
explain it as an indirect identity, as though Jesus is a
human individual through whom God speaks from time to
time. Barth states that Jesus Christ not only lives with
God, "He is Himself God." His reality, existence, and
being are "wholly and absolutely that of God Himself."
Barth does not make such claims about the Bible and the
creaturely media of proclamation. They can become the
Word of God, but they are not God himself, and their
existence is not absolutely that of God. Consequently, it
is unwise to conclude that Jesus is a mere man who is more
closely related to God than other men. Barth's terminology indicates that the difference between Jesus Christ and
other men is more than a matter of degree.[85]

Those who accept an Alexandrian interpretation of Barth
can admit that Barth's treatment of the relation of God
the Word to the Bible and proclamation is Antiochian. The
Bible and the creaturely media of proclamation have an
independent existence as other creatures. They persist in
time even though God may not be speaking through them at
every moment. On the other hand, the human nature of
Christ does not exist independently as it would if it were
a man. It is, as we shall see momentarily, God's mode of
operation as a man.[86] In this respect, the human nature
of Christ belongs to a class by itself, apart from the
Bible and proclamation.

Third, since Jesus Christ is directly identical with
God, it is difficult to see how there can be two involved
here, and Barth denies that there are two. We have seen
that the Antiochian interpreters assume that this denial
is intended to prevent the idea that the two persons, God
and Jesus, are related in an external manner, side by
side. However, Barth denies not only that there are two
side by side, but also that another is "in" God. He
states:

> We resume the discussion with the second
> statement in our description of the incarna-
> tion: (2) that the existence of the Son of
> God became and is the existence of a man.
> There are not two existing side by side or
> even within one another. There is only the
> one God the Son, and no one and nothing either
> alongside or even in Him.[87]

This statement clearly precludes the idea that Jesus is a
human person who exists in the existence of God.

The concepts of anhypostasis and enhypostasis, then,
affirm that the existence of the human nature of Christ is
identical with the existence of Jesus Christ and also the
existence of God. There is only one existence here, and
it is God's acting in the creaturely realm. As a result,
these two concepts should be interpreted in relation to
Barth's understanding of God's act as his being and his
concept of the two moments in the divinity of Christ. The
existence of Jesus Christ is God's act ad extra. This act
and existence are identical with the one divine person in
his relation to men.

God Is Subject

Now we come to the question of what Barth means when he
says that God performs the human actions of Jesus. This
topic is clarified by Barth's use of the concept of the
"bearer."[88] God is the subject of Jesus Christ's
actions because he is the bearer of the human nature of
Christ. Jesus Christ is fully identical with God because
he is also this one bearer, not a person distinct from God
in an Antiochian sense. He is the same agent God is.

Barth's concept of the bearer is Alexandrian in two
ways. In the first place, this concept emphasizes the
divinity of the agent who performs the actions of the man
Jesus. Divinity is an inherent quality of this agent, not
a predicate ascribed to him because of his association
with God. In the second place, Barth's concept of the
bearer is Alexandrian because it indicates that the human
nature of Christ lacks a strictly human bearer, and
therefore it neither was nor became an individual person

in itself. The bearer of this particular humanity is God himself, while the bearers of other instances of humanity in the world are simply human; thus, Jesus Christ is absolutely unique.

Barth's treatment of the bearer of the divine and human natures is found principally in his discussion of God's assumption of flesh in volumes 1/2 and 4/2 of the Church Dogmatics. He explains that the actor in the incarnation is God himself, God the Word, not the divine nature. The divine nature has no existence and cannot act in itself. It exists only in and through the existence of the divine subject, who is its bearer. Godhead, Barth says, "is only the modus" of God's being.[89]

In the same way, human nature is only the modus of a particular human being. It does not exist and act in itself. For that reason, it must be said that the human nature is not the agent of the incarnation and the atonement. Human nature consists of those characteristics which distinguish men from other realities, but it exists only in a bearer. Speaking specifically of Jesus Christ, Barth affirms, "But in itself and as such the humanity of Jesus Christ is a predicate without a subject."[90]

Individual men, Barth states, are bearers of the human essence. Since many men have existed, Jesus Christ is not the only bearer of human essence, although in his case both the bearer and the human essence which he bears are unique.

> Of human essence, on the other hand, we have to say that it, too, is actualized in as many cases as there have been and are and will be men. It is actualized, of course, as human essence: not of itself, but by the creative will and power and act of God, as the One who alone is actual originally and in Himself; and as a creaturely essence, absolutely conditioned and limited by His will and power and act. It, too, does not await the incarnation of the Son of God for its actualization. It is another matter that it is created with a view to this, and has in it its meaning and telos, and is only true human essence by it and in it. But, since the Son of Man Jesus

Christ is only one of countless other men who
also bear this essence, we cannot say that it
is actualized only in Him.[91]

The uniqueness of the bearer of the human essence of
Jesus Christ is that he is the Word of God.   In Jesus
Christ there is no purely human bearer of the human
nature, as is the case with other men.   When the Word
enters the creaturely realm and becomes man, he adds to
the divine nature, which is already his, fallen human
nature, bearing it and its sin.   Barth states:

> The Word became flesh--not just man, but the
> bearer of our human essence, which is marked
> not only by its created and unlost goodness
> but (in self-contradiction) by sin, so that it
> is a perverted essence and lost as such. . . .
> And we can and must say that He overcame it at
> the deepest level by not refusing to
> accomplish the humiliation of the Son of God
> to be not only a creature but a sinful
> creature, to become and be the bearer of human
> essence in its inward contradiction, to repent
> as such, to become the friend of publicans and
> sinners, to suffer and die as a malefactor
> with others.[92]

When the eternal Son or Word becomes the bearer of
human nature, he does not cease to be the bearer of the
divine nature.   Barth makes this point clear by stating
that the divine nature belongs to the Son originally, but
that the human nature is his through adoption.   As the
bearer of both natures, he acts through each of them, and
he determines each to the other.

> The Son of God is the acting Subject who takes
> the initiative in this event, and not either
> His divine or His human essence.   Of both
> these it is true that they are real and can
> act only as He exists in them: in Himself
> with the Father and the Holy Ghost in His
> divine essence; and per assumptionem in His
> human.   He Himself grasps and has and main-

> tains the leadership in what His divine
> essence is and means for His human, and His
> human for His divine, in their mutual partici-
> pation. . . . As His divine essence is that
> which is originally proper to Him, and His
> human is only adopted by Him and assumed to
> it, it is clear that we must see their mutual
> determination in the distinction in which we
> have described it.[93]

Barth coordinates the concept of the bearer with his understanding of Jesus Christ as a history. As the Son of God who bears the divine nature, Jesus Christ humiliates himself to become man. As the Son of Man he bears and exalts the human nature. The act in which he bears both natures is his history and his being. Barth states:

> It is in the actual occurrence of this history
> that we have seen that which particularly
> interests us in the present context--its
> movement from below to above, the exaltation
> of the Son of Man who in His identity with the
> Son of God comes to God as the bearer of our
> human essence.[94]

In the event of the incarnation, there are three principal elements: the divine agent, the divine nature, and the human nature. In the act which constitutes his being from all eternity, the divine agent adds human nature to his divine nature. For Barth, there is no need for any additional elements. The human nature is complete in itself, with its own will and personality, its soul and body. The divine agent, with his divine essence, is also complete in himself.[95]

Since there are only these three elements, it can be seen that there is no strictly human bearer of the human nature in Jesus Christ. Barth makes this clear by saying: "There was and is, therefore, no Son of Man who, conversely, has assumed divine essence to His human essence and thus become the Son of God." This statement means that there is no bearer of the human nature, called "Son of Man," who acted in and through the human nature and assumed divine nature to himself, becoming God. On the contrary, the one who is properly called "Son of Man" is already the one who bears the divine nature as well as the human nature.

> But the second, His exaltation as the Son of Man, does not mean that He became God. How could He just become that which He already was from all eternity as the Son of God, and which He did not cease to be even as the Son of Man?[96]

Barth's use of the concept of the bearer gives him a clear way to affirm that Jesus Christ is one person not two. He is one person in that he is the same subject both in eternity and in time, both in his divine nature and in the human nature which he adopts. Because he acts humanly as well as divinely, he has a human nature as well as a divine nature, and the characteristics of men can be attributed to him. Because the human nature has no strictly human bearer, it is not a complete man alongside or within the one Christ.

At the same time, the concept of the bearer indicates that the man Jesus is directly identical with the Son of God. Since the eternal Son is the single bearer of the human nature and since bearers of humanity are called "men," the man Jesus is the Son himself and not a human person united with him.

Because Jesus is directly identical with God, God is directly the subject of the acts of Jesus. Of course, God performs the actions of Jesus through his human nature, but the human nature is not an agent in itself. Because God bears the human nature, Barth can say that "God Himself is its human subject."[97] More specifically, he affirms that God is this subject "directly" rather than indirectly.

> Now it is no accident that for us the Virgin birth is paralleled by the miracle of which the Easter witness speaks, the miracle of the empty tomb. These two miracles belong together. They constitute, as it were, a single sign, the special function of which, compared with other signs and wonders of the New

> Testament witness, is to describe and mark out
> the existence of Jesus Christ, amid the many
> other existences in human history, as that
> human historical existence in which God is
> Himself, God is alone, God is <u>directly</u> the
> Subject, the temperal reality of which is not
> only called forth, created, conditioned and
> supported by the eternal reality of God, but
> is identical with it.[98]

The statement that God is alone the subject of Jesus' existence precludes effectively the supposition that God simply acts vicariously through a human person named Jesus who is distinct from God. Barth clearly rejects the Antiochian idea that there are two persons involved here, and that God is the prior and more important of the two, guiding, directing, and affirming the acts of Jesus. On the contrary, the identity between Jesus and God is an identity in the fullest sense of the word.

Because of the identity of Jesus with God, Barth is not compelled to distinguish two different subjects when he speaks of the divine and human actions which are attributed to Jesus Christ in the Bible. This freedom is most apparent when Barth uses the pronoun "he" to denote the one who obeys the Father in the inner-trinitarian life, descends to earth and is born of Mary, is baptized, calls his disciples, preaches, forgives sins, dies, is buried, and rises from the tomb. Barth gives no indication that he intends to differentiate a divine "he" who obeys the Father in eternity from a human "he" who eats, drinks, and sleeps. In each case, the "he" refers to the one bearer of both natures who acts divinely and humanly.[99]

In conclusion, Barth's doctrine of the incarnation gives support to an Alexandrian interpretation. There is a direct identity between Jesus Christ and God not only in the inner-trinitarian life but also in the creaturely realm. The existence of the man Jesus is directly identical with God's existence, and the subject who acts in the human nature is God, not a human person distinct from God. Once this conclusion has been reached, it is possible to understand Barth's treatment of the relation between God and the human nature, the union of the two natures, and the coordination of the divine and human aspects of the work of Christ in an Alexandrian manner.

God the Word and the Human Nature

In his discussion of this subject Barth considers the analogies which have been used to aid in comprehending the unity of God and man in Christ. He argues that there is a radical discontinuity between God's union with the human nature and other unities. We have already shown how Barth distinguishes this union from the unity of God the Word with the Bible and proclamation in the moment in which they witness to revelation.[100] Here we wish to make two points. The first is that the uniqueness of God's union with the human nature of Jesus can be demonstrated by showing how Barth contrasts it with God's relation to the individual and to the church. The second is that Barth has a preference for analogies which suggest that the human nature is not a complete person. Both these points support the Alexandrian conclusion that Barth conceives of the unity of God and man in Christ as a unity between the person God and a specimen of human nature which is not a person.

That Jesus Christ is not simply a religious personality who is related to God in a special way is implied by Barth's insistence that all other unions and thus all possible analogies have their ground in Jesus Christ himself.[101] As God's eternal decision, Jesus Christ is the all-embracing reality. As a result, all analogies are inadequate and, in the final analysis, misleading. Barth states:

> In Him (Jesus Christ) we have the basic reality which underlies the possibility of the basic relationship of the covenant, and therefore all the natural and historical relationships, and in them the analogies, and therefore His own connexion with His earthly surroundings and the comparisons which it invites. In Him we have their beginning, their meaning and their goal, the center which unites and carries the whole, both creation and the covenant.[102]

Because the hypostatic union is a union with the human nature of all men and not simply one man, the union of God

with all man is included in it. Thus, the presence of God
in the life of the individual, the so-called unio mystica,
does not actually correspond to the divinity and humanity
of Jesus Christ. Consequently, Barth argues, we should
not accept Donald Baillie's attempt to understand the
Chalcedonian formulation of the unity of Jesus Christ
along the lines suggested by texts such as Gal. 2:20,
"Nevertheless I live; yet not I, but Christ liveth in me."
The difficulty with this view is that individuals do not
have a direct relation to God as Jesus Christ does. Jesus
Christ is God himself, and he is also the mediator of all
human relations with God.[103]

Barth's discussion of the unity of the church with God
follows much the same pattern. He describes the church as
the second form of the existence of Jesus Christ. Since
we have seen that Jesus Christ's existence is directly
identical with the existence of God the Word, it might be
assumed that the church is identical with God in the same
way that the man Jesus is. However, Barth is not willing
to make this equation. Rather, the relationship between
God and man which occurs in the church is included in the
reality of Jesus Christ. Therefore, the relation of the
church to God is not parallel to that between the human
nature of Christ and God. Barth states:

> He carries and maintains it (the community) in
> this unity with Himself as the people which
> not merely belongs to Him but is part of
> Himself. In God's eternal counsel, in His
> epiphany, and finally in His revelation at the
> end of the age, He was and is and will be this
> totus Christus--Christ and Christians. And
> these two elements of His one being are not
> merely related to one another as He Himself as
> Son of God is related to His human nature.
> But, in this second form, His relationship to
> His body, the community, is the relationship
> of God and man as it takes place in this one
> being as Head and body.[104]

We turn to our second point; Barth notes that certain
analogies which were used by the church fathers have value
by way of illustration. Many of the ones included in this

list, such as "that the Word is in flesh like a man in his
clothes, or a sailor in his boat" have to do with a
personal reality and a nonpersonal one.[105] Interest-
ingly, when Barth uses analogies, these are the ones he
favors. For example, in his polemic against the Lutheran
doctrine that the human nature was divinized in the
incarnation, he states that it is better to think of the
human nature as a temple in which God dwells.

> Is temple or dwelling--a dwelling which is
> certainly filled with Godhead and totally and
> exclusively claimed and sanctified, but still
> a dwelling--not really enough to describe
> what we have to say of human essence in
> relation to Jesus Christ and this history
> which took place in Him? Do we have to deify
> this temple, this dwelling as such, in order
> that the dwelling of the Godhead in it may be
> a real one? If it is deified, does it not
> cease to be His temple?[106]

As we saw earlier, in his explanation of the notion of
appropriations, Barth indicates that the Father, Son, and
Holy Spirit are involved in the action of the incarnation,
but only the Son becomes flesh. His analogy is that the
Father and the Holy Spirit hold a coat for the Son to put
on. They participate, but they do not put on the coat.
[107] Barth's preference for analogies of this type
suggests that his view is Alexandrian, and that the human
nature involved in the incarnation is not a person. If
Barth were Antiochian, we might expect to find him using
analogies involving two persons, such as husband and wife,
more often.[108]

The Union of the Two Natures

Barth's understanding of the fellowship of the two natures
is not developed in such a way as to require the assumption that he thinks of the two natures as being two
persons, God and Jesus. In his treatment of the union of
the two natures, Barth does not use I-Thou terminology,
although he speaks of fellowship and confrontation. In

the union of the two natures, the human nature attests the divine nature, witnesses to it, and is obedient to it. In the Alexandrian view, this relationship of fellowship between the two natures should be understood as analogous to the kind of obedience and communication that Barth can locate within a single person, rather than that which is found in a relation between two persons, such as a parent and a child.

Barth describes the relationship between the Son and the Father in the inner-trinitarian life as a relation of obedience. The Son obeys the Father. Yet, this does not mean, for Barth, that the Son and the Father are two separate persons. Barth is quite explicit that it is the essence of the triune God which is a person. God is one subject, although he acts in different ways and although he has internal relations.[109] One of these internal relations can be described as obedience.

Since there are not two persons or "wills" in God, the obedience of the Son to the Father in the inner-trinitarian life should be understood to mean that God is true to himself. God as he is in his second mode of being is obedient to himself as he is in his first mode of being. His inner obedience is complete and perfect, and it cannot be adequately conveyed in the metaphor of Father-Son. Speaking of the term "Son," Barth states:

> But the term cannot bring out the ontological necessity in which this Father has this Son, and this Son this Father, the perfection in which this Father and this Son are one, i.e., are the different modes of being of one and the same personal God, the eternity of the fatherly begetting and of the being begotten of the Son, which is the basis of their relationship, their free but also necessary fellowship and love in the activity of the Holy Spirit as the third divine mode of being of the same kind, the self-evident fulfillment of that determination of a son to his father, the actual rendering of a perfect obedience, the ceaseless unity of the One who disposes and the One who complies, the actual oneness and agreement of that which they will and do.

The history in which God is the living God in
Himself can only be indicated but not
conceived by our terms son and father and
spirit.[110]

Barth makes it quite clear that when he talks of the
obedience of the Son to the Father he means an obedience
which is rendered by God to himself. Only God can render
perfect and complete obedience. Barth asserts:

In rendering obedience as He does, He does
something which, as in the case of that
lordship, only God can do. The One who in
this obedience is the perfect image of the
ruling God is Himself--as distinct from every
human and creaturely kind--God by nature, God
in His relationship to Himself, i.e., God in
His mode of being as the Son in relation to
God in His mode of being as the Father, one
with the Father and one of essence. In His
mode of being as the Son He fulfils the divine
subordination, just as the Father in His mode
of being as the Father fulfils the divine
superiority.[111]

The point to be emphasized is that Barth can attribute
to God himself relationships which we normally think of as
requiring more than one personal agent. Yet, in God,
these relationships occur within a single person, the one
true person. There is a dialectic in God, but not more
than one agent.

Barth can also attribute an obedience to the human body
of Jesus Christ. This body is obedient, Barth explains,
to the human soul within the human nature of Jesus Christ.
That Barth can speak of a human obedience of this sort
gives additional support for the contention that Barth's
personal ways of speaking do not necessarily require
separate persons in the strict sense. A statement of the
obedience of the body of Jesus is the following:

The interconnexion of the soul and body and
Word and act of Jesus is not a chaos but a
cosmos, a formed and ordered totality. There

is in it a higher and a lower, a first and a
second, a dominating and a dominated. But the
man Jesus Himself is both. He is not only the
higher, the first, the dominating, nor is He
both in such a way that the lower, the second,
the dominated is associated with him only
externally or accidentally. This would again
imply the destruction of that oneness and
wholeness. He is also the lower, the second,
the dominated. He is not only His soul but
also His body. But He is both soul and body
in an ordered oneness and wholeness. His
being is orderly and not disorderly. Nor is
He this in such a way that the order is
accidental and imposed from without. He is in
an order which derives from Himself. He
Himself and from Himself is both the higher
and the lower, the first and the second, the
dominant and dominated. He Himself is in both
cases His own principle. The meaning, plan
and intention, the logos of His life is thus
not exterior and accidental. It is no foreign
law to which He binds Himself but which comes
from elsewhere and is established over Him.
Rather He is His own law, and He is subject to
it in a free obedience arising in Himself and
proceeding from Himself. Jesus wills and
fulfils Himself. He is His own ground and His
own intention. He lives in such a way that
command and obedience, ordination and subordination, plan and execution, goal and aim
proceed from Himself and thus partake of an
equal inward necessity.[112]

The fact that Barth can use personal language to
describe a relation within a person in the examples just
given does not prove that his treatment of the relation of
the two natures is to be understood in a similar fashion.
Yet, it does make such an interpretation plausible.
Furthermore, it undermines the argument that the presence
of personal language implies that Barth's concept of the
relation between the two natures is a way of talking about
a relation between a person God and another person Jesus.

In these ways, Barth's use of personal language to explain a relation within a person rather than between persons contributes to an Alexandrian interpretation of Barth's christology.

The Coordination of the Work

In Barth's doctrine of reconciliation, the work of Jesus Christ as priest and as king should be understood in an Alexandrian rather than an Antiochian manner. It is the work of one divine agent, not two agents, one divine and the other human. If it is the case that the bearer of both natures is God himself, then there is not a sufficient reason to suppose that Barth means that the priestly work is carried out by the divine agent and the kingly work by a human agent. While it is true that the priestly work is more logically associated with the divine nature and the kingly work is more closely related to the human nature, it does not follow that Barth intends for the two natures to be understood as two distinct persons. Through his divine nature, the eternal Son humiliates himself and overcomes sin. Through his human nature he is exalted to a state of fellowship with the Father. The two aspects of his work are two moments, two movements, and two directions of one work performed by one agent. There can be no question of the human nature, or some human agent, exalting itself or himself.

Nor can there be any suggestion that the priestly work is exclusively related to the divine nature and the kingly work exclusively performed by the human nature. What God does, he does through both natures simultaneously. The humiliation of Christ in his priestly task involves his human nature, although the possibility of this act is grounded in his divine nature. Barth says: "It was to fulfil this judgment on sin that the Son of God as man took our place as sinners."[113] This statement indicates that the priestly work, in which God took our place, involves God's being "as man" as well as his being as God.

The exaltation also involves the divine nature as well as the human nature. It is through his divine nature and its power that the eternal Son of God can exalt the human nature, although the divine nature is already exalted and needs no additional honor. Barth clearly indicates that the work of exaltation is performed by God himself, and God does not act apart from his divine nature. "But it is also true that in and with His own abasement God has elected and achieved man's exaltation."[114] Thus, the saving work of Jesus Christ is performed by one divine agent through both natures. Barth's account of this work is not Antiochian, in our definition of Antiochianism. [115]

CONCLUSION

In this discussion of Barth's concepts of the divinity of Christ and the unity of his person, we have defended the claim that Barth's position is basically Alexandrian. Although the human nature which is united with God is capable of witnessing to the Word, and thus has some degree of agency, and although Barth develops the idea of the union of the two natures in Antiochian categories of fellowship and obedience, in the final analysis it seems clear that an Antiochian interpretation cannot be fully sustained. For Barth, Jesus Christ is essentially divine. As the act of God and also as the divine subject who acts in eternity and in time, he is directly identical with God himself. In the incarnation, he becomes the bearer of human nature, which has no independent existence and is not a person in itself. He is not merely a human person who is related to God in a special way, but the all-embracing divine reality in which all men have their being.

The Alexandrian interpretation of Barth is also supported by an analysis of his use of the name "Jesus Christ" and its variants. As we shall see next, Barth uses these names to denote God himself, not a human person distinct from God.

Chapter 4

The purpose of this chapter is to show that Barth uses the name "Jesus Christ" and its variants to denote the personal subject God rather than a human person distinct from God. As we have seen, according to an Antiochian interpretation of Barth, Barth uses some terms, such as "Jesus," "Jesus of Nazareth" and "Son of Man" to distinguish a human subject from the divine subject, who is usually designated by other terms, such as "Son of God" and "Word of God." In an Alexandrian interpretation, all these terms denote the one divine subject, although they have different connotations. Some of them, such as "Jesus," connote this subject in his being and action as man, while others, such as "Son of God," connote his being and action as God.

To substantiate the Alexandrian interpretation, we shall first consider the evidence which indicates that Barth understands "Jesus Christ" and its variants as names of God. This evidence can be divided into two general categories, one having to do with the theoretical aspects of Barth's christological language and the other with his actual uses of the names. Before turning to Barth's uses of the names, we shall discuss his explanation of the referent of "Jesus" and "Jesus Christ," his analysis of the identity statements called <u>propositiones personales</u>, his rejection of the use of "Jesus Christ" and its variants to denote a human person distinct from God, and his account of the basis for applying possible predicates to these names. Throughout this first section of the chapter we shall show that Barth indicates that even such terms as "Jesus" and "man Jesus" can be used for God himself. In this way, Barth distinguishes himself from the Antiochian theologians who prefer to use such terms only for the human person united with God. Nevertheless, "Jesus" and similar terms are not always used in exactly the same ways as "Jesus Christ" and "Son of God."

In the second major section of this chapter we shall show that one who accepts an Alexandrian interpretation of Barth can account for the differences in the ways Barth uses "Jesus Christ" and its variants without resorting to the Antiochian hypothesis that there are two agents involved. One can defend an Alexandrian interpretation of Barth's language by appealing to two basic principles which operate harmoniously in Barth's language. The first is that "Jesus Christ" and its variants connote as well as denote. The second is abstraction. Because Jesus Christ, as the act of God, is a comprehensive and complex reality, Barth finds it necessary to abstract from the whole Christ particular aspects of his being and action. When he talks of the divine nature of Christ, for example, he is abstracting from the total Christ. To draw attention to this process, Barth uses the connotations of the various names of Christ. For example, to abstract Christ's mode of being and action as man, Barth sometimes uses the title "Son of Man." In such cases, "Son of Man" should be understood as a shortened form of "Jesus Christ as man," not the title of a separate, human person.

"JESUS CHRIST" AND ITS VARIANTS AS NAMES OF GOD

"Jesus," "Jesus Christ," and Their Referent

Barth's belief that "Jesus" and "Jesus Christ" name God himself is expressed in a variety of ways. One of the most forceful of these is his claim that "Jesus" has the same "practical meaning" as "Yahweh." Commenting upon the fact that the early disciples prayed, taught, and baptized in the name "Jesus," Barth states:

> It is pretty much the same, comprehensive, pervasive meaning which . . . the name of Yahweh has in the OT: the n a m e of Yahweh is just Y a h w e h m a n i f e s t t o m e n. Who then is Jesus, if his name has the same meaning? Does it still need the express

declaration of Paul (Phil. 2:9) that God hath
given him the name which is above every
name?[1]

Barth also clearly affirms that "Jesus," "Jesus
Christ," and "Yahweh" have the same referent. "Yahweh" is
the Old Testament name for God, and "Jesus Christ" is the
New Testament name for God. In both cases, the names
denote the "Self-Utterer," the "utterly <u>simple</u>, the simple
reality of God." Barth explains:

> The answer of the New Testament to our ques-
> tion about the reality of God's revelation is
> to be found in the constant reiteration in all
> its pages of the name Jesus Christ . . . .
> That is precisely why we say that by the
> answer of the New Testament is meant the
> simple reality of God. The real fact, the
> fact meant, namely Jesus and, earlier, Yahweh
> did not admit of utterance, just because in
> both cases it was the simple reality of God.
> Any utterance of it by the witnesses could
> only hint, and was only meant to hint, that
> the One indicated by this name is the
> Self-Utterer, the Word. That is why all
> further utterances of biblical witness point
> back to this name. In so doing, of course,
> they point past the name to the bearer of it,
> whom man can no longer express, because He
> wills to express or utter Himself in the power
> of the truth . . . which he Himself is.[2]

In its capacity as a name for God, the name "Jesus
Christ" simply points to God without expressing an idea or
having any content. It is the symbol of the person who is
God.

> Ultimately only the name Jesus Christ, in what
> would appear to be its utter emptiness as a
> mere name, which by itself can express no
> content, principle, idea or truth, but is only
> the symbol for a person--this eternally
> inexpressible name, known and still to be made

known, alone represents the object which they
all signify and to which they all point.[3]

Similarly, this person God who bears the name "Jesus
Christ" is the sovereign "I."[4]
    While these passages might be fitted into an Antiochian
interpretation of Barth, making them fit would require
considerable qualification which is not supplied by Barth.
The direct and forceful way in which he affirms that
"Jesus" and "Jesus Christ" are names of God suggests that
they are not first of all names of some man and that they
can also be applied to God because of his relation to that
man. These names belong to God in the way that "Yahweh"
belongs to him in the Old Testament.
    Before leaving this topic, two points should be added.
The first is that when "Jesus" and "Jesus Christ" denote
God, they refer to an objective reality. This function of
these names is evident from the passages just mentioned.
God is the "object" to which the names refer; he is their
"bearer," and they "point to" him. For Barth, "Jesus
Christ" is not simply a name given to the sum total of all
particular truths. He is not merely a theoretical concept.[5] As God, Jesus Christ is the transcendent reality
who confronts us and to whom our language must conform in
order to be valid.
    Second, "Jesus" and its variants are not always used by
Barth to denote God himself. They may also be used to
refer to themselves or interpretations of Christ. For
example, the word "Jesus" has a certain number of letters,
a particular history, and a definite meaning. When Barth
says that "Jesus" means "Yahweh saves,"[6] he is speaking
primarily of the word, not the divine-human person. Also,
when Barth speaks of the "Johannine Jesus" or the "Christ
of Paul," he is speaking of interpretations rather than
the one who is interpreted. Yet, for our purpose, the
most important function of "Jesus" and its variants in
Barth's theology is to denote God himself.

Propositiones Personales

Barth's explanation of the meaning of the propositiones
personales indicates that he thinks such terms as "this
man, the Son of Mary" name God, rather than a human person

distinct from God. To show how Barth understands these propositions, it is necessary to report part of his account of how Reformed and Lutheran theologians have disagreed about their meaning.

The propositiones personales are equations which result from the unio hypostatica, the union of God the Word with the human nature in the incarnation. They affirm on the one hand "that the Son of God, and therefore God in His divine essence, is this man, the Son of Mary." On the other hand, they affirm "that this man, the Son of Mary, is the Son of God, and therefore God in His divine essence."[7] Barth explains that the emphasis is upon the second of these, which states that the man Jesus is by nature divine.

According to Barth, both the Lutherans and the Reformed accepted the propositiones personales, but they interpreted them differently. The Lutherans understood these propositions as statements about "the humanity of Jesus Christ which in themselves denote and describe only the divine and not the human essence." Because of the union of the two natures, the Lutherans believed that the predicates of the divine nature, such as "by nature divine," could be attributed to the human nature itself. Thus, when they stated that the Son of Mary is the Son of God and therefore divine by nature, they meant that the human nature is also divine.[8]

On the other hand, the Reformed tradition interpreted the propositiones personales as statements about the eternal Son who assumed human nature, not as statements about the human nature itself. Thus, when they said "this man, the Son of Mary, is the Son of God, and therefore God in His divine essence," they understood "this man, the Son of Mary" as denoting the eternal Son of God himself, not the human nature.[9] By interpreting the propositiones personales in this way, they evidenced a concern to emphasize the sovereignty of the divine subject in the incarnation.[10]

Barth's preference for the Reformed interpretation of the propositiones personales is explicit. "We, too, have accepted a similar orientation, and therefore attached ourselves to the Reformed tradition."[11] Consequently, when Barth proclaims his own version of the propositiones personales, he uses "the Son of Mary" to denote God.

Barth's statement of the propositiones personales, which occurs immediately following his discussion of the Reformed and Lutheran interpretations, takes this form:

> But in respect of the Subject acting in this matter we must also make a second differentiation. The Son of God becomes man. That is, He adopts and assumes human essence to His own divine essence. He becomes and is Jesus of Nazareth, the Son of Man. We have, therefore, to say quite unreservedly that J e s u s, the son of David and Mary, a s t h e S o n o f G o d, was and is very God, God by nature, of d i v i n e essence. The Son of God exists as Jesus exists, and Jesus exists as the Son of God exists. Jesus Himself is, as very man, the Son of God and therefore of divine essence, God by nature.[12]

"Jesus," and "Jesus of Nazareth," and "the Son of David and Mary" are used here to name the eternal agent who is the Son of God. When he becomes a man, he becomes Jesus of Nazareth. It is only because Jesus of Nazareth is also and primarily the Son of God that he can be said to be divine by nature. The names involved do not denote the human nature itself, as though Barth interpreted this human nature in a concrete sense, identifying it with a particular person. This subject is not a human person who is also divine; he is the divine person who is also human. Since in the propositiones personales Barth refers to God with "this man, the Son of Mary," and other terms which appear to be more directly related to Christ's humanity than his divinity, it is likely that he always uses similar terms in this way. If he were to use them to name a separate, human person as well, he would be using them equivocally, and this could generate considerable confusion. In the next section we shall show that in certain specific cases Barth rejects the practice of using "Jesus" and its variants to denote a person who is distinct from God.[13]

Improper Use of "Jesus Christ" and Its Variants

That Barth uses "Jesus" and its variants to denote God himself in his mode of being as the incarnate one is also indicated by his account of the incorrect interpretations of Jesus held by nonbelievers, ebionites, docetists, and the disciples before faith. Barth believes that these groups use "Jesus" and its variants improperly, as though they denote a separate, human person.

Barth makes this point in regard to nonbelievers by noting that they focus their attention upon Jesus' being as a man and that they fail to grasp that he is essentially and primarily God himself. Because the eternal Son became a man and existed in time, it takes no faith or revelation for people to be aware of him as a figure in world history. He can be known and studied as other historical realities are known, through historical investigation. Because he is "generally visible to His fellow-creatures, and may be generally located and interpreted, within the limits that this is possible to creatures" and because "no special eyes are needed to be aware of Him, nor is any special understanding needed to interpret Him," it is understandable "that there is hardly a historian who can simply ignore Him, or a philosopher who will fail to give Him appropriate consideration in a carefully subdued acknowledgment side by side with Buddha and Socrates."[14] However, it cannot be said that they truly know him. True knowledge of him is possible only through "the divine act of majesty" in which God speaks for himself and makes himself known. Barth states:

> But it is one thing to know, another to recognize. To recognize is to know Him as the One He--and He alone--is, as the One in whom, in virtue of His ground of being, God's act of majesty, there takes place and is that which is new and unique in the series of all other elements and figures in cosmic being and history--the fact that, without ceasing to be the Creator, the Creator Himself also becomes a creature, and therefore, without ceasing to be God, God also becomes man. To know Him as this--just this, no more and no less--is to recognize Him.[15]

In this passage Barth does not speak specifically of referents of the name "Jesus." However, it is clear that those who do not understand that Jesus is God himself use the name "Jesus" to refer only to Jesus in his being and action as a man. They assume that this is the totality of his being, while, according to Barth, it is only one aspect. Thus, they use the names of Jesus improperly, assuming that the humanity of Jesus is a complete person in itself.

Barth's interpretation of ebionitism and docetism indicates that he believes that followers of these views use "Jesus" and its variants to name a human person who is separate from God. Barth does not make this point as explicitly as he might, but what he says about these two positions makes it clear that he understands them in this way.

Barth states that modern ebionitism and docetism are not so different from each other as might be imagined. Both of them regard the New Testament statement about the divinity of Jesus Christ as "a manner of speaking loosely meant and loosely to be interpreted."[16] As a result, ebionites and docetists can say many of the same things that the New Testament says, but their words do not mean the same thing as the New Testament. The New Testament speaks of the God who became man and revealed himself, while the words of the ebionites focus upon "the historical form of a 'great man,'" and those of the docetists have to do with some "general truth" which becomes "personified" in Jesus.[17]

The ebionites and docetists interpret the New Testament concept of the divinity of Christ as the divinity of a man named "Jesus" who is an individual over against the person God. They defend concepts of the divinity of Christ which are based "on the assumption that the original outlook and declaration of the NT witnesses concerned a human being, who subsequently was either exalted as such to divinity, or appeared among us as the personification and symbol of a divine being." For Barth, there is "no possibility on this road of ending anywhere save in a blind alley."[18]

Both the ebionites and docetists begin with a "human being," and then they ask the question of how the knowledge of that human individual becomes transformed into faith.[19] The ebionites argue that Jesus of Nazareth was

such an impressive personality that he was venerated by
his disciples and elevated so highly in their minds that
"the equation between Jesus and God ceases to be impossible."[20] Of course, this equation might be made in
regard to other men as well.

The docetists, on the other hand, find some general
truth personified in the man Jesus. This truth can be
understood in numerous ways. It might be the "truth of
the community of godhead and humanity" or the "truth of
redemption by way of Die and Be born!" Whatever truth is
chosen, however, it is "more or less accidental" that it
becomes known through this human phenomenon.[21] It is
because the idea becomes known through the man Jesus that
he was called "Lord," "God's Son," and finally "God."

Both these views are idolatrous. Ebionitism is idolatrous because it idealizes and worships a mere man.
Docetism is idolatrous because it worships a human idea,
and since men actually created the idea, docetism also
worships man. Barth makes these accusations here:

> By their assumption that there is at the end
> of an ascending or descending reflection--
> reflection upon the man Jesus as such and
> reflection upon divinity in special connection
> with the man Jesus--simply a small or even a
> great exaggeration, as the case might be, by
> means of which the statement of the divinity
> of Christ would spring up, or could be made
> intelligible, the Ebionite and Docetic Chris-
> tologies impute to the thought of the Biblical
> witnesses a performance which the latter
> themselves could, of course, only have con-
> demned as the blasphemy of which Jesus Himself
> was accused, but really falsely accused. If
> Jesus had designated himself, or the oldest
> Church had designated him the Son of God, in
> the sense presupposed by both these concep-
> tions then he and his Church would have been
> rightly expelled from the community of the OT.
> For what else could such idealizing of a man
> or mythologizing of an idea be, but character-
> istically the thing regarded by the OT as
> setting up and worshipping an idol, one of

those unworthy and null rivals of Yahweh. How
little could the word "God" have been understood in the sense of the OT by one who could
imagine, or even hyperbolically pretend to
imagine, that a man could really become God,
or that the real God could have His copy in a
man![22]

It seems evident, then, that Barth believes that
ebionitism and docetism use "Jesus" and its cognates
incorrectly to denote a human person who is distinct from
the person God. Because of this misunderstanding of the
proper referent of these names, both these christologies
fail to grasp the meaning of New Testament language. The
New Testament affirms that Jesus is divine because he is
the person God himself. "The actual content in the NT
texts is at least this, that in Jesus it is God who is
found, because in fact Jesus himself cannot be discovered
as anyone else than God."[23]

Since Barth thinks that nonbelievers, neutral observers, ebionites and docetists use "Jesus" and its variants
to denote a human person distinct from God, it follows
that the original disciples practiced the same pattern
before they came to faith. However, when they were the
beneficiaries of God's revelation of himself in the
resurrection event, they became aware that Jesus really
was and is God himself. Therefore, they became aware of
the proper referent of "Jesus" and its variants.

Barth does not state this point explicitly, but it is
firmly implied in his account of the conversion of the
disciples from a state of nonbelief to a state of belief.
There was a time before they recognized who Jesus really
was. It was the resurrection event which revealed to the
disciples who Jesus was and is.[24] Since they did not
know who Jesus really was before the resurrection, they
did not know the proper use of his names. Barth states
that it is only because of Jesus' self-revelation in the
resurrection that "the men of the New Testament could
think and speak at all of Jesus Christ." Barth explains,
"In His resurrection and ascension He gave Himself to be
seen and heard and understood by them as the One He was
and is."[25]

In conclusion, it is clear that in these cases Barth

believes that it is improper to use "Jesus" and its variants to name a human person who is separate from the person God. This fact gives additional support to the hypothesis that Barth always uses these names to denote God.

Possible Predicates of "Jesus Christ" and Its Variants

Barth's discussion of the factors which determine what predicates can be assigned to "Jesus Christ" and its variants contributes to our investigation in two ways. First, his explanation of the basis for attributing divine and human predicates to the one Christ has an Alexandrian form. This suggests that Barth understands the names and predicates as belonging to one person, not two. Second, Barth prefers not to affirm all the statements which are made possible by his basic theory of predication, and this preference indicates that he does not always use all the names of Jesus Christ in exactly the same ways.

Barth states that the characteristics of the divine and the human natures are "unlimitedly and unreservedly proper" to Jesus Christ. Everything distinctive of each nature is "not merely verbaliter" but "realiter et verissime" proper to Christ.[26] These qualifications imply that Barth rejects the Antiochian category of relation. He does not suggest that the divine qualities can be assigned to the man Jesus because of his relation to God or that the human qualities can be attributed to the divine subject because of his relation to a separate, human person. These predicates belong directly to the one divine person because he is the bearer of both natures.

Because the predicates of both natures can be attributed to the one divine subject and because this subject can be denoted by so many different terms, striking combinations are possible. Barth admits this possibility, and he aligns himself with the Reformed theologians who refrain from taking advantage of it. He states:

> Where the Reformed were not willing to follow (the Lutherans) emerges supremely in the fact that they refrained from certain statements which were quite possible within this common

framework but seemed to be rather arbitrary
and without biblical foundation, as, for
example, that "God died" ("O ill most dread,
that God is dead"), or that "the man Jesus
Christ is Almighty."[27]

Barth does not explain why such statements appear
"arbitrary," but the reason seems clear. He thinks that
it is wise to be aware of the distinctive contributions of
each nature to the activity of the one divine subject.
For example, he notes with approval that

both Lutherans and Reformed emphasized that in
His work each nature does that which is
appropriate to its distinctive character:
dying, for example, in the case of the human;
and the establishment of the infinite and
universal significance of His death in the
case of the divine.[28]

However, the distinctions between the two natures are
obscured when predicates which belong to one nature are
combined with names which are usually associated with the
opposite nature.

In the second example which Barth gives above, "the man
Jesus Christ is Almighty," the first phase is more closely
related with the humanity of Christ than his divinity,
while the predicate is more directly associated with his
divinity. Consequently, the statement sounds odd.

In the next section, when we examine Barth's uses of
the names of Christ to denote the divine subject, we shall
encounter again some of the restrictions which Barth
places upon those names which are closely associated with
Christ's humanity. Then, in the following section, we
shall argue that these restrictions can be explained
without accepting the Antiochian hypothesis that they
denote someone other than God.

Uses of "Jesus Christ" and Its Variants

In the previous sections of this chapter we have concentrated primarily upon Barth's discussion of language about

Christ. Our purpose here is to give additional evidence that Barth actually uses "Jesus Christ" and its variants to denote God himself. Since Barth does not use all these names in exactly the same ways, we shall first consider "Jesus Christ" and then "the man Jesus."

Barth's use of "Jesus Christ" to denote God is made apparent in four principal ways. First, qualities and actions which can be predicated of "God," "Son of God," and "Word of God" can also be assigned to "Jesus Christ." Second, these four terms can be used in apposition to each other. Third, in discussion of a specific topic, for example, reconciliation, these four terms can be substituted for each other. Finally, Barth freely affirms identity statements using these four terms, without qualifying the identity as indirect. We shall give some examples under these four categories.

Barth states that all the qualities that belong to the divine nature, and are therefore shared by the three of the trinity, can be ascribed to Jesus Christ. In application of this principle, he speaks of Jesus Christ as being "transcendent," "free," and "sovereign," just as God is.[29] Furthermore, Jesus Christ performs actions which can only be performed by God. He elects man, he creates the universe, he humbles himself and becomes a man in the incarnation, he assumes flesh, he speaks and makes himself known in the event of revelation, and he justifies and sanctifies human beings, reconciling them to himself.[30]

Barth often uses "Jesus Christ," "Son of God," "Word of God," and "God" in apposition with each other. This usage is more common in relation to the first three of these terms, but it also occurs with "God." Barth uses "Jesus Christ" and "Son of God," in apposition in this statement: "Jesus Christ, the Son of God and Lord who humbled Himself to be a servant, is also the Son of Man exalted as this servant to be the Lord."[31] An example of "Jesus Christ" and "Word of God" used in apposition is the following: "Jesus Christ, the W o r d of God, meets us as n o t h - i n g o t h e r than God."[32] "God" is used in apposition with "Son" and with "this One," which apparently refers to "Jesus Christ," in the following statement: "It is, then, the secret of the becoming and being of the existence of Jesus Christ that it took place and is: (1) that this One, God, the Son, became and is also man."[33]

The substitution of these four terms for one another can be seen in Barth's discussion of the doctrine of reconciliation in volume four. The event of reconciliation contains two movements, a movement from God to man and, as a result, a movement from man to God. The first of these movements can be designated by Barth in a variety of ways. It is the moment in which God, the Son of God, the Word of God, or Jesus Christ becomes a man. It is the act in which the Word becomes flesh or assumes flesh. It is the event in which the Son of God, God himself, or Jesus Christ goes into a far country. It is the act in which the Son obeys the Father. It is the event in which Jesus Christ the Lord becomes a servant. Since this one event can be designated in all these ways, it seems clear that these four terms are used to name one agent.[34]

Finally, Barth uses the four terms under discussion in identity statements. He affirms that the Son of God and the Word of God are identical with God and that Jesus Christ is identical with the Son of God, the Word of God, and God himself. While these identities may appear difficult conceptually, particularly to an Antiochian theologian, Barth's affirmations of them are often quite simple and direct. "Jesus Christ is God."[35] "The Word of God is uncreated reality, identical with God Himself." [36] "God is God the Son just as He is God the Father." [37] "Jesus Christ is the Word of God."[38] "Jesus Christ is the Son of God."[39]

We turn now to "the man Jesus," "Jesus of Nazareth," and "Son of Man," terms which are more closely associated with Christ's humanity than his divinity. Barth seldom attributes divine qualities and actions directly to these grammatical subjects, nor does he often use them to substitute for, or in apposition with, "Son of God" and "Word of God." Yet, it is clear that he uses them to denote God.

In our discussion of the propositiones personales we noted that Barth uses "Jesus" and "this man, the Son of Mary" to denote the one who is God "by nature." This is also true of "the man Jesus" and "Jesus of Nazareth." Using the latter term, Barth states: "It was as this man that Jesus of Nazareth was 'the Father's Son, by nature God.'"[40] Similarly speaking of the divinity of the man Jesus, Barth asserts:

> But there can be no disputing the fact that,
> in the sense of those who gave it, this
> witness is to the simple effect that, prior to
> any attitudes of others to Him or statements
> of others about Him, the man Jesus did in fact
> occupy this place and function, that prior to
> any knowledge of His being or temporally
> conditioned confession of it, He actually was
> and is and will be what He is represented in
> the reflection of this witness, the Son of the
> Heavenly Father, the King of His kingdom, and
> therefore "by nature God."[41]

Because this one is divine by nature, he possesses all
the power that belongs to God alone. In his elaboration
of this point, Barth indicates that "the man Jesus" and
"Jesus of Nazareth" do not name the human nature of the
Logos. He states that all divine power is given "to this
man," not to his human nature. The human nature is the
organ of the divine agent who is called "Jesus."

> He, the Son of God, did and does and will do
> all these things. But He does not do them in
> the nakedness of His divine power, in which
> they could not have been done as the reconcil-
> iation of the world with God, but as the Son
> of Man, in His identity with the man Jesus of
> Nazareth. But this means that His divine
> power, all power in heaven and on earth, is
> given to this man in His identity with the Son
> of God. . . . It is to Him and not this organ,
> to His human essence as such, that there is
> given "all power in heaven and in earth"
> (Mt. 28:18). [42]

In this same context, Barth makes it clear that "Son of
Man" should also be understood as the name of God, not the
human nature itself. The human nature is the organ of the
Son of Man just as it is the organ of the man Jesus.
Barth states:

> There is no reason to mistake the pure human-
> ity of Jesus Christ in relation to the empow-

ering which comes to His human essence by the
electing grace of God. We insist that its
function is that of an organ of the Son of Man
who is also and primarily the Son of God.[43]

Because the man Jesus is God himself, he is the agent
of revelation. Barth is emphatic about the fact that only
God can reveal God.[44] Consequently, when he states that
Jesus reveals God, the identity between Jesus and God is
implied. In his act of revelation, the man Jesus reveals
himself and, at the same time, God. Barth states:

But this means that in the power and mercy of
the same divine act of majesty which is the
ground of His being the man Jesus speaks for
Himself, expounds Himself and gives Himself to
be known, so that He is no longer just confessed in a way, but known and recognized as
the One He is. This means that in and with
His self-disclosure He induces and initiates
the human seeing and interpreting which
attaches itself to the divine act of majesty
in and by which He has His being, following
and accompanying it, repeating the being which
He has on this basis, and therefore becoming
and being a relevant human seeing and interpreting (as that which is mastered by
Him).[45]

Because "the man Jesus" and "Jesus of Nazareth" denote
God himself in his second mode of being, it would be
possible for Barth to use these terms when speaking of the
first movement of reconciliation. Just as Barth speaks of
Jesus Christ assuming flesh and becoming man, he could
also say that the man Jesus elected to become man, that
the man Jesus humbled himself and went into the far
country, and that the man Jesus, the Lord, became a
servant. Barth usually refrains from such statements,
indicating that "the man Jesus" and "Jesus of Nazareth"
are not so flexible as "Jesus Christ." Nevertheless, on
at least one occasion, Barth says that the man Jesus
accepted human nature. This exception confirms that "the
man Jesus" denotes God himself. Barth states:

> Thus the man Jesus does not transcend the
> limits of the humanity common to Him and us,
> or become alien to us, when in His acceptance
> of human essence, even in its perversion, He
> does not repeat the perversion or do wrong,
> when in virtue of His origin He cannot will or
> do it.[46]

In this statement about the sinlessness of Jesus, Barth implies that the one called "the man Jesus" is originally divine. The fact that this agent could accept human essence presupposes that this essence was not already inherently his before he accepted it. If "the man Jesus" denoted the one who was already existing as a man in time, it would appear that he could not accept human nature, for he would already have it.

In conclusion, Barth's understanding of the names of Christ and his uses of them conform to his doctrine of Christ. Jesus Christ is directly identical with God, and therefore his names are also names of God. In the next section more needs to be said about the theoretical basis for the distinctive ways that the various names of Christ are used.

DENOTATION, CONNOTATION, AND ABSTRACTION

The purpose of this section is to provide an explanation of how Barth can use "Jesus Christ" and its variants differently, although all of these names denote one divine agent. We shall argue that the names of Christ have connotations as well as denotations and that Barth uses the connotations when he abstracts from the one whole Christ, calling attention to particular aspects of his being and action.[47] Then we shall examine some specific examples which seem to give strong support to the Antiochian view that Barth uses some of the names of Christ, such as "the man Jesus," to denote a human person other than God. We shall show that even in these cases the terms in question denote the divine subject, although they connote his being and action as man.

Our first task is to show that Barth recognizes the connotations as well as the denotations of the names of

Christ. "Jesus," Barth explains, is not merely a label which could be replaced at will. It means "Yahweh saves," and this meaning expresses the essence of Jesus Christ. [48] Similarly, other titles and names, such as "Messiah" or "Savior," have meanings which are fitting for the one who bears them.[49]

Barth relates the meaning of the titles "Son of God" and "Word of God" to their metaphorical character. Because of their places in the metaphors of father-son and speaker-word, "Son of God" and "Word of God" have different connotations, although both denote God in his second mode of being. These connotations enable the two terms to balance and correct each other. While "Word of God" suggests that in his inner fellowship and in revelation God is intellectually alive, eternally knowing himself, it is misleading in that it implies that God's Word is other than God himself. In the creaturely realm, words are essentially distinct from their speakers. On the other hand, "Son of God" indicates that the second of the trinity is of the same essence as the first, just as earthly sons are of the same essence as their fathers. Barth states:

> The two figures, that of the Son and that of the Word of God, point to an object for which they are not appropriate. But for that very reason each of them must be taken seriously for itself, and neither of them should be dispensed with because the other is suggested.[50]

While Barth can describe the terms "Son of God" and "Word of God" as metaphors, he sees no inconsistency in speaking of them also as names. "Under the name of Son of God Jesus took the very place which in the Old Testament has often enough been allotted to the 'children' of Israel in their relation with God."[51]

These examples indicate that Barth believes that names have meanings or connotations as well as referents. He does not explore systematically the significance of this two-sidedness of names; he simply accepts it and applies it.

Our next task is to show that Barth endorses abstrac-

tion in theological thinking. This endorsement might not
be apparent to the casual reader, since Barth so often
attacks abstraction. For example, he argues against
abstracting God from his act of revelation,[52] election
from Jesus Christ,[53] the election of the individual from
the election of the community,[54] the judgment of God
from the grace of God,[55] and the humanity of Jesus
Christ from his divinity. In the last of these examples,
abstraction can lead to false worship. Barth states:

> As God cannot be considered without His
> humanity, His humanity cannot be considered or
> known or magnified or worshipped without God.
> Any attempt to treat it in abstracto, in a
> vacuum, is from the very first a perverted
> undertaking. As Son of Man, and therefore in
> human form, Jesus Christ does not exist at all
> except in the act of God, as He is first the
> Son of God.[56]

Nevertheless, in spite of this polemic against abstraction in specific instances, Barth also admits that it is
necessary. For example, as we have seen, Barth argues
that the concept of a logos asarkos is an abstraction
which is "indispensable for dogmatic enquiry and presentation." In this instance, proper abstraction recognizes
that the Logos is always united with his human nature in
the eternal decision and being of God.[57]

While Barth does not often draw attention to his
abstracting by using the words "abstract" or "abstraction," on at least one occasion he does. Concerning an
abstraction of Christ's being from his resurrection and
ascension, Barth states:

> The being of Jesus Christ was and is perfect
> and complete in itself in His history as the
> true Son of God and Son of Man. It does not
> need to be transcended or augmented by new
> qualities or further developments. The
> humiliation of God and the exaltation of man
> as they took place in Him are the completed
> fulfillment of the covenant, the completed
> reconciliation of the world with God. His

being as such (if we may be permitted this
abstraction for a moment) was and is the end
of the old and the beginning of the new form
of this world even without His resurrection
and ascension.[58]

In this quote, Barth calls attention to the fact that
he is abstracting by using the word "abstraction," and
also by using the phrase "as such." The latter of these
two methods is by far the more common. Barth often speaks
of the man Jesus "as such" when he is abstracting his
being and action as a man, and he often speaks of the Son
of God "as such" when he is abstracting his being and
action as God. Barth does not wish to refer to Jesus
Christ "in words that refer exclusively to His divine or
exclusively to His human essence," but sometimes he wishes
to speak of Jesus Christ in words that refer specifically
to his human nature or his divine nature.[59]
    Abstraction is a crucial element in Barth's christo-
logical language; therefore it merits more clarification
than Barth himself has given it. We shall provide some of
the necessary clarification by indicating how abstraction
and the connotative function of names influence Barth's
language about Christ.

Jesus Christ's Being as God and as Man

When speaking of Jesus Christ, Barth often abstracts
particular aspects of his being and action for clarification and emphasis. He abstracts the divine nature, the
human nature, the agent himself, the act which he performs, his being and action as God, and his being and
action as man. The most important of these, for our
purpose, are the last two. In these instances the connotations of the various names become apparent.
    Our principal purpose is to show that the names of
Christ which are more closely related to his divine
nature, such as "Son of God," denote the one divine agent
while they connote his being and action as God. On the
other hand, the names of Christ which are more closely
associated with his human nature, such as "Son of Man,"
denote the one divine agent and connote his being and

action as man. Before we consider the abstractions of
Christ's being and action as God and as man, it is wise to
mention the simpler abstractions of the human nature, the
divine nature, the agent, and the act.

Barth abstracts each of the two natures from the total
Christ when he specifies their characteristics, their
relation to each other, and their relation to Christ
himself. For example, he is abstracting the divine nature
when he states that it is characterized by holiness,
mercy, wisdom, and so forth. Similarly, he is abstracting
the human nature when he lists its temporality, mortality,
and responsibility before God.[60] He abstracts the two
natures when he states that the two are not transformed
into each other in their union but that they maintain
their integrity and proper function.[61] Further, he
abstracts the two natures from the divine agent when he
says that they do not exist apart from him.[62]

From the one whole Christ Barth also abstracts the
divine agent and his act. This occurs, for example, when
Barth states simply that the act of the incarnation is
performed by God rather than man.[63] It also occurs when
Barth explains that even after the initial moment of the
incarnation the actions of Jesus Christ are the actions of
God himself.[64] Although many of Jesus' acts, such as
his washing the disciples' feet or taking children into
his arms, "might well have been performed by others," they
are important because of Jesus' divinity. "The significance of all His acts is finally and decisively to be
sought in the fact that they are His acts."[65]

We turn now to Barth's abstraction of Christ's being
and action as God and his being and action as man. Barth
abstracts Christ's being and action as God when he draws
attention to the qualities which Christ possesses and the
actions he performs through his divine nature. Conversely, Barth abstracts Christ's being and action as man when
he focuses upon the qualities which Christ possesses and
the actions he performs through his human nature. By
abstracting in these ways, Barth attempts to convey the
distinctions between the two natures without dividing
Christ into two persons.

When he wishes to specify Christ's being and action
through his human nature, Barth often uses such phrases as
"as man," "as the Son of Man," or "in his human nature."

To accomplish the same purpose he also omits the preposition "as" and uses such terms as "Jesus," "Jesus of Nazareth," and "Son of Man." Similarly, when he draws attention to Christ's being and action through his divine nature, Barth often uses such phrases as "as God," "as the Son of God," "in his divine nature," or simply "Son of God." Some examples should be mentioned.

Barth states that "as the Son of God" Jesus Christ shares all the attributes of God, such as his omnipotence and omnipresence.[66] On the other hand, Christ "had human wants, was subject to human temptations and influences, shared only a relative knowledge and capacity, and learned and suffered and died as a man."[67] As the Son of God Jesus Christ elects, and as man he is elected.[68] As man he prays to God, but as the Son of God he is the answer to his own prayer.[69] In these examples, Barth clearly intends for "as man" to indicate what Christ does through his human nature and "as the Son of God" to indicate what he does through his divine nature.[70]

In his discussion of the concepts of humiliation and exaltation, Barth explains that when Jesus Christ becomes man the divine nature is humiliated and the human nature is exalted.[71] Since everything that can be attributed to each of the two natures can also be attributed to the agent who acts through both natures,[72] it is possible to say that Jesus Christ is exalted and that he is humiliated. However, in order to clarify that he is exalted through his human nature and humiliated through his divine nature, Barth uses "as God" and "as Son of God" to modify the humiliation and "as Son of Man" and "as man" to modify the exaltation. "As God He was humbled to take our place, and as man He is exalted on our behalf."[73] Similarly, Barth states: "As the Son of God he goes into the far country. As the Son of Man he returns home."[74] He adds: "In and with His humiliation (as the Son of God) there took place also His exaltation (as the Son of Man)."[75]

Using these qualifying phrases, Barth makes it clear that Jesus Christ cannot be exalted as the Son of God, for as the Son of God he already participates in the being and essence of God himself. He can be exalted only in his being as the Son of Man. As the Son of Man, he is not divinized nor does he become God, but he is exalted into fellowship with God. Barth states:

In His Godhead, as the eternal Son of the
Father, as the eternal Word, Jesus Christ . .
. did not stand in need of exaltation, nor was
He capable of it. But He did as man--it is
here again that we come up against that which
is not self-evident in Jesus Christ.[76]

In His identity with the Son of God, when He
was lifted up into heaven, He was not deified,
or assumed into the Godhead (for this was
unnecessary for Him as the Son of God and
impossible for Him as the Son of Man), but
placed as man at the side of God, in direct
fellowship with Him, in full participation in
His glory.[77]

Barth makes these same points about the humiliation and
exaltation of Christ by omitting the preposition "as" and
relying upon the connotations of the various names and
titles. The statement that Jesus Christ, as the Son of
God, humbled himself and became man can be simplified into
the statement that the Son of God humbled himself and
became man. Similarly, the claim that the Son of Man is
exalted without being divinized is another way of affirming that Jesus Christ, as the Son of Man, is exalted but
not divinized. For example, Barth states: "The atonement
as it took place in Jesus Christ is the one inclusive
event of this going out of the Son of God and coming in of
the Son of Man."[78] Further, Barth affirms: "The Son of
Man is not deified by the fact that He is also and primarily the Son of God."[79] In addition, Barth asks: "What
else can the Son of God who humbled Himself as man become
and be but the Son of Man who is not divinized but exalted
to the side of God?"[80]
     In these instances, it is clear that the titles and
names which Barth uses to denote Jesus Christ also connote
information about him. The titles "Son of God" and "Word
of God" imply that Jesus Christ has a divine nature and
that he performs divine acts. The title "Son of Man" and
the name "Jesus" imply that Christ has human qualities and
performs human acts. Even when these names and titles
stand alone, without the preposition ."as," it is not
necessary to conclude that they denote two different
agents.

Whether "Jesus" Names a Person Who Is Only Human

Our purpose in this section is to determine whether Barth ever uses some of the names of Christ to denote a human person who is distinct from God. Although we have demonstrated that he uses such terms as "the man Jesus" to denote the divine subject and to connote his being and action as man, it is possible that he might use them also in an Antiochian manner to denote a person who is only human. We shall look at some specific instances which appear to support an Antiochian interpretation, and we shall argue that even in these cases Barth speaks of the Christ who is divine by nature.

The recognition of Barth's use of the connotative function of the names of Christ opens up an alternative to the Antiochian interpretation of Barth's account of the two types of christological statements.[81] While statements of both types, "God's Son is Jesus of Nazareth" and "Jesus of Nazareth is God's Son" are intelligible if they are understood on the basis of the Antiochian assumption that "Jesus of Nazareth" denotes a complete human person distinct from God, they are also intelligible on the basis of the Alexandrian view that both terms denote the divine Christ.

In the Alexandrian interpretation, although "Jesus of Nazareth" and "God's Son" denote the same agent and the "is" indicates a direct identity rather than an identity of becoming, the two types of statements are not merely tautological. Because of the connotative function of the two terms, the statements convey more information than simply that this person is this person. The first type affirms that the Son who is divine by nature also exists as a man, having human characteristics and performing human actions. The second type states that the one who exists as a man is also and primarily God himself.

The Alexandrian interpretation of the two types of christological statements is consistent with Barth's explanation of their characteristics. He asserts, for example, that the two types move in opposite directions, "from above downwards or from below upwards." Because of the connotations of the terms "God's Son" and "Jesus of Nazareth," the first type of statements suggests a movement from the Son's eternal being as God "above" to his being as man on earth. Similarly, "Jesus of Nazareth" can exalt human nature "from below upwards" because he exists as a man "below" but is fully identical with God and therefore has divine power.[82]

That the two types of statements move in opposite directions is also indicated by Barth's explanation of the way divinity and humanity are involved in them. The first type presupposes the divinity of Christ and moves toward his humanity. The second type presupposes his humanity and moves toward his divinity.[83] This explanation indicates that "God's Son" connotes the divinity of Jesus Christ and that "Jesus of Nazareth" connotes his humanity.

We turn now to some instances in which Barth seems to substitute names such as "Jesus" for "human nature," implying that the human nature is a complete person in itself. Our view is that these occasions should be understood as inferences rather than substitutions. For example, Barth can say that the human nature of Jesus is limited and then add that the man Jesus is limited. Following an Antiochian interpretation of Barth, one might understand the second statement simply as a way of saying the same thing as the first statement, using "the man Jesus" to denote the human nature. On the other hand, since Barth believes that what can be attributed to the human nature can also be attributed to the bearer of that nature,[84] the second statement can be understood as an inference from the first. The human nature is limited, therefore, the man Jesus is limited. In the second case, "the man Jesus" does not denote the human nature itself but its bearer.

When Barth discusses the knowledge of God, he speaks of both the human nature and also the man Jesus as the form of revelation. This identification raises the question whether "Jesus" names the human nature. For example, in his argument that the form of revelation does not have the power to reveal but that this power belongs to God alone, Barth seems to equate "the humanitas Christi" and "the man Jesus of Nazareth" with "this form." Barth states that in the New Testament

> the humanitas Christi comes under the reserva-
> tion of God's holiness, i.e., that the power
> and the continuity in which the man Jesus of

> Nazareth . . . was in fact the revealed word,
> consisted here also in the power and continu-
> ity of the divine action in this form and not
> in the continuity of this form as such.[85]

While it seems prima facie that "Jesus of Nazareth"
names the human soul and body which are the form of
revelation and therefore different from God, it is also
possible to interpret this name as denoting the divine
agent in his being and action as man. Since God, as a
man, is the form as well as the content of revelation,
what can be said of the form can also be said of him.
Consequently, to say that Jesus of Nazareth has no power
to reveal is an inference from the statement that the
human nature has no power to reveal, not simply another
way of denying that humanity has that power.
    Another example in which Barth seems to personify the
human nature of Christ is found in his statement that the
form of revelation can be known by neutral observers.

> What the neutral observer of these events
> might apprehend or may have apprehended of
> these events was the form of revelation. . . .
> Thousands may have seen and heard the Rabbi of
> Nazareth. But this historical element was not
> revelation.[86]

Since the form of revelation is other than God[87] and
since it is also a rabbi, it seems to follow that this
rabbi is a human person distinct from God. However, this
interpretation is not the only option. The statement
about the rabbi of Nazareth can be understood as an
inference from what can be said about the human nature of
Christ. Since the human nature itself is not revelation
and since "Rabbi of Nazareth" connotes Jesus Christ in his
being and action through the human nature, Barth's point
can be paraphrased in this way: "Thousands saw and heard
Jesus Christ in his being as a man, but his being as a man
was not revelation."
    A similar example is found in Barth's polemic against
viewpoints which advocate worshipping the human nature of
Jesus Christ apart from his divine nature. This dangerous
deviation, Barth states, is not escaped by the pietism of

Zinzendorf, the "Heart of Jesus" cult of Catholicism, or the historicism of modern Protestantism with its emphasis upon the hero Jesus. In his criticism of these three movements, the clearest apparent use of "Jesus" as a name for the human nature itself is found in the sentence quoted below. After affirming that the eternal Logos is superior to the flesh which he assumes and to which he gave reality, Barth states:

> Likewise from this point there results the inevitable rejection of any abstract Jesus-worship, i.e., any Christology or christological doctrine or practice which aims at making the human nature, the historical and psychological manifestation of Jesus as such, its object.[88]

In this passage, worship of Jesus seems to be identified with worship of the human nature. As in previous cases, however, the statement about Jesus can be understood as an inference. Since the human nature in itself should not be worshipped, it is also improper to worship Jesus only in his being as a man. Further, Barth appears to be relying upon the connotations of the name "Jesus" to make his point. To say that one should reject "any abstract Jesus-worship" is to say that one should not restrict one's worship to "Jesus as a man."

Other examples concerning the human nature as the form of revelation involve the grammatical construction of apposition. In the first of these, Barth places "Jesus of Nazareth" in apposition with "the human being of Christ." Speaking of the Word of God who descended from heaven in the incarnation, Barth states:

> There is no other form or manifestation in heaven or on earth save the one child in the stable, the one Man on the cross. This is the Word to whom we must hearken, render faith and obedience, cling ever so closely. Every question concerning the Word which is directed away from Jesus of Nazareth, the human being of Christ, is necessarily and wholly directed from Himself, the Word, and therefore from God

Himself, because the Word, and therefore God
Himself, does not exist for us apart from the
human being of Christ.[89]

There is a difficulty with this example. Since Barth
speaks of the human being rather than the human nature of
Christ, the question arises whether he makes a distinction
between the human being and the human nature. That is a
theoretical possibility, but in this passage Barth seems
to identify the two. The point he is making is that the
Word cannot be known apart from his human being or nature.
For support he appeals to Luther, and in his explanation
of Luther he uses Menschheit, Menschsein, and menschliche
Natur synonymously. He states:

This assertion of Luther's was then built up
doctrinally by Lutheran orthodoxy in the form
of an idea which expressly maintained a
perichoresis between the Word of God and the
human being of Christ (Menschsein Christi),
i.e., a reversal of the statement about the
enhypostasis of Christ's human nature (mensch-
lichen Natur Christi), to the effect that as
the humanity (Menschheit) only has reality
through and in the Word, so too the Word only
has reality through and in the humanity
(Menschheit).[90]

Even if Barth identifies human being and human nature
in this context, it does not follow necessarily that
"Jesus of Nazareth" is the name of the human nature of
Christ. Items in apposition need not be identical. They
may merely explain or define more precisely what is meant.
Consequently, Barth may be paraphrased in this way:
"Every question concerning the Word which is directed away
from Jesus of Nazareth, that is, from his being and action
as a man, is necessarily and wholly directed away from God
himself." The phrase "from his being and action as a man"
makes a further, more narrowly specified point. It does
not simply identify Jesus of Nazareth.

Another case of apposition should be mentioned. Here
Barth places "Jesus" in apposition with "the historical
existence of Jesus of Nazareth." In a discussion of

docetism, Barth states: "It can upon occasion abandon
Jesus, the historical existence of Jesus of Nazareth, and
yet retain Christ, i.e., its Christ."[91]

A question which this example raises is whether "the
historical existence of Jesus of Nazareth" is identical
with "the humanity of Jesus." Without definitely deciding
this question, we can say that Barth often seems to use
these phrases synonymously.[92] However, even if Barth
identifies the existence of the man Jesus with his human
nature, it is not necessary to conclude that Barth uses
"Jesus" to denote that human nature in such a way as to
imply that the human nature is itself a separate person in
its own right. As stated above, items in apposition are
not necessarily identical, although they might be. Here,
by adding the phrase "the historical existence of Jesus of
Nazareth," Barth gives an additional explanation of his
meaning. He does not simply refer to Jesus using different words. His sentence might be paraphrased in this way:
"Docetism can upon occasion abandon Jesus; that is, it can
abandon Jesus' existence as a man, and yet retain Christ,
its Christ."

Barth leaves himself open to a misinterpretation of his
Alexandrian position when he seems to state explicitly
that he is naming the human nature "Jesus Christ." He
says that in the event of grace, the human nature

> acquires even in its pure creatureliness
> divine exousia, even in its human weakness
> divine power, even in its human meanness
> divine authority, even in its human par-
> ticularity (for individuality with all its
> limitations belongs to its humanity) divine
> universality--and all this in the occurrence
> of this event, or, to put it more simply, as
> Jesus Christ (for we are speaking of His human
> essence) lived and lives and will live.[93]

Even here, however, as in the cases involving apposition, Barth should not be understood as giving the human
nature itself the name "Jesus Christ" and thereby person-
alizing it. He is simply emphasizing Christ's life as a
man, for it is in Christ's human existence that his human
actions and qualities acquire divine power. The words in

the parenthesis give additional information; they do not
indicate that the human essence bears the name "Jesus
Christ."

Barth also appears to personify the human nature of
Christ in his discussion of election. He argues that
Jesus Christ is not only elected as a man, he is also the
Son of God who elects. In support of this point, Barth
attacks the view of Thomas Aquinas. According to Barth,
Thomas reserves the role of Christ in election to that of
recipient. It is the human nature as such which is
elected. Rephrasing the point, Barth states that according to Thomas only "the man Jesus as such" is elected.
This substitution of the two ways of speaking seems to
imply that here Barth uses the phrase "the man Jesus as
such" to name the human nature. The important sentences
are the following:

> But Thomas would restrict the election of
> Christ to this passive relationship, and thus
> to His human nature. . . . If we say only what
> Thomas would say, then we have knowledge only
> of the election of the man Jesus as such, and
> not of the election and personal electing of
> the Son of God which precedes this elec-
> tion.[94]

In this example, not only do we have an apparent
substitution of "the man Jesus as such" for "the human
nature," we also seem to have a dichotomy between the man
Jesus and the Son of God. "Son of God" seems to name the
one divine agent, while "the man Jesus as such" seems to
denote a separate human being who is elected by God.

However, it is possible to conclude that Barth is not
actually substituting "the man Jesus as such" for "the
human nature" and that he does not mean that Jesus is a
human person separate from the person God. Since what can
be stated about the human nature as such can also be
stated about the eternal Son as a man, the statements here
about the man Jesus can be understood as inferences from
the statements about the human nature. Since the human
nature has a passive role in election, Jesus Christ as a
man also has a passive role. Barth admits that Christ has
a passive role in election, but he does not want to limit

Christ's involvement to the passive role. As the eternal Son of God, Jesus Christ takes part in election as the elector; as Son of Man he is elected. Again, it is not necessary to resort to an Antiochian hypothesis.

The apparent substitution of "human nature" or "human essence" for the names "Jesus," "Jesus of Nazareth," and so forth, also occurs when Barth is speaking of kenosis. In order to understand the various controversies which have taken place over the way the kenosis should be understood, it is necessary to make a distinction between the divine subject as he is in himself and the human element which he assumed in the incarnation and with which he is subsequently related. Some proponents of the theory of kenosis have argued that the divine subject himself either abandoned his divine attributes or suspended their use when he became a man. Others argued that the kenosis meant only that the human nature did not possess those attributes.

In his discussion of the Calvinistic and Lutheran positions on this question, Barth apparently uses the term "man Jesus" to designate the same reality designated by "human nature." Calvin, Barth explains, makes a point that had been made previously by Augustine, Origen, and Gregory of Nyssa: the humanity of Christ conceals the glory of God for men, but the humanity does not include absolutely the Word of God. Barth can state this position by saying that the essence of the Word of God is united with the human nature but not included in it. He can also make this point by saying that the Logos cannot be included "in the creature, the man Jesus."

Barth's willingness to state the point in the two different ways is evident in the quotation below. When phrasing it in the terminology of the two natures, Barth quotes Calvin in Latin. Immediately afterward, Barth uses language involving "the man Jesus."

> It was the same basic thought which many years later Calvin was trying to express in his well-known statement: Etsi in unam personam coaluit immensa Verbi essentia cum natura hominis, nullam tamen inclusionem fingimus. An absolute inclusio of the Logos in the creature, the man Jesus, would mean a subordi-

nation of the Word to the flesh, a limitation
and therefore an alteration of His divine
nature, and therefore of God Himself.[95]

In explaining the Lutheran position, Barth again uses
both ways of talking. According to the Lutheran position,
the two natures are united in such a way that the attributes of the divine nature can be attributed to the human
nature. This interpretation should be called, Barth
thinks, "the divinisation of the man Jesus as such." On
the basis of the doctrine of the communication of properties, particularly of the divine nature to the human
nature, it can be said not only that the human nature is
omnipresent, but also that the man Jesus as such is
omnipresent. One example is the following:

> The Lutherans rejected it (the <u>Extra Calvinis-</u>
> <u>ticum</u>), because they thought they could see in
> it a "Nestorian" separation of the divine and
> human natures, because on their doctrine of
> the communication of the attributes the fact
> that He "filled the whole world" had also to
> be said of the man Jesus as such on the basis
> of His union with the Logos.[96]

Barth indicates that there are at least three alternatives on the question of Christ's omnipotence. It is
possible to say that the human nature or the man Jesus, in
the state of humiliation, refrained from the use of the
divine powers which he possessed. This was the view of
the Giessen theologians. Another possibility is that the
human nature or the man Jesus as such refrained from the
visible use of those powers. This was the view of the
Tuebingen group. A third alternative focuses upon the
divine agent and his essence rather than the human nature
or the man Jesus. According to it, there was an "abstention not only on the part of the man Jesus as such but on
the part of the Son of God, the Logos Himself, from the
possession and therefore the power to dispose of His
divine glory and majesty."[97]
In this discussion of <u>kenosis</u>, it appears on the
surface that Barth uses "Jesus" to name the personality of
the human nature itself. However, it is possible to

interpret these occurrences of "Jesus" as denoting the divine agent in his unity with his human form. If Barth's statements are read with the assumption that "Jesus" denotes the divine agent, the statements which apply divine attributes, such as omnipresence, to "the man Jesus as such," can be paraphrased in the form "Jesus Christ, as a man, is omnipresent," or "the Son of God, in his human form, is omnipresent." Such statements can be read as inferences from the premise that the human nature itself is omnipresent.

In regard to the question of whether the Son of God divested himself of divine power in the incarnation, if one interprets the name "Jesus" as the name of the divine subject in his unity with the human nature, the three alternatives can be paraphrased as follows: (1) Jesus Christ as man refrained from using his divine powers; (2) Jesus Christ as man refrained from visibly using his divine powers; and (3) Jesus Christ as God surrendered the possession and use of the divine powers when he became a man. Even though, at first glance, "Jesus" or "the man Jesus" seem to name the human nature as such, the language is still understandable if these names actually denote the divine person in his human form.

Some final examples in which Barth appears to use "Jesus" and its variants to name the human nature as such are found in his discussion of the unity of human nature with God. Barth often affirms that the Son of God united human nature with himself. For example, he states:

> For the moment, however, it is enough to maintain that Lutheran and Reformed were at one in their starting-point, that the unity involved, Jesus Christ, is originally and really the unity of the divine Word with the human being assumed by Him. But this unity also implies the unity--a unity to be thought of neither as identity nor as duality--of the divine being of the Word with the human being assumed by Him, the unity of the two natures.[98]

On the other hand, Barth also often speaks of the unity of the Son of God, the Word of God, or God himself with

Jesus. Here are some examples: (1) "In the person of His eternal Son, He (God) has united Himself with the man Jesus of Nazareth."[99] (2) "Everything which comes from God takes place 'in Jesus Christ,' i.e., in the . . . union of His Son with Jesus of Nazareth."[100] (3) "It was in this way, . . .in the unity of His Son with the Son of Man, Jesus of Nazareth (Jn 3:16), that God willed to demonstrate His love to the world."[101] (4) "The Son of God in His unity with this man exists in solidarity with the humanity of Israel suffering under the mighty hand of God."[102] The question which such statements raise is this: When Barth speaks of the unity of God with Jesus is he simply using different words to speak of the unity between God and the human nature of Jesus? If so, the human nature of Christ is apparently a person in its own right.

If Barth intends for "Jesus of Nazareth" and "this man" to denote a human person who is distinct from God, the sentences above are quite simple and direct. Because God has united himself with one man, he is also united with all men. In this union between the divine person and the human person, God's love is revealed and he participates in the suffering of his children.

On the other hand, if Barth intends for "Jesus of Nazareth" and "this man" to denote not simply the human nature but the divine subject in his unity with human nature, the statements are perplexing, but they are still understandable. In this interpretation, the unity which is established by God's grace is a unity between Jesus Christ "as the Son of God" and Jesus Christ "as the Son of Man." Jesus Christ as he is in his divine nature is united with himself as he is in his human nature. This unity might more appropriately be designated as an identity, for Barth does want to maintain that Jesus Christ as God is identical with Jesus Christ as man. However, an identity is also a particular kind of unity.[103]

To summarize, in this section we have argued that Barth apparently does not use "Jesus" and its variants to name a human person who is distinct from God. While all occurrences of "Jesus" in the Church Dogmatics cannot be examined here, we have noted that significant examples which appear prima facie to denote a separate, human person can be interpreted quite differently. They can be understood as denoting God himself in his second mode of being.

An Antiochian interpreter of Barth might object, however, that we have not demonstrated that Barth does not use "Jesus" and its variants to name a human person distinct from God. While we have shown that it is possible to understand many controversial instances of "Jesus" as denoting the person God, we have not shown that it is impossible to interpret them in an Antiochian manner, as denoting a human person distinct from God. Consequently, the two interpretations remain on equal footing, neither having vanquished the other.

In response to this objection, two points can be made. First, the evidence that Barth uses "Jesus" and its variants to denote God must be evaluated in relation to the Alexandrian interpretation of Barth's christological doctrine. When both Barth's doctrine and also his language are taken into account, the Alexandrian interpretation appears to be more formidable than the Antiochian.

Second, once it has been demonstrated that Barth uses such terms as "the man Jesus" to denote the divine subject, the Antiochian hypothesis becomes increasingly difficult to sustain. This is true because if Barth uses the same terms, such as "the man Jesus" and "Jesus," to denote two different persons, one divine and one human, he is using them equivocally. Since Antiochian theologians have traditionally tried to distinguish between the two persons by using different terms to refer to them, Barth betrays that ideal if he uses some terms equivocally. Further, the idea that Barth uses the terms equivocally implies that he tries to hold onto two different theologies, the Alexandrian and the Antiochian, without making a clear choice between them. If so, Barth falls short of his ideal of solid theological achievement. He states: "A theology worthy of respect is always one-sided."[104] Consequently, it seems more reasonable to assume that Barth chooses either the Alexandrian or the Antiochian position and works out its logical consequences, rather than trying to hold onto two opposing alternatives.

CONCLUSION

In this chapter we have argued that Barth's understanding
and use of "Jesus Christ" and its variants should be
interpreted in an Alexandrian rather than an Antiochian
manner. Although all the terms which denote Christ are
not used by Barth in exactly the same ways, the differences can be accounted for by abstraction and the connotations of the various names and titles, without recourse to
the Antiochian hypothesis that some of them are used to
denote a human person separate from God. Barth clearly
uses even such terms as "the man Jesus" and "Son of Man"
to denote God himself in his being as man, and the evidence indicates that he considers this their proper use.
     When Barth's use of "Jesus Christ" and its variants is
considered in relation to his development of the doctrines
of the divinity of Christ and the unity of the two natures, the superiority of the Alexandrian interpretation
over the Antiochian is apparent. The features of Barth's
thought which appear to support an Antiochian interpretation can be accounted for within an Alexandrian framework,
while the reverse is not always the case. For example, as
the Antiochians emphasize, Jesus Christ is the form of
revelation, and therefore he is, in some respects, distinct from God. Yet, as the Alexandrian perspective
maintains, this distinctness from God does not preclude
the essential divinity of the man Jesus, a fact which the
Antiochian view can scarcely incorporate.

The purpose of this chapter is to consider briefly some of the major implications of Barth's Alexandrian development of the divinity of Jesus Christ, the unity of the person of Christ, and the meaning and use of the name "Jesus Christ" and its variants. Our observations will be organized under four headings.

First, we shall indicate the importance of the Alexandrian character of Barth's thinking on these issues by showing how it influences his understanding of some other principal doctrines. Since this influence is extensive, a recognition of Barth's Alexandrianism contributes to a clear understanding of his theology as a whole

Second, we shall note the advantages of Barth's Alexandrian christology. Barth's position is formidable for many of the same reasons that have allowed Alexandrian theology to maintain considerable appeal throughout the history of Christian thought. It guarantees the true divinity of Christ, it accentuates the uniqueness of his divinity, and it emphasizes the oneness of the person of Christ. At the same time, Barth's account incorporates many Antiochian elements, and the presence of these features contributes to a well-balanced and subtle position.

Third, we shall mention some of the major problems that Barth's construction of this doctrine entails. We shall argue first that Barth's thoroughgoing emphasis upon the divinity of Christ tends to mitigate the significance of his humanity. Second, while the uniqueness of Christ's divinity is preserved, the fact that Barth attributes divinity to the Bible and proclamation deprives him of a possible argument to use against Antiochian thinking. Third, the significance of the lives of human persons in time seems to be undercut by Barth's claim that all men have their true being only in Christ. Finally, since revelation and reconciliation occur within God's act ad intra, the necessity and importance of God's act ad extra are brought into jeopardy.

Fourth, we shall discuss the question of whether Barth's entire dogmatic theology should be considered an Alexandrian theology. As we shall see, a surprisingly strong case can be constructed for the conclusion that Barth's dogmatics should not be classified as Alexandrian. Barth's approach to the issue of the relation between theology and philosophy, for example, seems to be quite different from the stance of classical Alexandrian theologians on that topic. However, our principal contention is that since Barth's christology is Alexandrian and since Barth's Church Dogmatics is christologically centered and determined, it is proper to consider his entire theology Alexandrian.

THE IMPORTANCE OF BARTH'S ALEXANDRIAN CHRISTOLOGY

While we have focused upon three principal issues in our investigation of whether Barth is Antiochian or Alexandrian in his christology, we have necessarily encountered many other crucial doctrines in Barth's theology, such as revelation, the trinity, election, and reconciliation. What we have said about these topics indicates that there is an inherent relation between them and Barth's Alexandrianism, particularly his understanding of the direct identity of Jesus Christ with God. Although it is not our purpose either to repeat what we have said or to present a detailed explication of all the ways in which Barth's Alexandrianism influences his treatment of the other doctrines in his dogmatics, we can mention briefly some of the connecting links that are present in, or implied by, what we have said previously. We shall begin with the concept of revelation.

Barth affirms that God's revelation through Christ is the revelation of God, not merely one among God's revelations.[1] This claim seems to make much more sense within an Alexandrian interpretation of Barth than an Antiochian interpretation. If Jesus Christ is directly identical

with God and not merely indirectly identical with him, it
is clear that God's presence in the human nature of Christ
is ontologically different from his presence anywhere else
in the created order. In this case, the existence of
Jesus is the existence of God, and the actor is God
himself. Barth does not mean simply that God is somehow
more present in the man Jesus than in other creatures, or
that his character is revealed here more adequately than
in other sources. The difference between Jesus Christ and
other modes of God's presence is a difference in kind, not
merely in degree.

If God's presence in Jesus differed only in degree from
his presence elsewhere in creation, it would be more
difficult for Barth to sustain his polemic against natural
theology. If it were merely a question of whether our
knowledge of God is restricted to the ordinary man Jesus,
understood in an Antiochian sense as a person distinct
from God, there would seem to be little justification for
denying that God can be known just as readily through
other media, should he decide to reveal himself. In fact,
to deny that God might reveal himself just as fully
through other media seems to restrict his freedom.
Consequently, it is not surprising when interpreters who
think of Barth as Antiochian are puzzled by his
restricting revelation to Christ.[2]

On the other hand, since the Alexandrian interpretation
of Barth emphasizes that Jesus Christ is both the agent
God and also the act which constitutes God's being in its
dimensions ad intra and ad extra, it follows that God does
not reveal himself either to himself or to men apart from
Jesus Christ. By definition, Jesus Christ is the act of
revelation in which all the moments which witness to that
revelation have their being. Consequently, even if God
reveals himself through various creaturely media, and
Barth admits that he can, this does not mean that he
reveals himself apart from Jesus Christ.

It should be added immediately that God's revealing act
always involves the human nature of Christ. Both ad intra
and ad extra, God's revelation has direct reference to his
life as a man in time, in which he makes himself known to
men as the God who takes man's plight upon himself and
reconciles man to himself. If it were otherwise, Barth
believes that the uniqueness of the revelation through the

human nature of Jesus would be threatened, and the danger of natural theology would be increased.[3]

Another topic which is related to Barth's concept of revelation and his polemic against natural theology is his famous rejection of analogia entis. While Barth's treatment of this concept is much too complicated for us to pursue in detail here, we can indicate one way that Barth's Alexandrianism appears to be related to it. One of the reasons that Barth rejects analogia entis is that he thinks that it requires a higher concept of being in which both God and creation participate. Such a concept impugns the glory of God.[4] Since a theology which emphasizes the independence of the created order from God seems to need a higher concept of being to unite God and creation, the Antiochian interpretation, which claims that Jesus is a person who exists in a relative degree of independence from God, might conclude that Barth is unsuccessful in ridding himself of the analogia entis.[5] On the other hand, those who see Barth as an Alexandrian can better understand his rejection of the analogia entis. Since Jesus Christ is fully identical with God, he is not so independent from God that a higher concept of being is required to unite him with God. Jesus Christ and the creatures who have their true being in Christ participate in God's knowing and loving of himself. They are united with God through God's own act of being, not a neutral being which includes them and God.[6]

Barth's Alexandrian thinking also contributes to his development of the doctrine of the trinity from the event of revelation. Because God is directly identical with the self who is present in a human form in Jesus Christ, it is clear that his presence here is radically different from his presence elsewhere in creation. Consequently, the doctrine of the trinity is derived from this one event of revelation, not just any revelatory event. If the Antiochian interpretation of Barth were correct, and God were merely more present in Christ than elsewhere, it would be difficult to maintain that the concept of the trinity is derived from this particular revelation rather than others.[7]

Barth's important concept of election can also be better understood when the Alexandrian character of his thought is recognized. Jesus Christ can elect to become

man and he can elect other men because he is fully identical with God himself. While he does not elect apart from
his humanity, it is his divinity rather than his humanity
which enables him to elect. As the Son of God, he participates in God's eternal decision before time, and this
participation is the foundation for his sojourn as a man
in the creaturely realm. He is not only the one who obeys
the Father, he is also the Word which he obeys. He is the
act of election itself, and as such he is the reality
which embraces all people.

Similarly, when Barth's treatment of reconciliation is
understood in an Alexandrian sense, his emphatic rejection
of any form of synergism is made clear. Since the human
nature of the divine Christ is not a person in its own
right, it is not so independent of God that it can make a
positive contribution to God's reconciling work. The
human nature which is united in fellowship with God is
able to respond in obedience and gratitude to God because
of God's grace, not its own power. Without this grace,
the creature would not be able to exist or avoid evil.
While it might be possible for an Antiochian theology to
avoid the conclusion that man cooperates with God in the
work of reconciliation, the emphasis which this theology
places upon the independence of Jesus and other men from
God makes it more susceptible to the danger of synergism.
If one were to accept the Antiochican interpretation of
Barth, concluding that Jesus is a complete person distinct
from God and that all other men exist in and through him,
Barth's radical emphasis upon the grace of God would be
obscured.[8]

These examples indicate that Barth's Alexandrianism
exerts considerable influence upon some of the most
important and distinctive themes in his theology. We turn
now to the advantages and disadvantages of Barth's version
of this way of doing theology.

THE ADVANTAGES OF BARTH'S ALEXANDRIAN CHRISTOLOGY

By defining Christ's deity as the act which constitutes
the being of God, Barth emphasizes that Christ's deity is
his being and also the being of God. Christ is not divine
because of his faith, his God-consciousness, his obedi-

ence, his courage, his concern for others, his sacrifice
of himself, or any other aspect of his greatness as a man.
Nor is he divine because he is the occasion of faith for
others, because he reflects God, or because others interpret God's being and nature through clues found in his
existence. He is divine because he is fully and completely God himself, just as the Father and the Holy
Spirit are also God.

The affirmation of the divinity of Christ is not the
last in a series of propositions, as the conclusion of an
argument or an interpretation. According to Barth, we do
not believe that Christ is divine because he makes a
particular kind of impression, or because of something
about him that can be known in an ordinary, empirical and
historical fashion. The idea of the divinity of Christ is
not the result of human discovery or creative thought. It
is based upon the recognition, granted by God himself,
that Christ is who he is, namely God himself in and
through a human form. Christian thought begins simply by
acknowledging that God himself is present in this revelatory act; and because this act is identical with Jesus
Christ, to begin with revelation is to begin with the
divinity of Christ.[9]

The divinity of Christ is guaranteed by Barth because
Christ is God's act <u>ad intra</u> as well as his act <u>ad extra</u>.
Jesus Christ is not simply the act of God in the sense
that God called a human person into existence and guided
him through his life, accomplishing a unique goal. Jesus
Christ in both his divine and his human natures is present
eternally in God's act of being.[10]

By conceiving Christ's deity in this manner, Barth
precludes any accusation of idolatry. He is not guilty of
advocating the worship of a man who is simply declared to
be divine. In Barth's construction of this doctrine,
divinity is not predicated of Christ in a "loose" manner;
it is his essence.

Barth's concept of the divinity of Jesus Christ also
emphasizes the uniqueness of Jesus in relation to all
other creaturely realities. The directness of Jesus'
identity with God is safeguarded by the claim that the
existence of Jesus is also the existence of God himself.
In the case of Jesus, the bearer of the human nature is
not simply an ordinary man but God himself. Although God

is present with other creatures, and even though he can be nearer to them than they are to themselves, he is not identical with them.

While Barth's concept of the divinity of the Bible and proclamation is similar to his treatment of the divinity of Jesus Christ in certain respects, the uniqueness of the divinity of Christ is not undermined. While Christ's essence is divine, the Bible and proclamation become divine when God speaks through them. They are not essentially divine; unlike Christ, they maintain an independent existence of their own over against the existence of God.

Barth's treatment of the concept of the divinity of Christ also emphasizes the oneness of the person of Christ. This oneness can be seen in the identification of act with being. God's person is his act, and insofar as he is one act, he is one person. Barth explains that God is constituted by one act and that this act is his eternal positing of himself in his inner life. In the same way, Christ's work is his being, and it is also the work of God. Christ is the act of God and the person God. Since the act of God which is identical with Christ is, in essence, one act, it is clear that Christ is one person.

The oneness of the person of Christ is also seen in that he is the agent who reveals himself and reconciles men to himself. Even the movement upward to God, which is traversed by the human nature, is not traversed by the human nature in abstraction from God himself. It is Jesus Christ who exalts his human nature. Both the movement downward toward the creature and the movement upward toward God are performed by the one agent Jesus Christ. As the Son of God he humiliates himself, and as Son of Man he exalts human nature. There is only one agent involved here, and therefore Jesus Christ is one person, not two.

Finally, although Barth's concept of the divinity of Christ is a vigorous and innovative reformulation of the classical Alexandrian perspective, it incorporates significant elements from Antiochian thought. Barth affirms that Jesus Christ is fully human. As a man, Christ was subject to the conditions of all men. He had a soul and a body, he was conditioned by his environment, he had limited knowledge, he was anxious.[11] Further, Barth conceives of the human nature of Christ as both a subject of attribution and also a subject of action.[12] That is, he attributes qualities and actions to the human nature. The human nature is active in relation to the divine nature; it obeys, serves, and attests the divine. The fact that Barth grants this degree of independence to the human nature contributes to the hypothesis that he is an Antiochian thinker.

Barth's emphasis upon the concepts of fellowship and confrontation in his treatment of the union of the two natures also makes him similar in some respects to such Antiochian thinkers as Theodore, for whom the harmony of the two wills was of special importance. Barth's use of these categories grants a degree of independence to both natures, since fellowship implies a certain "distance" between participants. Further, Barth sides with the Reformed tradition in refraining from attributing the qualities of the divine nature to the human nature. In agreement with the Reformed, he prefers to stress the distinction of the two natures rather than their insepa-rability, although he does not deny the latter.

Although Barth has incorporated significant elements of Antiochian thought in his christology, it appears that his perspective is still basically Alexandrian. Barth has not found a genuine synthesis which avoids making a choice between the two theologies. Some of the grounds for this conclusion will be made clearer as we turn from the advantages of Barth's thought to some of the problems which it encounters, for these problems are similar to those which have traditionally plagued Alexandrian theolo-gians.

THE PROBLEMS OF BARTH'S ALEXANDRIAN CHRISTOLOGY

The limitations of Barth's concept of the divinity of Christ are most apparent at the point of his greatest strengths. It must be asked whether Barth's emphasis upon the divinity of Christ does sufficient justice to his humanity. While it is clear that Barth insists upon the affirmation that the eternal Son became man, it is not clear to what extent Barth can say that Jesus Christ is an ordinary man as other men are,

Because God is identical with Christ in the full sense

of the term "identical" and because the bearer of the human nature of Jesus is God himself and not simply a man, the full humanity of Christ is brought into question. Although it is difficult to know precisely all that Barth intends by the concept "bearer," it is clear that other men are the bearers of their human nature, while in the case of Jesus Christ there is no purely human bearer. The bearer is God and only God.

Although Barth does not follow Apollinarius by abstracting some "part" of human nature, such as the mind, and arguing that the mind of the human nature was replaced by the mind of God in the incarnation, his claim that Jesus Christ is the divine rather than the human bearer of his human nature has an Apollinarian appearance. A human element that normally is found in existing men is not present in Jesus Christ.[13] Further, the human element which is not present in Jesus Christ seems to be an important dimension of human beings. In Barth's formulation, the bearer appears to be the principal locus of human individuality and the foundation of each human being's independent existence. Consequently, Barth's denial that the human nature of Jesus Christ has its own human bearer threatens the complete humanity of Jesus Christ.[14]

Barth's tendency toward Apollinarianism is also evidenced by his use of "Jesus Christ" and its variants to denote God rather than an independently existing human individual who is inseparably united with God. Since, in the case of Jesus Christ, the divine bearer of the human nature is the subject and agent to whom the name "Jesus" and its variants refer, the human nature of Christ does not possess its own name. Barth's use of "Jesus" and its variants in this manner might be described as "terminological Apollinarianism" because this usage does not grant to the human nature of Christ what all other human individuals have--a personal name. In Barth's thought, the fact that other individuals possess their own names appears to be dependent upon their independent existence and the fact that they are the bearers of their human nature. In theory and also in linguistic practice, Barth is consistent; in both areas the complete humanity of Jesus Christ appears to be undermined.[15]

In addition to the question of whether Barth maintains

the full humanity of Jesus Christ, it should also be asked
whether Barth protects sufficiently the independence of
the• human nature of Jesus Christ. Although Barth does
grant to the human nature of Christ a certain degree of
independence, in that the human nature can obey and serve
the Son and his divine nature, it is difficult to see how
this human nature can fail to obey and serve God. Since
the human nature comes into being only because God begins
to act humanly and since the human nature exists only as
the form of revelation, without having an independent
existence, it seems to be merely an aspect or a part of
God's being and act. It is so integrally taken up and
assumed into God's being that its purely human existence
is denied. In the final analysis, the degree of independence which the human nature has is extremely slight. It
serves and attests God because God determines it to be
that which serves and attests him.[16]

The obedience of the human nature to the eternal Son,
as we have noted, is analogous to the obedience of the
body to the soul of a human person and also to the obedience of the Son to the Father in the inner-trinitarian
life. In these instances, two distinct individuals are
not necessary. The obedience is the obedience that occurs
within one person. Concomitantly, the independence of the
"two" which is presupposed by this inner obedience is
considerably less in degree than the independence of one
person from another. The human nature of Jesus Christ is
so inherently related to him and so disposed to his
control that we cannot conceive how it could be said that
he was really tempted, much less actually moved to commit
sin. Thus, for Barth, the claim that Jesus Christ was
tempted cannot be systematically correlated with the fact
that he is the Son of God.[17]

Barth also seems to slight the humanness of Christ in
other ways. Although he states that Jesus Christ has
limited knowledge and can be anxious, these features of
Jesus play no significant role in Christ's revealing
activity. While the one Jesus Christ reveals through both
natures, he reveals in spite of his human nature. The
human nature actually veils God's revelation. It is
basically the same story with respect to reconciliation.
God performs this function primarily through his divine
nature. It is because God is present that man is justi-

fied.   Justification and reconciliation occur because of
God's decision that the human nature be exalted.   The
human nature simply acquiesces with God's action.

Jesus'   human   characteristics   contribute   little   to
Barth's understanding of Jesus' life as a man.   There is
no significant attention given, for example, to Jesus'
growing awareness of God in his life or to the fact that
his beliefs and ideas about God may have changed over
time.   Jesus' faith is treated as a constant, and it is
interpreted   through   the   claim   that   the   human   nature
attests and serves the divine nature at every moment.   The
actual form of the service of Jesus' human nature is not
related specifically to the ideas, teachings, feelings or
actions of Jesus as a man.

Similarly, the humanity of Christ appears to play a
minimal role in the relation of Christians to Christ.
Barth's affirmation that Jesus Christ is always "for" men
rather than merely "with" them seems to make it difficult
for Christians to feel that he is completely their brother.   Further, since Christ cannot really be tempted, it is
clear   that   he   cannot   experience   the   human   situation
exactly as other people who can be tempted.   The relation
of Christians to Christ is characterized more by obedience
and worship than by comradeship.[18]

We have looked now at the problem of the importance of
the human nature in Barth's Alexandrian christology.   At
this point, we turn to the question of the theoretical
justification for predicating divinity to a creaturely
reality.   Although Barth places an extraordinary emphasis
upon the divinity of Christ and the uniqueness of that
divinity, the fact that he speaks of the divinity of the
Bible and proclamation in the way that he does poses a
threat to his treatment of the divinity of Christ.   If it
is proper to affirm the divinity of the Bible and proclamation because of their participation in revelation, it
would apparently also be proper to affirm the divinity of
a purely human person if he were to become the medium
through which God speaks.   As a result, if Jesus were
considered to be a purely human person in an Antiochian
sense, it would appear to be permissible, even on Barthian
grounds, to ascribe divinity to him, should God speak
through him in a moment of revelation.

By speaking of the divinity of the Bible and procla-

mation in the way that he does, Barth deprives himself of
an argument that defenders of Alexandrian theology might
wish to use to oppose Antiochian formulations. That is,
he cannot argue that it is improper to speak of the
divinity of creatures who merely participate in revelation. By incorporating this element of Antiochian thought
in respect to the Bible and proclamation, he raises the
question whether divinity should be attributed to Jesus on
the same basis.

The fact that divinity can be ascribed to the Bible and
proclamation because of their participation in God's
speaking indicates that Barth's polemic against ebionitism
and docetism does not necessarily apply directly to
Antiochian thought. Barth argues that ebionitism attributes divinity to a mere man with an impressive personality. Because of the disciples' veneration of this man,
ebionitism supposes, the equation of this man with God
becomes a possibility, although it is a slight exaggera-
tion. Docetism is willing to call Jesus "Son of God" and
"God" because he is the vehicle of a lofty idea. In both
cases, divinity is ascribed to a mere man, according to
Barth, and therefore they are guilty of idolatry.[19]
This might appear to be a devastating criticism of Antiochian thought, since Antiochian thought conceives of
Jesus as an ordinary man. However, if Barth's polemic
against ebionitism and docetism is effective opposition to
the attribution of divinity to any finite reality, it is
also effective opposition to Barth's own attribution of
divinity to the Bible and proclamation.

Barth's emphasis upon the divinity of Christ and the
way he conceives the human nature of Christ also seem to
mitigate the significance of the existence of other
people. Barth states that Jesus Christ is a man, but he
is a man in a unique sense. He is the one man who is the
true actualization of human essence and in whom all other
people have their true being. Other people do not exist
so much alongside of Jesus Christ as within him. Furthermore, their existence in him is a transformed existence;
they are brought into conformity with God's will and
therefore into fellowship with God.[20] In the first
analysis, sin is rejected. This raises the question of
the reality and value of the lives of men now, as they are
influenced by sin. Put another way, this question asks

whether Barth provides sufficient distinctions within
the one whole reality which is Jesus Christ.   For
example, is the theologically necessary distinction
between God and men finally collapsed through the notion
that men have their being only in Christ?[21]
   The significance of the existence of all men is threatened not only by the fact that they have their true
existence in Christ, it is also obscured by Barth's claim
that the human nature which the Son assumed in the incarnation has no independent existence.   Since the human
nature which the Son assumed is the human nature of all
men, and since this human nature has no independent
existence, it is difficult to see how the many persons who
are assumed in and with the assumption of the human nature
of Jesus can have an independent existence.[22]   Barth
does affirm that other men, in contrast to Jesus, exist
independently of God.   This is how other men differ from
Jesus.   But since all men exist in and through the particular humanity which has no independent existence, the
grounds for affirming that all men other than Jesus exist
independently remain unclear.   In other words, if all
people exist in a humanity that has no independent existence, how can these people exist independently?
   Not only does Barth's concept of the divinity of Jesus
Christ as the act which includes all men threaten the
independent reality of men, the claim that this act occurs
eternally in God seems to make its occurrence ad extra in
time unnecessary.   Because God's decision is his being,
his decision to become a man is not a mere plan in the
manner of the plans of men.   God's plan is executed in its
planning, and therefore it is real in the strictest sense.
Thus, Jesus Christ is already present as man before
creation.   Of course, Barth's distinction between God's
act ad intra and his act ad extra is not intended to be a
distinction between two acts.   It is intended rather to
guarantee God's freedom.   Nevertheless, the positing of
this distinction renders it difficult to supply a reason
for God's act ad extra.   Everything has already happened
in God, and therefore God's act ad extra seems to have no
inherent value.   If Jesus' real life, and ours as well, is
lived eternally with God prior to his becoming a man in
time, how could his life in time be very important?[23]

BARTH'S THEOLOGY AND THE ALEXANDRIAN THEOLOGICAL TRADITION

If the principal contention of this book is correct, and it is proper to characterize Barth's christology as Alexandrian, an important but difficult question inevitably arises. Should Barth's entire theology, and not simply his christology, be considered Alexandrian? One way to approach this complex question would be to engage in a thorough comparison of Barth and leading Alexandrian theologians on both doctrinal and methodological issues. However, such a study is beyond our present purpose. On the other hand, since our investigation has led us unavoidably to the problem of the relation of Barth's dogmatics to Alexandrian theology, we would prefer not simply to dismiss the topic on the grounds of its difficulty. What we propose, therefore, is to mention both some of the evidences which suggest that Barth's theology should not be classified as Alexandrian and also some of the factors which support the view that Barth's dogmatics is Alexandrian. By constructing a tentative case for these two opposing alternatives, we can illustrate the complexity of the problem, we can point out specific issues which should be confronted in deciding the question, and we can help the readers formulate tentative judgments regarding the strength of each case. We shall look first at the arguments which might be marshalled to contest the assumption that Barth's theology is Alexandrian.

An opponent of the view that Barth's theology should be classified as Alexandrian might direct our attention, first of all, to the limitations of the label "Alexandrian." This opponent might argue that the term "Alexandrian" should apply directly to christology rather than to an entire systematic theology. If "Alexandrian" should be limited in this way, it would be improper to characterize an entire dogmatic theology as Alexandrian, even if its christology were Alexandrian. Our hypothetical opponent could defend this stance by pointing out that the classical debates between Antiochian and Alexandrian theologians in the fourth, fifth, and later centuries revolved around christological issues. Consequently, the Alexandrian and Antiochian traditions became differentiated from each other primarily on the basis of their christologies.

Further, our hypothetical opponent could continue, during those classical debates there were only minimal differences between major Alexandrian and Antiochian theologians on issues other than christology and the most direct and immediate implications of christology, such as might be found, perhaps, in soteriology. To substantiate this last claim, it could be pointed out that both Alexandrian and Antiochian theologians have accepted orthodox doctrines of the trinity, that both have emphasized the aseity and the impassibility of God in his divine nature, and that both have admitted the validity of allegorical interpretations of scripture.[24]

A second argument based on the limitations of the term "Alexandrian" is that Barth's theology is more appropriately characterized by other labels, such as dialectical or neo-orthodox.[25] According to this claim, while there may be Alexandrian elements in Barth's thought, they are not as significant as his attempt to correct the humanistic tendencies which he saw in Protestant liberalism or his adherence to the Protestant emphases of Calvin and Luther. To support this conclusion, it might be mentioned, for example, that the early Alexandrians were Catholics, while Barth is noted for his attacks upon Catholic theology. The term "Alexandrian," to those who defend this argument, does not seem sufficiently broad to suggest either the traditional or the novel elements in Barth's distinctively Protestant dogmatics.

Other arguments opposed to classifying Barth's theology as Alexandrian focus more on the presuppositions and content of Barth's theology than upon the limitations of the term "Alexandrian." We shall confine our discussion to three such arguments: (1) Barth and the early Alexandrians confronted different problems and, as a result, their theolgies are different; (2) Barth's understanding of the relation between philosophy and theology is diametrically opposed to that held by influential Alexandrian theologians, and (3) Barth's theology avoids the dangers to which the classical Alexandrians succumbed.

It is not difficult to support the contention that the classical Alexandrians concentrated upon issues which differ significantly from those which occupied Barth's energy. Clement of Alexandria and Origen faced challenges from gnostics, stoics, non-Christian Platonists, and Roman polytheists, and their concern to engage in dialogue with such opponents influenced the character of their theologies.[26]   Clement of Alexandria and Origen, for example, stressed against the stoics that God is not a material but rather a spiritual reality.   On that issue they sided with the Platonic tradition, and they borrowed arguments from that tradition to use against philosophical materialists. This emphasis upon the spiritual and intellectual nature of God, with its corollary that God is transcendent over all creaturely reality, was perhaps the most important element   in   Clement's   and   Origen's   theologies.   This concept   of   God   had   important   implications   for   other aspects of Clement's and Origen's theologies, such as their high evaluation of human reason and the intellectual contemplation   of   God.   This   concept   of   God   was   also important historically in that it undermined a literal, anthropomorhpic understanding of God, and it also provided a necessary foundation for the orthodox doctrine of the trinity, which presupposed the immateriality of God.[27]

In contrast, Barth found himself engaged in dialogue with Protestant liberalism, represented by such figures as Friedrich Schleiermacher, Wilhelm Herrmann, and Adolph von Harnack; existentialist philosophers and theologians, such as Martin Heidegger and Rudolph Bultmann; Roman Catholic theologians, represented by such figures as St. Thomas and Erich Pryzwara; and perhaps most important of all, atheistic humanists such as Ludwig Feuerbach.   All of these schools of thought, according to Barth, share one serious defect; they attempt to build affirmations about God upon claims about humanity and the created order.   Because of that tendency, they are all subject to Feuerbach's charge that their claims about God are only projections of human wishes, with no foundation in reality outside the human mind.   Consequently, Barth concluded, these schools of thought would lead the church down a dead-end street, and at the end of that street await both Feuerbach's atheism and also world war.[28]

The principal task of Barth's theology, it can be said, was to find a solid foundation for theology, a foundation which   would   protect   theology   from   atheism   and   moral bankruptcy.   This foundation, he concluded, was not the order in nature, or human consciousness of dependency, or human consciousness of God, or human awareness of the categorical imperative, or even the greatness of Jesus; it was God himself in his revelation, God speaking his Word in Christ, scripture, and proclamation.[29]

Not only did the early Alexandrians face problems which were different from those which confronted Barth, but also Clement of Alexandria and Origen had to face those problems without the benefit of having available a systematic statement of the entire body of Christian belief.[30] Clement and Origen stood at the beginning of a long line of systematic theologians, and their theologies reflect that handicap.[31] On the other hand, Barth followed many systematic theologians, including St. Thomas, Calvin, and Schleiermacher, and he profited from their efforts. Further, the availability of these resources helped make it possible for Barth to concentrate so much of his effort upon questions of theological method, that is, upon questions of the nature of theology, its relation to the church and secular disciplines, and the relationship of doctrines to each other. Clement and Origen were not ignorant of questions of theological method, but they did not devote so much attention and reflection to them as Barth did.

A defender of the conclusion that it is improper to classify Barth as an Alexandrian theologian can also point out that Barth and the early Alexandrians differ from each other on the question of the relation between philosophy and theology. The contrast between Barth and the early Alexandrians can be stated succinctly: the early Alexandrians, especially Clement of Alexandria and Origen, emphasized the continuity between philosophy and theology while Barth stressed the discontinuity between them. This contrast requires a brief elaboration.

Patristic scholars have recognized that both Clement of Alexandria and Origen had a deep appreciation for the works of leading philosophers, both ancient and contemporary. Clement and Origen studied philosophy carefully; they concluded that many philosophers, especially Plato and other Platonic thinkers, taught truth; and they relied upon philosophical thought and philosophical arguments in their theological work.[32] Three results of Clement's and Origen's reliance upon philosophy, and particularly Platonic philosophy, should be mentioned here. First, they believed that the truths which had been discovered by

philosophers had been made available to those philosophers, directly or indirectly, through God's initiative.
The philosophers had learned some of those truths from
Moses and the Old Testament, but in addition to that fact,
all people have a natural knowledge of God and God's basic
moral laws. Since Clement and Origen believed that God
had created human beings with an intellectual nature which
has a natural affinity to God's intellectual nature, they
did not find it surprising that non-Christian thinkers can
recognize elements of truth.[33]

Second, Clement and Origen believed that philosophical
learning could provide valuable contributions to Christians and Christian theology. While philosophy does not
teach the whole truth and needs to be completed and
corrected by teachings from the Bible, and while philosophers usually fail miserably to communicate the truths
which they discover to any people other than the intellectuals, it seemed obvious to Clement and Origen that the
study of philosophy could prepare one for, and even lead
one toward, the study and acceptance of Christian belief.
In this sense, philosophy and theology are in continuity
with each other.[34]

Similarly, Clement and Origen thought that philosophical thinking could help Christians progress from the
level of faith to the level of knowledge. While some
Christians might remain at the level of faith and simply
accept Christian teachings on the basis of their obedience
to authorities who tell them what to believe, other
Christians may attain a higher and more joyful state
characterized by knowledge. In this state, one believes on
the basis of reasonable convictions and understanding, not
simply because of fear of authorities. The tools which
lead to this knowledge include the philosophical tool of
rational and orderly thinking, secular learning, and study
of the Bible.[35]

Third, both Clement and Origen produced theologies
which combine Platonic and biblical elements into an
admirable synthesis. These two men had an overarching
vision of the fundamental unity of Christianity and
Platonism which allowed them to rely heavily upon the
underlying presuppositions and terminology of the Platonism of their day. Conversely, biblical terms and thought
patterns added to and transformed the meaning of Platonic

concepts. The result, in each theologian's work, is a synthesis which resists the efforts of those who would like to separate out the philosophical and theological elements. Speaking specifically of Origen, Norris states:

> In his thought, these two elements are so wedded as to be indeed one flesh. Origen is the continual despair of those who try to impugn his Christianity by pointing to his Platonism, or to minimize his philosophical leanings by calling attention to the scriptural and ecclesiastical elements in his thought. In Origen, Christian faith and philosophical understanding are no longer exterior to each other.[36]

In contrast to the early Alexandrians, Barth insists that theology should maintain its own integrity and unity apart from any philosophical consideration. Theology, declares Barth, has its own subject matter and its own methods which are determined by God's revelation of himself in Jesus Christ, not by philosophical principles or systems. In order to be reliable, Barth argues, theology must conform to its ultimate object, God in his revelation. Theology should not allow philosophical principles to function as norms or criteria for theological method or theological formulations. Nor should theology ally itself with any one philosophical system.[37]

Barth indicates that philosophy, philosophical concepts, and philosophical principles pose a serious danger for theology because they tend to distort theological thinking. On the other hand, it is not possible for theology to exist without making use of philosophical terms, concepts, and principles. Insofar as theologians think conceptually and use language to communicate, they are being influenced by philosophical presuppositions. Further, each individual has assumptions about the fundamental nature of things in the universe, and these assumptions color one's perceptions of theological issues and one's formulations of theological conclusions. The problem is to keep philosophical presuppositions subordinate to theological criteria, and that is an extremely difficult task, for philosophical principles tend to function as tyrants, usurping their superiors. In Barth's view, theologians should be on constant guard against allowing their work to be undermined by philosophical subversives. To guard against this danger, theologians should continuously seek the guidance of the scripture and proclamation. Because God's revelation is mediated to us through these sources, theologians should use them, not philosophy, as their tutors.

Barth's suspicion of philosophy is directly related to his assessment of human intellectual abilities. According to Barth, it is not possible for the human mind to create a world view or a metaphysics which provides a complete and consistent explanation of all reality and also God. Human thought can approach reality by thinking either realistically or idealistically, by beginning with nature or the requirements of thought. However, the philosophical "systems" which are produced by these approaches, realism or idealism, are inconsistent with each other, and they also have internal difficulties. Consequently, we cannot expect philosophy to provide a foundation or a norm for theology.

A theology which recognizes the limitations of human thought will utilize both realistic and idealistic modes of thought, but it will not attempt to provide a "system" in which these two modes are synthesized into a final, absolute unity. In theology, as in philosophy, these two modes of thought are in tension with each other, and their conceptual harmony is not apparent to us. This limitation of human thought is perhaps most apparent with regard to revelation, since revelation involves both God and a creaturely medium or form. If we deal with revelation realistically, by focusing upon the creaturely element, what we observe is a phenomenon similar to other phenomena; there are no special characteristics which point unmistakably toward God and thereby demonstrate that the phenomenon in question is in fact a form of God's revelation. On the other hand, if we deal with revelation idealistically, focusing upon the divine element, there is no systematic connection between the content and that particular form. Why did God choose that particular form, or any form? Further, to affirm that God chose a form appears to deny certain attributes of God normally assumed to be required by an idealistic concept of God, such as his impassability. Consequently, Barth states that when we deal with revelation, we can discern either the form or the content, but not both in a unity. Nevertheless, although we can think or speak only realistically or idealistically, we believe in faith that the unity of these two modes of thought rests in God himself.[38]

There is another sense in which Barth's theology can be called realistic. Barth affirms that theology must conform to an objective reality which freely makes itself available for human knowledge and analysis. That object is God's Word, and insofar as theology conforms to that reality it is a realistic theology. Further, Barth clearly rejects a theology which is idealistic in the sense that claims about human beings or human consciousness are thought to entail claims about God. A concept of God which conforms to the God who reveals himself in Christ is not, according to Barth, a necessary element in, or an implication of, human self-understanding or human intellectual activity. On the other hand, Barth's theology is not realistic in the same sense as the Thomistic tradition. Barth opposes the view that philosophy, under the label of natural theology, can provide a foundation upon which theology can build. It is not the case, Barth teaches, that human reason can attain, through its reflection upon the natural order, a concept of God which is basically correct but limited and which, therefore, must be supplemented by revelation to become adequate. Rather, theology has its own foundation, and that foundation is God's revelation in Christ, scripture, and proclamation. [39]

Barth's attempt to ground theology in itself rather than in philosophy has stimulated criticisms from thinkers who hold a higher estimate than Barth of the potential of philosophy. Such critics have accused Barth of de-emphasizing excessively the value of philosophy, human reason, and everything human.[40] Also, Barth has been accused of compartmentalizing philosophy and theology into two separate realms, so that they can have nothing to do with each other. This compartmentalizing, it is alleged, undermines the possibility of discussion and understanding between philosophers and theologians and also between individuals who have different commitments, different

faiths, and different experiences.[41] Similarly, others
have stated that because Barth is unwilling to ground his
starting point in philosophy or upon some kind of rational
defense or foundation, his starting point becomes arbitrary. Why start with Christ? Why not start with Buddha
or some other religious authority?[42] Although Barth's
supporters contest the claims that Barth is arbitrary,
that he is an irrationalist, or that he compartmentalizes
philosophy from theology,[43] the widespread persistence
of such criticisms is, in itself, evidence that Barth's
position regarding the relation of philosophy and theology
is different from that of the classical Alexandrians. One
would not be likely to accuse Origen or Clement of depre-
ciating the importance of philosophy and human reason.
Further, even if one agrees with Barth's defenders and
concludes that Barth is not an irrationalist and that he
does not separate philosophy from theology in an unreason-
able manner, it is nevertheless apparent that Barth's
evaluation of philosophy is quite different from that of
the classical Alexandrians.

To conclude this discussion of the relation of philosophy to theology, one who opposes classifying Barth as an
Alexandrian theologian can argue that there is a substantial difference between Barth's approach to philosophy and
the approach to philosophy found in Clement and Origen.
Clement and Origen have a profound appreciation for
philosophy, and they focus upon the harmony between
philosophy and theology. On the other hand, Barth is
suspicious of philosophy, he opposes any synthesis of
theology and philosophy, and he attempts to keep
philosophical considerations from distorting theological
method and theological conclusions.

The final topic we shall discuss in our consideration
of the view that Barth should not be classified as an
Alexandrian theologian involves the weaknesses of Alexandrian theology. A case can be made for the conclusion
that Barth avoids the errors of the early Alexandrians and
that, therefore, the label "Alexandrian" does not fit his
thought. We shall begin our discussion of this point of
view by mentioning some traditional criticisms of Alexandrian theology, and then we shall indicate some of the
evidences which suggest that Barth is not subject to these
criticisms.

Alexandrian theology has been subject to two principal objections. The first is that the Alexandrians were so influenced by philosophical and Platonic modes of thought that important, distinctively biblical beliefs were overshadowed or altogether eliminated from their theologies.[44] This criticism includes opposition to many specific assertions of the Alexandrian thinkers and therefore it requires some elaboration. The second major objection, which is more readily understandable and needs less clarification in this context, has to do with the Alexandrians' approach to the interpretation of scripture. According to it, the Alexandrians' emphasis upon the allegorical method of interpreting scriptural texts allowed them both to overlook the meaning which was actually in the text and also to read their Platonic ideas into the text.[45]

The charge that the Alexandrians allowed their Platonism to dominate their theologies can be defended by focusing upon the Platonic distinction between being and becoming. As is well known, Platonism, following Plato's lead in the Timaeus, emphasized that being is eternal, unchanging, invisible, incorporeal, intelligible, not composite, and not generated. On the other hand, the realm of becoming is temporal, changing, visible, corporeal, composite, and generated. Becoming is perceived by the senses, but knowledge of being is true and proper knowledge because it is knowledge of underlying, permanent truth. In this dualistic approach, the realm of being is granted more value than the realm of becoming, which is considered inferior and questionable.[46] The early Alexandrians were profoundly influenced by these Platonic presuppositions, and some of the implications of this influence should be noted.

Perhaps the most dramatic impact of Platonism's dualism on Alexandrianism has to do with the Alexandrians' understanding of the goal of Christian life. For them, the human soul is an intellectual substance with a natural kinship to God. In its earthly life, which is characterized primarily by becoming, the soul has become united with a physical body alienated from its original nature. Consequently, the soul has become distracted from its original purpose of knowing intelligible being. The goal of the Christian life is to lead the soul to higher levels of spiritual understanding until the soul is united with God. In contrast with Tertullian, who stressed the crucial importance of obedience to God's will, the Alexandrians stressed the value of contemplative knowledge which restores the soul to its original likeness to God. For example, speaking of Origen, Norris states that "his conception of the point and purpose of Christian teaching is shaped by the Platonist idea of the soul's intellectual quest for union with intelligible Reality."[47]   This understanding of the goal of the Christian life appears to give insufficient attention to the importance of the eschatological dimension of Jewish and early Christian thought, according to which God has a purpose not just for intellectual souls to be united with God in some spiritual realm beyond the lower regions of becoming but rather for the transformation of nature and the perfection of history.

In order to achieve this knowledge of God and the realm of true being, the Alexandrians added, the soul must turn its attention away from the realm of becoming. One does not find fulfillment by seeking it through bodily or material existence, through things which are visible or available to us through sense perception, or through things with are temporal. Earthly existence is characterized by error, and the soul, if it is to progress to a higher state of existence, must repudiate the bodily, material realm of becoming. One way to repudiate the world of becoming, of course, is to practice asceticism, to overcome the desires and passions of the body.[48]

The Alexandrians' acceptance of the distinction between being and becoming, according to critics, led them to a devaluation of creaturely existence which is contrary to the biblical understanding of creation. If the Bible is accurate when it affirms that the world is good, one might ask the Alexandrians, why should one have to repudiate temporal existence in order to attain salvation?

Other features of Alexandrian thought which imply an unbiblical devaluation of the goodness of creation should be mentioned in passing. Prominent among them is Origen's doctrine of the creation of matter and the material world. According to Origen, this present, visible world is a result of the sin and fall of rational spirits who existed before this world was created. Some souls fell farther than others, and the inequalities and disharmonies of the world are a consequence of that fact. Matter is the principle of differentiation, so matter was created by God to mark the varying depths of the fall of rational souls. Although Origen does not conclude that the material world is evil, the fact that it is the product of sin raises serious questions about its inherent goodness and importance. If the rational spirits had not sinned, there apparently would have been no reason for God to create the physical, material world in which we now live.[49]

Even if Origen had not concluded that the material world must be the result of a pretemporal fall, his claim that human souls are eternal suggests a devaluation of physical, created existence. By affirming that human souls are eternal, Origen safeguards their natural kinship to God and the realm of being, their intelligence, and their value. On the other hand, by denying them their creation in time, Origen implies that human souls are too valuable to be included in the realm of becoming. If human souls were created as trees, for example, are created, their value and the possibility of their salvation would be seriously threatened.[50]

Similarly, Origen's devaluation of nature is implicit in his denial of the resurrection of the flesh. The idea of a resurrection of the flesh was repugnant to pagan Platonists, who had such a low regard for matter that they could see no value whatsoever in a physical resurrection. Origen could not deny the claim of resurrection in the New Testament, but he thought that the New Testament really meant the resurrection of a spiritual, not a physical body.[51]

At the opposite end of the spectrum, Alexandrian theologians have been accused of holding an unbiblical view of God. According to this criticism, the Alexandrians' concept of God was excessively influenced by Platonic affirmations of the superiority of being over becoming. Platonic dualistic thought patterns led the Alexandrians to emphasize God's perfection, eternality, incomprehensibility, and unchangeability. God became identified with reality itself, and the effort to maintain his transcendence "above" the realm of becoming and even above the realm of other intellectual substances such as human souls, prevented the Alexandrians from giving sufficient support to God's personal characteristics. In order to concentrate upon God's perfection, they said God is absolutely simple, as a mathematical point from which all qualities have been extracted, not extended or composite as material realities which can decompose. Since God is a purely simple unity, pure being and pure act, he is incomprehensible and beyond our categories. We approach him through the via negativa, by stating what God is not, and we also hope that we shall ultimately be united with God in a direct, intuitive vision. Further, God does not change, and no passions or emotions can disturb him. In the Alexandrian interpretation, the biblical view of a personal God who loves, acts, knows, and decides seems relegated to the misconceptions of the uninstructed common people, while the abstract God who is radically absolute is recognized by those who progress from mere faith to knowledge.[52]

The Alexandrians' emphasis upon God's transcendence had trinitarian and christological implications which should be mentioned briefly. Both Clement and Origen seem to have been guilty of a certain subordinationism in the trinity, according to which the Logos or Son was accorded reduced status. Origen stated, for example, that the Son was a "second god," and therefore was accused of providing a foundation for Arianism.[53] Further, since God was so much more worthy than realities in the realm of becoming, it was difficult for the Alexandrians to avoid various forms of docetism. Clement suggested that the incarnate Logos was not really subject to the frailties of the flesh, so he could not be hungry or tired.[54]

While the objections against Alexandrian thought which we have mentioned here do not exhaust all the possibilities, they provide a sufficient platform from which we can look again at Barth. Those who conclude that Barth avoids the errors of Alexandrian thought can support their views by speaking about Barth's position with regard to the objections we have noted.

Although Barth often draws upon philosophical concepts or arguments, and although there are many idealistic or Platonic elements in his theology,[55] one might argue that Barth's dogmatics is true to his explicit ideal of relegating philosophy to theology. In his method and in his dogmatic formulations, these Barth supporters might contend, Barth is consistently guided primarily by the event of revelation rather than by philosophical principles or arguments.[56] One might defend this contention by appealing to Barth's understanding of the relation between God and the world, his understanding of the goal of Christian life, and his emphasis upon the personality of God. We shall discuss briefly each of these three points.

Although Barth clearly stresses the transcendence and sovereignty of God, Barth's sympathizers can argue that Barth is not significantly influenced by the Platonic and Alexandrian dualism of being and becoming. Rather, for Barth, the relationship between God and the world is determined by God's election, that is, by God's decision to become human and to gather human nature, human beings, and the entire created order into fellowship and unity with God himself. In this view, the world exists "within" God's graceful act of rescuing humans and nature from the threat of nothingness. For Barth, there is no created order which exists "outside" or "below" God's being.[57] God's transcendence is not a matter of God's "distance" from the world, and therefore the concept of God's transcendence should not be understood as a spatial metaphor. Rather, Barth's emphasis on God's transcendence has to do primarily with God's freedom. Although God is nearer to the created order than the created order is to itself, the created order has no claim on God, and it has no ability or means to reach God through its own efforts. However, created beings do not have to reach God through their own efforts, for God has already reached them and embraced them in his act of being.[58]

At this point in the discussion, a critic of the above interpretation of Barth's understanding of God's relation to the world might raise an interesting question. If Barth maintains that the world is "near" to God because God has "taken" the world "up" into his act of being, why does Barth attack so vehemently those theologians who stress a "point of contact" between creatures and God? If God and world are in close proximity to each other, it would appear that there are many points of contact, so why should Barth question a point of contact? The answer to this question has to do both with theological method and also with the way Barth interprets his opponents' use of the phrase "point of contact." According to Barth, Emil Brunner uses "point of contact" to refer to some quality or attribute of humanity which makes it possible for God to make contact with humans through revelation. This human capacity for God was given by God through creation, and it persists in spite of sin. Thus, Brunner can argue that a theological anthropology can provide a foundation and starting point for dogmatics. In contrast, Barth argues that theology must begin with the Word of God, not with theological anthropology. For Barth, there is no human capacity for God which was given in creation and persists in spite of the fall. If "point of contact" means such a capacity, Barth rejects it. On the other hand, Barth is willing to reinterpret "point of contact" and use it in his dogmatic theology. In the reconciling act of the Word of God, the lost "point of contact" is reestablished, and man is able to acknowledge God's Word in faith. In the moment in which God speaks to people, he also grants them the faith to hear him speaking. This faith, this possibility for hearing God's Word, is the real "point of contact," and it is recreated in the moment of revelation and reconciliation.[59]

In the controversies between Barth and the advocates of theological anthropology, then, the phrase "point of contact" was used when discussing the human response to revelation. The phrase did not have direct relevance to the relation between God and the world or to God's omnipresence in the world. If we were to broaden the implications of the phrase "point of contact" to include God's relation to the world,[60] it would be fair to Barth to say that God is in contact with every dimension of the created order and with every individual of every species in creation. In this sense, there are countless points of contact, but all of them are dependent upon God's freedom. No individual of any species can hear and know God, unless God wills to reveal himself to that individual and grant to that individual the faith to hear and know God's Word. In still another sense of the phrase "point of contact," it would be fair to Barth to say that there is only one point of contact, and that is Jesus Christ, who includes in his electing act all the moments which witness to him. Jesus Christ is the point of contact because he initiates and embraces all other points of contact.[61]

With regard to the goal of the Christian life, Barth interpreters who decline to classify Barth as an Alexandrian theologian may argue that Barth does not rely primarily upon the Platonic ideal of the individual's contemplative, mystical knowledge of God but rather upon the social and eschatological dimensions of biblical thought. Although Barth's volume on redemption was never completed, and what we say on this topic must therefore be tentative, Barth has given us clues regarding his thinking on this question. One of these clues is Barth's christological emphasis in his doctrines of justification and sanctification. Man's relationship to God, according to Barth, is determined primarily by God's act in Jesus Christ. In his justifying and sanctifying act in Jesus Christ, God exalted human nature, all human beings, and all creaturely reality into fellowship with himself.[62] This exaltation has an ontological dimension which is the basis of all creaturely knowledge and love of God. It is the foundation of a new direction for humans, a new direction characterized by obedience and by fellowship with other Christians in the church. For Barth, it is not merely the case that Jesus Christ teaches us about God and we can build upon and complete this knowledge through a life of contemplation.[63]

Barth's concept of God also provides ammunition for those who consider Barth's theology to be significantly different from the theology of the Alexandrians. In contrast to Clement and Origen, Barth does not emphasize God's transcendence above personal qualities. For Barth, God's deity is not characterized by his impassibility or his noninvolvement in the creaturely realm. Rather, God's deity is constituted by his decision to become a participant in creation and to suffer for the benefit of his creatures. God's being is defined as the being of a person because God freely decides to condescend to his creatures. We do not simply apply the category "person" to God because God has some similarities to humans. On the contrary, God is the one true person because only he is completely free in his deciding and acting. Barth's emphasis upon the claim that God is a loving, living, acting person appears to free him from the accusation that his doctrine of God is determined primarily by Platonic categories.[64]

Those who defend the view that Barth's theology should not be classified as Alexandrian might also want to point out that Barth's explication of the doctrine of the trinity rules out any subordination of the second person to the first. As we have seen earlier, Barth stresses that the act which constitutes God's being is the second person of the trinity. The deity of the Son is equal to the deity of the Father, and it is also the same, identical deity.[65] Similarly, Barth explicitly denies both docetism and also monophysitism, dangers to which the traditional Alexandrians tended to succumb.[66]

It appears, then, that a rather impressive case can be presented in defense of the conclusion that Barth's theology is not Alexandrian. Not only are there legitimate questions regarding the applicability of the term "Alexandrian" to an entire theology, especially a theology as rich and complex as Barth's theology is, but Barth and the Alexandrian theologians faced different problems and had different attitudes toward the relation between philosophy and theology. Further, Barth's theology seems to have avoided many of the defects of Alexandrian thought. On the other hand, arguments can also be presented for the conclusion that Barth's theology should be classified as Alexandrian. It is to these arguments that we now turn.

The most persuasive argument, in our view, for classifying Barth's theology as Alexandrian is that his christology is Alexandrian according to the definition of Alexandrianism we have presented in this book. We want to reemphasize that this definition is credible and defensible, although it is not the only definition which might be proposed. According to this definition, a christology is Alexandrian if it (1) identifies Jesus Christ as, first and foremost, the second person of the trinity who existed with the Father and the Holy Spirit, in some sense, prior to his incarnation and existence as a creature in time; (2) understands the divinity of Jesus Christ as his original nature which he possesses apart from and prior to his life in time as a man; (3) understands the unity of the person of Jesus Christ as a unity of the complete and fully personal eternal Son with a human nature which is not a complete person; in this unity the human nature is an instrument of the Son; and (4) uses "Jesus" and its variants to name the eternal Son. If our arguments that Barth's christology conforms to these criteria are correct, his christology should be considered Alexandrian.

Because of the crucial importance of christology within a comprehensive, systematic theology, we believe that if a theologian maintains a christology which is Alexandrian according to the criteria we propose, that fact is sufficient ground for categorizing that theologian's entire theology as Alexandrian. The use of the term "Alexandrian" in this manner can be justified on the basis of (1) the historical importance of christological issues in the classical debates between ancient Alexandrian and Antiochian theologians, and (2) the systematic implications of a christological stance upon other theological questions. The use of the term in this manner is especially appropriate in the case of Barth, of course, because Barth stresses the importance of christology and uses his interpretation of God's act in Christ as the foundation and criterion of all his theological formulations. In fact, because Barth develops the implications of an Alexandrian christology in such an orderly manner, it might be said that he is actually the first full-fledged, successful Alexandrian theologian, while the earlier Alexandrians failed to work out the logical implications of their christologies so consistently.[67]

Our delineation of the meaning of the term "Alexandrian" has two notable consequences. First, our application of this adjective to Barth's entire theology does not depend simply upon how many similarities there are between Barth and the early Alexandrians. For example, the extent to which Barth is Platonic would have little or no relevance to the question of whether he is Alexandrian, unless it could be shown that the constitutive elements of Alexandrianism, as we have defined it, are in some important sense Platonic. However, since christological affirmations have important implications, it would be surprising if theologians who satisfy the criteria for Alexandrianism which we propose do not manifest significant similarities. Second, our classification of Barth as Alexandrian does not preclude the utility of other labels as well. To say that Barth is Alexandrian is not to deny in advance that he is also Protestant, Reformed,

dialectical, or even existentialistic. When we say that
Barth's theology is Alexandrian we do not say everything
that can be said about Barth, although we do say something
important.

Although our claim that Barth is Alexandrian is not
dependent upon quantifying the similarities between Barth
and major Alexandrian thinkers, we believe that there are
important similarities between them. One of these, which
we have already mentioned, is that both Barth and
Alexandrian theology were influenced by Platonic concepts
and terminology. In fact, a careful analysis of the
Platonic elements in Barth and a comparison of the way
Barth and Alexandrian theologians used Platonic concepts
would be a significant contribution to Barth scholarship.

Careful investigation would also, we believe, disclose
some important similarities between Barth and the major
Alexandrian theologians in the area of hermeneutics. Both
Barth and the Alexandrians stressed the spiritual and
theological meaning of scriptural texts. This point needs
a brief elaboration.

Barth's controversial commentary on Romans brought him
into conflict with the liberal theologian, Adolph von
Harnack, regarding biblical hermeneutics. As the debate
between Harnack and Barth illustrates, the liberal theologians were committed to conducting their biblical
investigations "scientifically." They attempted to
determine the historical situation of the writer, the
problems he faced, and the meaning of the terms he used.
Barth, on the other hand, wanted to understand and explain
the "point" the author was trying to make. For Barth, the
goal was to enter the mind of the author and explain his
thoughts as well as, or better than, he had been able to
explain them. Harnack and other liberals thought Barth
was ignoring the necessary, scientific ground work of
biblical investigation, the historical-critical study of
the words and the texts, and they concluded that Barth was
reading his own ideas into the text.[68] Harnack and
others also claimed that Barth was preaching, not engaging
in scholarly exegesis.[69] Barth, on the other hand, was
not attempting to deny the importance of the historical
dimension of Christianity or the validity of the historical-critical method of biblical study. Rather, he wanted
to move the goal of historical-critical investigation to a

higher level.[70] He thought that the liberals were
losing sight of the forest in their determination to
scrutinize every tree, and he also thought that many
exegetes were reading their own humanistic or existentialistic presuppositions into the Bible.[71]
   With this brief background data we can proceed to our
principal point, that Barth tends to stress the spiritual
or theological meaning of the text rather than the literal
meaning of the text. In this respect Barth is more like
the ancient Alexandrian than the ancient Antiochian
theologians. One dramatic example of this point is
Barth's debate with Brunner over the virgin birth.[72]
Brunner states that moderns can be indifferent to the idea
of a virgin birth because it is a "biological
interpretation of a miracle" which reflects a "biological
inquisitiveness" about how God became man.[73] That
conclusion indicates that Brunner stresses the literal,
biological meaning of the biblical story of the virgin
birth. Barth, on the other hand, affirms the virgin birth
as a sign of God's grace and power. Humans, through their
creative power, even through their reproductive power, are
unable to reach God. The virgin birth is a sign of the
limitations of human power, because it indicates that
Christ's coming into the world depends on God's initiative
and God's creativity. In defending the virgin birth in
this manner, Barth demonstrates that his primary concern
is with the theological meaning of the text, not with its
biological or literal dimension.[74] In his attempt to be
open to the biblical writers' intentions, Barth often
refuses to get bogged down with questions about the
literal meaning of the text.[75]
   A third similarity between Barth and the early
Alexandrians has to do with the weaknesses of these
theologies. Although Barth is not guilty of a Platonic
dualism in the same way as some of the early Alexandrians,
and although Barth is not docetic or monophysitic in the
same way some Alexandrians were, his theology can be
accurately criticized, we believe, for not giving
sufficient emphasis to the importance of creaturely
reality. As we have stated previously, Barth's emphasis
upon God's act ad intra undermines the value of God's act
ad extra and the creaturely realm which the act ad extra
requires.[76]

To conclude this section, although a persuasive case can be made for the view that Barth should not be classified as an Alexandrian theologian, we believe that it is more reasonable to recognize that his theology is Alexandrian according to the definition we have proposed. Barth's theology is unique and creative, and it is influenced by the situation in which Barth found himself, but it is also distinctively Alexandrian.

CONCLUSION

In this book we have argued that Barth's christology is Alexandrian rather than Antiochian. To show that there is a need for investigating the issue, we have demonstrated that reputable scholars disagree over it, and we have specified considerable evidence which can be given for each hypothesis. To provide a basis for determining which view is correct, we have proposed criteria for recognizing Alexandrian and Antiochian ways of thinking, and we have shown that these characterizations can be given historical support. Further, we have focused upon three issues which have been crucial in past debates between these two ways of doing theology and which are also involved in current debates over Barth's theology; they are the deity of Christ, the unity of the person of Christ, and the use of the name "Jesus Christ" and its variants.

According to an Antiochian interpretation, Barth understands the man Jesus as a complete, human person who is distinct from God. Jesus is said to be divine because he participates in God's revelatory event as the medium through which God speaks. Because of his unique relation to God, the characteristics of God can be ascribed to him, although they actually belong only to God. In the Antiochian view, although the man Jesus does not exist before the incarnation, in that event he comes into existence as a creature distinct from God but united with him in a personal unity. This unity is personal in the sense that it involves two persons, Jesus of Nazareth and the Son of God. Similarly, according to an Antiochian perspective, Barth normally uses such terms as "Jesus" and "Son of Man" to denote the human person and such terms as "Son of God" and "Word of God" to denote the divine person.

The evidence for the Antiochian interpretation of Barth revolves around those factors in his thought which seem to emphasize the independence of the man Jesus and his human nature from God. Chief among these are Barth's characterization of the human nature as possessing its own will, personality, and self-consciousness; his inclusion of the man Jesus and his human nature among the forms of revelation which are creaturely and not God; his emphasis upon the concepts of fellowship and confrontation in his treatment of the doctrine of the union of the two natures; and his apparent use of "Jesus" and its variants to denote a person who is distinct from God.

According to an Alexandrian interpretation, Barth maintains that Jesus Christ is essentially divine as the Father and the Holy Spirit are divine. As the second "person" of the trinity, Jesus Christ is God's act of speaking and also the Word which God speaks to himself and to mankind. Jesus Christ elects to become man and reconcile men to himself, and in the incarnation he assumes the human nature of all men. While this human nature has a degree of independence and is related to God in obedience and fellowship, it is not an individual person in itself. Further, in the Alexandrian interpretation, "Jesus Christ" and its variants refer to one person not two, although they connote various aspects of his being and action.

The evidence for the Alexandrian interpretation of Barth revolves around the factors in his thought which emphasize the oneness of Jesus Christ with God. The most important of these are Barth's identification of Jesus Christ's act and being with the act and being of God, his development of the concept of the trinity from the event of revelation, his account of the two moments in the deity of Christ, his denial that the human nature has an independent existence, his claim that the bearer of Christ's human nature is God, and his use of "man Jesus" and similar terms to denote one who is by nature divine.

The Antiochian interpretation of Barth can scarcely incorporate Barth's claim that the man Jesus is by nature divine without resorting to the assumption that Barth uses "Jesus" and similar terms equivocally, to denote both God and a man. This conclusion strains credulity, however, for it suggests that Barth attempts to avoid making a choice between two alternatives by resorting to obscurities.

On the other hand, the Alexandrian interpretation of Barth can assimilate both the claim of Christ's essential deity and also the basic elements of the Antiochian view. The Alexandrian interpretation can admit, for example, that Jesus Christ is completely a human person, that he has limited resources, that he responds to God in obedience, and that he is the form through which God reveals himself. However, the Alexandrian view stresses that although Jesus Christ is all these things as man, he does not abandon his original and eternal divinity. While as man he is other than God, as God he is by nature divine. In Barth's christology, the Antiochian elements are found within a perspective that is basically Alexandrian. For Barth, Jesus is God himself, and therefore "Jesus" is God's name.

Notes

NOTES TO CHAPTER ONE

[1] See the section entitled "The Alexandrian and Antiochian Traditions" in the second chapter, pp. 20-29.

[2] We use the terms "divinity" and "deity" interchangeably. Barth uses a variety of terms for this concept: Gottheit, Goettlichkeit, Gottsein, goettliches Wesen, goettliche Natur. In this note and throughout the book, the umlauts have been transliterated.

[3] For an example of an important work in each of the eight areas mentioned above, see the following: Daniel Leo Migliore, "The Problem of the Historical Jesus in Karl Barth's Theology" (Ph.D. dissertation, Princeton University, 1964); Thomas W. Ogletree, Christian Faith and History: A Critical Comparison of Ernst Troeltsch and Karl Barth (New York: Abingdon, 1965); George Harry Kehm, "The Christological Foundation of Anthropology in the Thought of Karl Barth" (Th.D. dissertation, Harvard University, 1966); Hans Urs von Balthasar, The Theology of Karl Barth, trans. John Drury (New York: Holt, Rinehart and Winston, 1971); Hans Wilhelm Frei, "The Doctrine of Revelation in the Thought of Karl Barth 1909-1922" (Ph.D. dissertation, Yale University, 1956); Hans Kueng, Justification: The Doctrine of Karl Barth and a Catholic Reflection, trans. Thomas Collins, Edmund E. Tolk, and David Granskou (New York: Thomas Nelson, 1964); Donald G. Bloesch, Jesus is Victor! Karl Barth's Doctrine of Salvation (Nashville: Abingdon, 1976); and Joseph E. Hathaway, "The Structure of the Grace of God in the Church Dogmatics of Karl Barth" (Th.D. dissertation, Harvard University, 1969).

[4] For example, see Warren Frederick Groff, "The Unity

of the Person of Christ in Contemporary Theology" (Ph.D. dissertation, Yale University, 1954); and William Richard Barr, "The Enactment of the Person of Christ: The Relation of Conceptions of Christ's Person and Work in Some Twentieth Century Christological Discussions" (Ph.D. dissertation, Yale University, 1969).

[5] Walter Guenther, Die Christologie Karl Barths (Mainz: Gutenberg Universitaet, 1954), p. 27, believes that Barth's acceptance of the concepts of enhypostasis and anhypostasis places him in the Cyrillian-Alexandrian tradition and accentuates his dependence upon Luther rather than Calvin. Herbert Hartwell, The Theology of Karl Barth: An Introduction (Philadelphia: Westminster, 1964), pp. 185-86, states that Barth denies that the human nature of the Logos is a person. Wolfhart Pannenberg, Jesus--God and Man, 2d ed., trans. Lewis L. Wilkins and Duane A. Priebe (Philadelphia: Westminster, 1977), p. 33, says that Barth is the foremost representative of Alexandrian thinking in modern Protestantism. Pannenberg bases this conclusion on the claim that Barth's christology begins "from above" rather than "from below." John Thompson, Christ in Perspective: Christological Perspectives in the Theology of Karl Barth (Grand Rapids: Eerdmans, 1978), pp. 16-18, accepts Pannenberg's contention that Barth's christology begins "from above," although he adds that in Barth's christology there is also a "movement from man to God" which is "wholly determined by God's movement to and for man and is in fact identical with it." According to Thompson, Barth's christology is thoroughly Chalcedonian. For a view similar to Thompson's, see Berthold Klappert, Die Auferweckung des Gekreuzigten; Der Ansatz der Christologie Karl Barths im Zusammenhang der Christologie der Gegenwart (Neukirchen, 1971), pp. 3-5. Hathaway, pp. 115-16, argues that Barth's position is Cyrillian because it emphasizes that Jesus Christ is man rather than a man. Similarly, Friedrich-Wilhelm Marquardt, Theologie und Sozialismus; Das Beispel Karl Barths (Munich, 1972), pp. 265-75, concludes that in the incarnation the Son of God became the species man. For a criticism of Marquardt, see Thompson, pp. 28, 148-49.

[6] Henri Bouillard, Karl Barth: Parole de Dieu et Existence Humaine, 2 vols. (Aubier: Editions Montaigne,

1957), 1:122. Here Bouillard concludes that Barth is
Nestorian because of the way he emphasizes the separation
of the two natures. Regin Prenter, in "Karl Barths
Umbildung der traditionellen Zweinaturlehre in lutherisch-
er Beleuchtung," Studia Theologica 11, Fasc. 1 (1957):
1-88, presents what is perhaps the most comprehensive
defense available of the claim that Barth is Nestorian.
Although Prenter does not explain thoroughly what he means
by Nestorianism, it is clear that he thinks that Barth
understands Jesus in the way that we have defined as
Antiochian. According to Prenter, Barth thinks of Jesus
as a human person, distinct from God. This is seen,
Prenter thinks, in the way Barth depicts the concept of
the unity of the two natures as the historical development
of the covenant between God and man. The relation of the
two natures appears to be, first of all, a relation
between two persons, Jesus and God. Then it is, secondarily, a relation between God and all other men as well. In
this union, God and Jesus confront one another and have
fellowship with one another. They are two partners in the
covenant. The distinction between Jesus and God is also
seen, Prenter argues, in the way Barth assigns the priestly function and humiliation to the divine nature, and the
kingly function and exaltation to the human nature. It is
God who reconciles, and man who is reconciled. See
especially pp. 10-30.

Fred H. Klooster, The Significance of Barth's Theology:
An Appraisal, with Special Reference to Election and
Reconciliation (Grand Rapids: Baker, 1961), pp. 94-95,
argues in a way that is similar to Prenter. Since Barth
obliterates the distinction between the person and the
work of Christ, and since he assigns humiliation to God
and exaltation to man, it is impossible for him, in
Klooster's view, to maintain a viable doctrine of the
unity of the person of Christ. Consequently, Barth is
guilty of a radical Nestorianism.

Barr also follows Prenter's arguments. He states that
the hypostatic union seems to be interpreted by Barth as a
union of the "thou" of God with the "thou" of the man
Jesus. See especially p. 337.

Groff chooses Barth as a representative of Antiochian
theology in contrast to representatives of Alexandrian
thinking. He argues that since Barth assigns a will and a

personality to the human nature which God assumed in the incarnation, this human nature must be understood as an individual person in his own right. Although Jesus is a complete person, he only becomes so in his unity with God. Therefore, it is not proper, Groff argues, to criticize Barth as Nestorian, as though the two persons, Jesus and God, were related only in an external manner, by association. Since Jesus and God are related as "I" and "Thou," the love between them has ontological depth. See especially pp. 172, 209, 235-43.

Daniel Lee Deegan, "The Doctrine of the Person of Christ in the Theology of Karl Barth" (Ph.D. dissertation, Yale University, 1958), also thinks that Barth falls principally in the Antiochian school. Like Groff, he emphasizes that the human nature of the Logos has its own will. He adds that the human nature has its own proper activity in relation to God, and therefore it is an acting person. See especially pp. 75-81.

[7] Hartwell, p. 185, states that Barth wants to stress the identity of the Son of God with Jesus Christ but that "the language used by him to that end is, theologically, open to question."

[8] More attention will be given to this topic in the fifth chapter in the section entitled "The Importance of Barth's Alexandrian Christology." See below, pp. 166-69.

[9] John McIntyre, The Shape of Christology (Philadelphia: Westminster, 1966), p. 154.

[10] Ibid. In this formula, B represents God and C represents the recipients of revelation.

[11] Ibid., p. 169.

[12] Ibid., pp. 153-55. McIntyre draws upon A.A.M. Fairweather, The Word as Truth (Lutterworth, 1939), p. 7, to support his claim that the medium of revelation must be different from the revealer.

[13] Ibid., p. 150. The significance of the man Jesus as the revealer of God is best expressed in McIntyre's model number two, A(x) reveals B(A) to C(H.S.). This model can be translated as follows: the man Jesus (A), pointing beyond himself (x), reveals God (B) as he is present in Jesus (A) to man (C), through the aid of the Holy Spirit.

[14] Karl Barth, Church Dogmatics, ed. G.W. Bromiley and T.F. Torrance, vol. 1: The Doctrine of the Word of

God, part 1, trans. G.T. Thomson, part 2, trans. G.T.
Thompson and Harold Knight; vol. 2: The Doctrine of God,
part 1, trans. T.H.L. Parker and others, part 2, trans.
G.W. Bromiley and others; vol. 3: The Doctrine of Creation, part 1, trans. J.W. Edwards, O. Bussey, and Harold
Knight, part 2, trans. Harold Knight and others, part 3,
trans. G.W. Bromiley and R.J. Ehrlich, part 4, trans.
A.T. Mackay and others; vol. 4: The Doctrine of Reconciliation parts 1-4, trans. G.W. Bromiley; 4 vols. (Edinburgh: T. & T. Clark, 1936-69). In the following pages,
references to this work will use the letters CD accompanied by the number of the volume and part. The corresponding page(s) in the original Kirchliche Dogmatik will
be stated in parentheses. For example, a reference to the
first page of the work will be designated CD 1/1, p. 1
(KD, p. 1).
    [15] McIntyre, p. 157. McIntyre thinks that Barth's
statements about revelation in CD 1/1 are misleading and
dangerous. There Barth speaks of the medium of revelation
as "God as He is in Jesus Christ." This implies that God
is both the medium and the subject of revelation, a notion
which McIntyre finds nonsensical. It also leads to a
neglect of the fact that revelation is based "upon a
historical person, Jesus of Nazareth." Nevertheless,
these statements by Barth about revelation, although
dangerous, are not exactly false, for they presuppose the
revelatory function of the man Jesus. McIntryre thinks
that Barth's position in CD 4/2 is clearer and less
confusing.
    [16] Ibid., p. 160. "Within the framework of very
strong assertions that no dualistic thinking must be
allowed to divide the human from the divine, Barth says
quite clearly that 'the divine essence (nature) expresses
and reveals itself wholly in the sphere of the human
nature.' Also, 'the saving act of God takes place in the
man Jesus of Nazareth. The power and authority of God are
revealed by him and to him, in his words and in his
actions.' These quotations are definitely not against the
run of play. Three times on earlier pages Barth has
spoken about the human essence of Jesus Christ being the
organ of the nature or work of the Son as the Mediator."
There is an omission in McIntyre's note pertaining to the
first quotation from Barth above; no page number is

indicated. The note states only "Church Dogmatics (ET),
IV/2, 1958. Cf. II/1, pp. 16f." The second quotation from
Barth is documented by McIntyre as follows: "Op. cit., p.
99." The note referring to Barth's speaking of the human
nature as the organ of the Son states "Namely, pp. 96ff."

[17] See the previous note, where McIntyre's speaks of
God acting in Jesus and of the divine nature revealing
itself in the human nature. Later we shall show that
Antiochian theologians tend to personify the human nature
which is united with God in the incarnation.

[18] CD 4/2, p. 100 (KD, p. 111), for example.

[19] McIntyre, p. 160.

[20] Ibid.

[21] McIntyre defines Nestorianism rather narrowly. In
our view, if McIntyre's interpretation of Barth were
correct, Barth would be Antiochian.

[22] Ibid., pp. 166-67.

[23] For a more detailed discussion of McIntyre's
critique of Barth and also his alternative suggestion that
the concept of the divinity of Jesus Christ should be
based upon redemption rather than revelation, see my
article "Revelation, Redemption, and the Divinity of Jesus
Christ," Scottish Journal of Theology 31 (1978): 501-15.

[24] Claude Welch, In This Name: The Doctrine of the
Trinity in Contemporary Theology (New York: Charles
Scribner's Sons, 1952), pp. 163-64.

[25] Ibid., pp. 169-70.

[26] Ibid., p. 174.

[27] Ibid., p. 175. Welch quotes from CD 1/1, pp.
469-70 (KD, p. 431).

[28] Ibid., pp. 182, 187, 191.

[29] Several other features of Welch's thought indicate
that he thinks of Jesus Christ primarily as the incarnate
Lord and not merely as the human person who is the medium
of revelation. For example, the fact that the oneness of
God is conceived as the oneness of a personal agent means
that the Son who acts to reveal himself is the one agent
God, not merely the human nature. Again, Welch speaks of
Jesus Christ as the object of faith and the content of
revelation, terms which he can apply just as readily to
God. (For Jesus Christ as the object of faith and the
content of revelation, see pp. 176, 223-24. For God as
the same, see pp. 169, 178.) Welch also indicates that

Jesus Christ is the second in God from eternity, and as such he is the "possibility" of revelation. See p. 183.

[30] Welch, p. 222. Here Welch seems to use these names to denote the human person as well as the divine agent. He says that the trinity affirms three different "him's," the "him who stands above and apart as the one to whom Jesus points . . . ; him who confronts man in Jesus Christ . . . ; and him who seizes and possesses man." In the second phrase, the "him" seems to denote the divine agent, while "Jesus Christ" appears to refer to the creaturely medium of revelation. See also p. 184 where Jesus Christ is explicitly called the form of revelation in which God acts.

[31] To support our contention that Barth's language is not always crystal clear it can be mentioned that many commentators have expressed exasperation over the difficulty of comprehending Barth's statements. Adolph von Harnack, for example, in his famous exchange of letters with Barth, states that Barth's answer to his first question regarding revelation is "totally obscure" and "wholly incomprehensible to me," in spite of "much hard effort" trying to understand it. See H. Martin Rumscheidt, Revelation and Theology: An Analysis of the Barth-Harnack Correspondence of 1923 (Cambridge: Cambridge University, 1972), pp. 35-36. Another example is provided by the contemporary American theologian, John B. Cobb, Jr., Living Options in Protestant Theology (Philadelphia: Westminster, 1962), p. 192. In reference to Barth, Cobb states that there are "inconsistencies, ambiguities, and simply meaningless sentences scattered throughout the thousands of pages of his Dogmatics."

There are several factors which contribute to the ambiguity of Barth's language. One of the most important of these, in our view, is Barth's failure to explain clearly how he uses "Jesus" and its variants. Consequently, our clarification of this facet of Barth's language will alleviate some of the difficulty involved in understanding Barth. However, our study will not deal directly with the other factors which contribute to the obscurity of Barth's writings, so we shall note some of them here. One cause of confusion is Barth's style. He writes in long sentences filled with dependent clauses and pronouns. It is often difficult to determine the

antecedent of the "it" or the "that." Another factor is
Barth's dialectical thinking, one feature of which is the
use of paradoxical and even apparently contradictory
statements to point to the truth which, in Barth's view,
lies beyond human powers of comprehension or description.
On this point, see Balthasar, especially pp. 68-73. Still
another factor, which is directly related to Barth's
dialectical thinking, is Barth's use of the language of
German idealism. For confirmation of this usage, see Hans
W. Frei, "Revelation and Theological Method in the
Theology of Karl Barth," in Faith and Ethics: The
Theology of H. Richard Niebuhr, ed. Paul Ramsey (New York:
Harper, 1957), p. 40 The dialectical and idealistic
elements in Barth's thought and language make his theology
especially difficult for those who approach him with
Thomistic or Aristotelian presuppositions. A final factor
which we believe should be mentioned is the sheer
originality of Barth's ideas. One of the reasons Harnack
did not understand Barth, we believe, is that Barth's
framework, starting point, terminology, and conclusions
were so different from his own.

[32] See, for example, CD 1/1, p. 443 (KD, p. 406),
where Barth defines Jesus' divinity as his capacity to
reveal and represent the Father.

[33] Welch is also aware that Barth defines the divinity of Jesus as his capacity to reveal the Father. How
this concept of divinity is related to a concept of
divinity as essence is unclear.

[34] Paul Lehmann, "Changing Course of a Corrective
Theology," Theology Today 13 (October 1956):332.

NOTES TO CHAPTER TWO

[1] Several reputable scholars argue that Antiochian
theologians did not conceive of the reality related to God
in the incarnation as a complete human person, but as a
human nature which was less than a person. These interpreters tend to think of the differences between the two
schools of thinkers as being primarily matters of terminology and emphasis. For example, J.N.D. Kelly, Early
Christian Doctrines, 2d ed. (New York: Harper, 1958), p.
317, states that Nestorius did not conceive of the human

nature as a distinct person. R.V. Sellers in his two
works, Two Ancient Christologies (London: SPCK, 1940) and
The Council of Chalcedon (London: SPCK, 1953) stresses
that these two theologies are in agreement on the basic
questions. For a survey of the scholarship, see Richard
A. Norris, Jr., Manhood and Christ; A Study in the Christology of Theodore of Mopsuestia (Oxford: Clarendon,
1963), pp. 246-61.

[2] W. Norman Pittenger, The Word Incarnate (New York:
Harper, 1959), pp. 12-13. Pittenger makes it clear that
he prefers the Antiochian view.

[3] For example, Aloys Grillmeier, Christ in Christian
Tradition from the Apostolic Age to Chalcedon (451)
(London: A.R. Mowbray, 1965) and Kelly use the terms
"Word-flesh" and "Word-man" to indicate the Alexandrian
and Antiochian theologies respectively. Kelly points out,
however, that they must be used with care because they can
be misleading (p. 281). The term "Word-flesh" is more
appropriate, he thinks, for the thought of Origen and
Apollinarius than it is for Cyril. This is the case
because Origen and Apollinarius held that what was united
to the Word was flesh, not a complete human nature.
Apollinarius, as is well known, argued that the flesh had
no human soul or mind, while Cyril thought that the human
nature involved in the incarnation had its own soul and
mind (Kelly, pp. 289-95, 317). Since Cyril and his modern
defenders (for example, see Herbert Maurice Relton, A
Study in Christology: The Problem of the Relation of the
Two Natures in the Person of Christ, with a Preface by
Arthur C. Headlam [New York: Macmillan, 1934]) conceive
the human nature as complete, perhaps the terms "Word-
nature" or "Person-nature" are more appropriate for the
Alexandrian position than "Word-flesh." "Person-nature"
is used by Karl Rahner, Theological Investigations, trans.
with an Introduction by Cornelius Ernst, 6 vols.
(Baltimore: Helicon, 1961-67), 1:149-200. In this formula, "Person" designates the divine person, the Word.
Throughout his discussion, Rahner makes it clear that he
thinks that the Chalcedonian solution affirmed a relation
between the divine Word and a human nature. He understands this human nature to be something other than an
individual person.

[4] For brief summaries of Alexandrian christology,

particularly as it is elaborated by Cyril of Alexandria, see Kelly, pp. 317-43, and Grillmeier, pp. 400-417. For a more thorough study of Cyril, and a comprehensive bibliography, see Robert L. Wilken, Judaism and the Early Christian Mind (New Haven: Yale University, 1971), pp. 201-21.

[5] For brief summaries of the Antiochian christology, see Kelly, pp. 301-17, and Grillmeier, pp. 338-88. In our interpretation of the basic characteristics of Antiochian thought we have relied heavily on the work of Norris and Pittenger. Both of these sympathetic commentators upon Antiochian theology argue that it is characterized by an emphasis upon the separate individuality of Jesus the man in his unity with God the Word. Norris, in Manhood and Christ, p. 196, says that Theodore understands the two natures as two agents in a single work. See also pp. 199-201.

[6] Pannenberg, pp. 286-87, states that christologies which affirm that the two realities united in the one Jesus Christ are complete in themselves encounter insoluble difficulties. Two whole beings cannot come together to form a complete whole. As a result christologies "have either combined the two natures to form a third or split the two natures and oriented the concrete picture exclusively to one or the other."

[7] For example, in his famous third letter to Nestorius, Cyril stated that "All the terms used in the Gospels are to be referred to one Person, the one incarnate hypostasis of the Word." This proposition is recorded in Edward Rochie Hardy and Cyril C. Richardson, eds., Christology of the Later Fathers, Library of Christian Classics, vol. 3 (Philadelphia: Westminster, 1954), p. 352. The editors also comment that Cyril was just as willing to speak of one nature after the union. He used the phrase "one nature of the Incarnate Word." This wording originated with Apollinarius and was later emphasized by Eutyches. It became a monophysite slogan. (See Hardy and Richardson, p. 352, and Kelly, pp. 319, 330-34.)

The commitment to the claim of one nature or one hypostasis is present in Cyril's fifth anathema. He said: "If anyone dares to say that Christ was a God-bearing man, and not rather God in truth, being by nature one Son, inasmuch as the Word became flesh, and is made partaker of blood and flesh precisely like us, let him be anathema." Nestorius took up the challenge on this point, producing his counter anathema. "If anyone dares to say that after the taking of manhood, the Son of God is one by nature, when he is also Emmanuel, let him be anathema." For this interchange between Nestorius and Cyril, see Hardy and Richardson, p. 353.

[8] Francis Aloyisus Sullivan, The Christology of Theodore of Mopsuestia, Analecta Gregoriana, vol. 82 (Rome: Pontificia Universitas Gregoriana, 1956), p. 263. Another implication of the term prosopon, when it was used by the Antiochians in reference to the unity of the two natures, had to do with the external form or appearance of a thing. Thus, since God is invisible, the prosopon of the God-man would appear as that of a man, although God was present in a unique way. See Kelly, p. 313. Prosopon could also be used by the Antiochians in much the same sense as hypostasis, to indicate an existing being. For example, an individual human person could be properly designated as an hypostasis and also as a prosopon. Using the term in this way, Antiochians such as Theodore and Nestorius said that the human nature united to the divinity had its own hypostasis and its own prosopon. In the same way, it was proper to speak of the divine nature as an hypostasis and a prosopon. Thus, the unity of the two natures was a unity of two hypostases and two prosopa.

[9] Norris, Manhood and Christ, pp. 212-13.

[10] Kelly, p. 314.

[11] Ibid., pp. 314, 320-21.

[12] Wilken, pp. 216-17. "To Cyril's way of thinking, the chief difficulty with Nestorius' view of Christ was that it could not account for the uniqueness of Christ. Nestorius could not show why this one man overcame death when others did not. If Christ were an ordinary man linked to God, he would hardly be unique. He would have been like other great men--Abraham, Moses, the prophets-- who were incapable of meeting the challenge of death. The typology of the second Adam establishes that Christ is the unique and extraordinary man, because he has come from heaven. He is God's Son. In the controversy with Nestorius Cyril returns to this point over and over again. Nestorius' Christology does not explain the redemption of

mankind, nor does it take into account the biblical data concerning Christ."

[13] Norris, Manhood and Christ, p.221.

[14] Ibid., pp. 219-27. The following comment, from p. 222, is especially instructive: "First, then, Theodore simply asserts that in the case of Christ, the indwelling is a union of the Word and the Man. He does not allude to the idea of 'co-operation' as in any sense constitutive of this union. What is to the fore here is not any mutual or reciprocal action of God and the Man, but simply the action of the divine Son, who himself, by the disposition of his will, unites the human nature to himself. It is this fact which, as Theodore sees it, distinguishes the divine indwelling in Christ from other instances of his indwelling. The union is logically prior both to the prosopic unity which it effects, and to the sort of co-operation to which, as we have seen, Theodore alludes in other passages."

[15] Kelly, pp. 317-23, especially pp. 319-21.

[16] Not all Antiochian theologians accepted Theodore's view of the two types of predication. Some of them held that the only proper predication is based upon the nature of the subject involved. Thus, only that which belongs to the Word "by nature" can be attributed to him, and only that which belongs to the man Jesus "by nature" can be attributed to him. Wilken, pp. 205-9, discusses this position. His comments about Eustathius are particularly instructive, p. 206. "Take the case of Eustathius of Antioch. He . . . did not think it was possible to distinguish two types of predication. What is predicated of the Logos is predicated kata physin. If this were so, then predicates such as passibility, hunger, thirst, etc. would limit the deity and make him something less than God. The Arians would be correct: the son is not God. Eustathius answered that the 'Word' is not the subject of the human actions or suffering of Christ. Passages in the Scriptures which speak of Jesus' suffering must not be attributed to the Logos, either by nature or according to the flesh; they must be ascribed to the man Jesus. It is Jesus who advances in wisdom, who hungers and thirsts, and who suffers."

[17] Norris, Manhood and Christ, p. 232.

[18] Ibid., p. 216. Norris explains how Theodore

justifies applying the predicates of divinity to Jesus and the predicates of humanity to the Logos. He states that Theodore "denies not that the Word can be called the Son of Mary, or that he may be said to have suffered, but that these properties can be predicated of him by nature. They are his only in a derivative sense--only by reason of his relation to the Man of whom they are predicated directly. Just as, because of the union, the Man shares in the honour of the divine form, so, for the same reason, what belongs to the humanity may be attributed to the Word 'by relation.' The Word associates Himself with the assumed Man: and therefore what happens to the man has reference also to the Word who indwells him. But it does not 'happen to' the Word. He is in no sense the natural subject of these properties, any more than the Man is naturally possessed of divine Sonship."

[19] Ibid., p. 215. I have transliterated the two Greek words.

[20] Pittenger, p. 181. See also pp. 32, 87, 194, 221.

[21] Ibid., pp. 91, 187. In the first of these references Pittenger reports that Nestorius thought "Jesus" should be used to denote the man, "Lord" the uncreated Word, and "Christ" the union of the two, the incarnate savior. In the second, Pittenger states that he prefers to use "Son" to denote the man Jesus rather than the agent God. "If we should speak of Jesus as the 'Son,' meaning the humanity of our Lord; of the divinity which was his, or in him, as the Word or Logos or Self-Expressive Activity of God; and of the unity of these in the one total life as Jesus Christ or Emmanuel (as Nestorius himself would have wished)--if we do this, we shall (I think) have come to some manageable terminology, at any rate."

[22] Norris, Manhood and Christ, pp. 190, 198, speaks of Theodore's exegetical practice of "dividing the sayings" about Christ in scripture. Theodore says: "When . . . we hear the Scripture saying either that Jesus was honoured or glorified . . . let us not understand God the Word, but the assumed Man." See our earlier discussion of Eustathius, p. 212, n. 16.

[23] Hardy and Richardson, p. 353.

[24] William Telfer, ed., Cyril of Jerusalem and Nemesius of Emesa, The Library of Christian Classics, vol.

4 (Philadelphia: Westminster, 1960), p. 104. Cyril of Jerusalem states: "Christ was twofold. As to what was visible, he was man, as to what is invisible, he was God. As man, he ate genuinely as we do, for he had the same fleshly needs as we have, but as God he made five loaves feed five thousand men. As man he truly died, and as God, on the third day, he raised to life his body that was dead. As man he was really asleep in the boat, while, as God, he came walking upon the waters."

[25] Wilken, p. 184. See also pp. 189-90. Here Wilken reports that Cyril, in his commentary on Luke 5:12, stated, "Divinely the Son is said not to suffer, but humanly he is said to suffer."

[26] There is a sense in which God, and therefore divinity, participate in the creaturely realm. In fact, it is because of God's act ad extra and his participation in creaturely existence that creatures can be said to participate in divinity. Our term "participatory divinity," however, is intended to direct the reader's attention to the resulting participation of the creatures in God's divinity, not the originating participation of God in the creaturely realm.

[27] CD 1/1, p. 443 (KD, p. 406).

[28] Ibid., p. 442 (KD, p. 405). Barth's emphasis.

[29] CD 1/2, p. 501 (KD, p. 555). See also pp. 463, 685 (KD, pp. 512, 768), where Barth speaks of the "divinity of Holy Scripture."

[30] Ibid., p. 752 (KD, p. 841).

[31] Ibid., p. 513 (KD, p. 569). See also p. 530 (KD, pp. 588-89). Jesus of Nazareth is not divinized by his unique relation to God. CD 4/2, p. 153 (KD, p. 171). Nor does he exercise divine sovereignty. CD 4/2, p. 161 (KD, p. 180).

[32] CD 1/2, p. 21 (KD, pp. 23-24).

[33] Ibid., pp. 508-9 (KD, pp. 564-65).

[34] CD 4/2, pp. 91, 95 (KD, pp. 100, 105).

[35] Later in this chapter we shall discuss in more detail the basis for concluding that Barth names the human nature "Jesus" and thereby indicates that it is a complete human person. See pp. 81-85. We shall also discuss in more detail the personality, will, and self-consciousness of the human nature. See pp. 52-64.

[36] Norris, Manhood and Christ, p. 200. "In the

Interpreter's terminology, 'human nature' essentially means 'the assumed Man' (i.e. Jesus), just as 'divine nature' essentially means 'God' . . . . Such phrases signify not merely the totality of human or divine properties, but concrete human or divine subjects." "The Interpreter" refers to Theodore of Mopsuestia.

[37] Barth might also speak of human nature in a general sense, with regard to the nature of all men. But when he speaks of the human nature of the Logos, those who follow the Antiochian reading of Barth assume that he equates that human nature with the man Jesus

[38] CD 1/1, p. 151 (KD, p. 138). If it were not so, says Barth, the Word would not be real for us. For a clear statement that this "physical event" involves a creaturely form, we quote from p. 188 (KD, p. 171-72): "We do not possess the Word of God otherwise than in the mystery of its worldliness. . . . we always have it in a form which as such is n o t the Word of God and as such, moreover, does not betray that it is the f o r m precisely of the Word of God."

[39] Ibid., p. 60 (KD, p. 55).

[40] Ibid., p. 365 (KD, p. 335).

[41] Ibid., pp. 364-65 (KD, pp. 334-35).

[42] Ibid., pp. 365-66 (KD, pp. 335-36). Note especially these words: "Into the place--not of Yahweh on Sinai or in heaven, but certainly of the name Yahweh . . . --there now comes the existence of the man Jesus of Nazareth."

[43] Ibid., p. 188 (KD, p. 171).

[44] Ibid., p. 373 (KD, p. 343).

[45] Ibid., p. 369 (KD, p. 339).

[46] Ibid., p. 371 (KD, p. 341).

[47] Ibid., p. 448 (KD, p. 411). See also p. 457 (KD, p. 419).

[48] Ibid., p. 344 (KD, p. 315). See also p. 342 (KD, p. 314).

[49] Ibid., p. 344 (KD, pp. 315-16).

[50] Ibid., pp. 364-65 (KD, pp. 334-35). Barth's statements about God's relation to the angel of Yahweh and the name "Yahweh" will become clearer when our discussion of Barth's understanding of how God reveals himself through creaturely media is complete. However, we can add at this juncture that Barth's views can be supported by

scholarship in the history of religions, a fact which
Barth himself notes in the passage cited here. Some
historians of religion speak of the divine or holy manifesting itself through some creaturely form or medium.
When the holy manifests itself through some particular
form, that form becomes in some sense sacred or holy. For
example, see Mircea Eliade, The Sacred and the Profane,
trans. Willard R. Trask (New York: Harper & Row, 1959),
pp. 11-12. Eliade states that the sacred or the holy
manifests itself to people through ordinary objects, such
as stones or trees. Eliade terms such an act a hierophany, and he adds that each hierophany involves a paradox.
"By manifesting the sacred, any object becomes something
else, yet it continues to remain itself, for it continues
to participate in its surrounding cosmic milieu. A sacred
stone remains a stone; apparently (or, more precisely,
from the profane point of view), nothing distinguishes it
from all other stones. But for those to whom a stone
reveals itself as sacred, its immediate reality is
transmuted into a supernatural reality." Eliade also
notes that the supreme hierophany for Christians is the
incarnation of God in Jesus Christ.

Barth's statements about the relation of God to the
angel of Yahweh can also be clarified by noting that
Barth makes them to support his contention that revelatory
acts of God imply the doctrine of the trinity. In himself, his first mode of being, God is invisible to humans.
In his second mode of being, God is manifest to humans in
a form. Even the Old Testament, according to Barth,
implies the doctrine of the trinity because it indicates
that God manifests himself in various forms. In Barth's
view, the Old Testament does not mean simply that humans
make inferences about God's nature or his acts on the
basis of human experiences or historical events. Rather,
in Barth's view, the Old Testament teaches that God is
actually present in a specific medium before specific
individuals. In these media, which include the angel of
Yahweh, the name "Yahweh," and even such concepts as God's
wisdom or glory (CD 1/1, p. 363; KD, p. 334), Barth
states, "Yahweh Himself is there, subsists, has
objectivity for those to whom He is manifest" (CD 1/1, p.
364; KD, p. 334). For Barth, the statement that the angel
of Yahweh is identical with God means that Yahweh is

objectively present when his angel is present. The angel conveys the message or Word of God, and in that event the angel becomes a part of that message or Word. Since God's Word is identical with God himself, the angel becomes, in some sense, identical with God.

Barth's interpretation of God's relation to the angel of Yahweh and other creaturely forms can be supported by exegesis of relevant Old Testament passages. In Genesis 22:1-18, for example, the angel of Yahweh speaks God's words to Abraham. When the angel speaks, God is objectively present in his words. Similarly, Genesis 18:1-15 implies an identity between Yahweh and one or all of the three men who speak to Abraham. In verse 10 the speaker is identified as one of the men, in verse 13 the speaker is identified as Yahweh, yet the words of promise are the same. When the men are present before Abraham, Yahweh is also present before him.

[51] CD 1/1, pp. 98-140 (KD, pp. 89-128).

[52] Ibid., p. 349 (KD, p. 321). See also CD 1/2, pp. 368, 492, 500, 736, 743, 755 (KD, pp. 405, 545, 554, 826, 831, 844).

[53] CD 1/2, p. 499 (KD, pp. 553-54). Since in this passage Barth speaks of an indirect identity between "God and man" in Christ, perhaps we should add the following quote in which Barth speaks explicitly of an indirect identity between the humanity and divinity of Christ. "If the humanity of Jesus is the image of God, this means that it is only indirectly and not directly identical with God." CD 3/2, p. 219 (KD, p. 261). See also CD 2/1, p. 486 (KD, p. 547).

[54] CD 1/1, p. 124 (KD, p. 113).

[55] Ibid., p. 57 (KD, pp. 52-53).

[56] Ibid., p. 155 (KD, pp. 141-42). "'God's Son' in the language of the doctrine of the Trinity does not differ from 'God's Word.'" See also p. 493 (KD, p. 453), where Barth states that these terms point to one object.

[57] CD 1/2, p. 16 (KD, pp. 17-18).

[58] Prenter, "Zweinaturlehre," pp. 30-32, proposes an interpretation of Barth's identification of Jesus Christ with the Son or Word of God which is similar to the one presented above. He argues that the "is" in such statements as "Jesus Christ is the Son of God" should be understood analogously. Jesus Christ is God's Son,

Prenter explains, in the sense that he reflects and illustrates the Son. The "is" expresses conformity rather than identity. Since Prenter bases his conclusion upon Barth's doctrine of reconciliation in CD 4/2 and the interpretation presented above is based upon Barth's treatment of revelation in CD 1/1 and 1/2, one might conclude that Barth understands the "is" in a technical sense, to express something less than a complete, direct identity, throughout the Church Dogmatics.

[59] CD 1/2, p. 22 (KD, p. 24).

[60] CD 4/2, p. 67 (KD, p. 72).

[61] CD 1/2, p. 535 (KD, p. 595).

[62] See p. 34.

[63] CD 1/1, pp. 98-140 (KD, pp. 89-128). See especially p. 127 (KD, p. 116).

[64] CD 1/2, p. 513 (KD, p. 570).

[65] Ibid., pp. 506-7 (KD, p. 562).

[66] See Barth's doctrine of election, especially "The Election of Jesus Christ," CD 2/2, pp. 94-194 (KD, pp. 101-214). We shall discuss this topic later; see pp. 107-8.

[67] See pp. 49-69, 108-20.

[68] The identity of Christ with his history, act, and work will be discussed in more detail in the third chapter. See especially pp. 88-101.

[69] The concept of the logos asarkos means that the Logos exists apart from the flesh which he assumes. Conversely, logos ensarkos means that the Logos exists in the flesh.

[70] CD 3/2, p. 464 (KD, p. 557).

[71] In our consideration of the Antiochian interpretation of Barth's development of the logos asarkos and the preexistence of Jesus, we shall utilize the analysis of Kehm, pp. 237-39, 313-19.

[72] CD 3/1, p. 54 (KD, p. 58). "It has to be kept in mind that the whole conception of the logos asarkos, the 'second person' of the Trinity as such, is an abstraction. It is true that it has shown itself necessary to the christological and trinitarian reflections of the Church. Even today it is indispensable for dogmatic enquiry and presentation, and it is often touched upon in the New Testament, though nowhere expounded directly." I have transliterated the two Greek words in this quotation.

[73] CD 4/1, p. 52 (KD, p. 54). See also CD 1/2, p. 169 (KD, p. 185); CD 3/1, p. 54 (KD, pp. 57-58).

[74] CD 4/1, pp. 52-53 (KD, pp. 54-56).

[75] See for example, CD 4/2, pp. 32-33 (KD, pp. 34-35), where Barth uses the categories of God's "will" and his "resolve" to explain the presence of Jesus with God from all eternity. See also CD 3/1, p. 54 (KD, p. 58); CD 3/2, p. 477 (KD, pp. 572-73).

[76] Barth speaks of the eternal Son as the Word who will become incarnate, the verbum incarnandum. See CD 4/1, p. 66 (KD, p. 70); CD 4/2, p. 683 (KD, p. 773); CD 2/2, p. 108 (KD, p. 116).

[77] In his defense of an Antiochian view, Kehm attacks the claims of Gerhard Gloege, "Zur Praedestinationslehre Karl Barths, Fragmentarische Erwaegungen ueber den Ansatz ihrer Neuauffassung," Kerygma und Dogma 2 (1956):212 and "Zur Versoehungslehre Karl Barths (Kirchliche Dogmatik IV, 3)," Theologische Literaturzeitung 85 (1960):161-86; Robert W. Jenson, Alpha and Omega: A Study in the Theology of Karl Barth (New York: Thomas Nelson, 1963), pp. 66, 73; Regin Prenter, "Glauben und Erkennen bei Karl Barth; Bemerkungen eines lutherische Boso zum theologische Methode Karl Barths," Kerygma und Dogma 2 (1956):176-92; and Daniel L. Deegan, "The Christological Determinant in Barth's Doctrine of Creation," Scottish Journal of Theology 14 (June 1961):128. All these interpreters, Kehm reports, argue that Barth makes Jesus' preexistence so real that the significance of his existence in time is threatened. See Kehm, pp. 314-18.

[78] CD 1/2, p. 147 (KD, p. 161).

[79] Kehm, pp. 235-36. Kehm indicates that such a view of Jesus' time leads to docetism.

[80] CD 4/2, p. 33 (KD, p. 34). Ogletree, pp. 177-78, relies heavily on this point, using it to show that Barth means that Jesus is eternal only in the sense that he exists in God's eternal decision and foreknowledge. He points out that Barth, in the passage noted, implies that Jesus is before all time only in the sense that "this is what God sees and wills."

[81] CD 4/2, pp. 119-20 (KD, pp. 133-34).

[82] CD 3/2, pp. 475-78 (KD, pp. 570-74). See Kehm, pp. 237-39.

[83] This is the view of Kehm, pp. 240-47. He relies

on Barth's discussion in CD 3/2, pp. 448, 624 (KD, pp. 537, 759-60).

[84] The last two of these concepts, defended most conspicuously in their formative years by Leontius of Byzantium (485-543), have often been used to indicate that the human nature assumed in the incarnation was not itself a person. See H.R. Macintosh, The Doctrine of the Person of Christ, 2d ed. (Edinburgh: T. & T. Clark, 1913), pp. 217-18. Pittenger seems to assume that any theology which accepts these concepts is Alexandrian; for example, see p. 133.

[85] CD 4/2, p. 45 (KD, pp. 47-48).

[86] Ibid., p. 37 (KD, p. 39).

[87] Ibid., pp. 43-44 (KD, pp. 46-47).

[88] Deegan, "Person of Christ," pp. 81-82, in his argument that Barth is basically Antiochian, relies heavily upon the idea that Barth understands the union of the two natures established by the incarnation as based upon grace.

[89] Sellers, Two Ancient Christologies, pp. 182, 205-11. Sellers reports that Cyril emphasized the statement "The Word became flesh" as a polemic against the notion that there were two Sons. For him, this proposition indicated that the Son on earth was the same Son who had been in heaven previously. Cyril said that the Antiochians did not really accept this verse. "He who divides the natures posits two sons; he does not believe the Scripture which says 'the Word became flesh'" (p. 207).

Theodore thought that the verb "became" implied a transformation of the Logos, and therefore it led to the notion that the divine nature was passible and mutable. He appealed to Phil. 2:7 and used the verb "took up" or "assumed" (labon) to interpret the meaning of "became" in "the Word became flesh" (pp. 205, 211). He said, "The Word 'became' can be interpreted only as meaning 'according to appearance.' . . . In appearance the Logos became flesh, and by 'appearance' we mean, not that the Logos did not take real flesh, but that He did not 'become' flesh. For when the Scripture says He 'took', it means that He took not in appearance but in truth. But when it says He 'became', then it is speaking 'according to appearance'; for He was not transformed into flesh" (p. 182).

Cyril thought that use of "took" or "assumed" implied

that there was a mere association between the Logos and the man who was taken. Therefore, he opposed it (p. 211).

[90] G. Wingren, "Gott und Mensch bei Karl Barth," Studia Theologica 1 (1948):31-32, states that it is the central concept in Barth's theology.

[91] CD 1/2, p. 159 (KD, p. 174).

[92] Ibid., p. 160 (KD, p. 175).

[93] Ibid.

[94] Ibid. In support of this claim, Barth refers to Phil. 2:7, Heb.2:16, Tertullian, Origen, and Hippolytus. He also states that the standard term in medieval and early Protestant scholasticism is assumere or assumptio.

[95] Ibid., p. 161 (KD, p. 176). In his discussion of the incarnation in CD 4/2, Barth indicates that he still prefers to interpret the Word's becoming as an assuming. See pp. 45, 47-48 (KD, pp. 48, 50-51).

[96] Theodore characteristically spoke of the assumptus homo, the assumed man, rather than the assumed human nature. For example, see Kelly, p. 305, and Norris, Manhood and Christ, p. 200.

[97] CD 1/2, p. 149 (KD, p. 163).

[98] Ibid., p. 149 (KD, p. 164). "But precisely this concrete reality of a man, this man, is itself the work of the Word, not His presupposition. It is not (in the adoptionist sense) as if first of all there had been a man there, and then the Son of God had become that man."

[99] CD 4/2, p. 48 (KD, p. 51).

[100] CD 1/2, p. 149 (KD, p. 164). This is Barth's standard teaching on the issue, not an isolated observation. See CD 4/2, pp. 48-51, 54 (KD, pp. 51-55, 58).

[101] CD 1/2, p. 150 (KD, p. 164).

[102] CD 4/2, p. 49 (KD, p. 52).

[103] CD 1/2, p. 153 (KD, p. 167).

[104] Ibid., p. 158 (KD, p. 173).

[105] Austin Farrer, Finite and Infinite: A Philosophical Essay, 2d ed. (London: Dacre, 1959), p. 229.

[106] Groff, pp. 148, 170, 209, 215. Barth does not explicitly argue that a will must be a person, but what he says about the relation of God's personal being to his decision seems to be consistent with Groff's view. God is the only true person, Barth explains, because only he is determined solely by his decision to be who he is. Since this decision presupposes God's will, it is clear that

God's will is an essential, if not the essential, aspect of his being and act. See CD 2/1, p. 271 (KD, p. 304).

[107] CD 1/2, p. 163 (KD, p. 178). I have transliterated egeneto, anhypostatos, and enhypostatos from the Greek. See also CD 4/2, pp. 49-50 (KD, pp. 52-53) where Barth gives another complete statement of the meaning of these concepts.

Barth usually employs Natur, Wesen, or Sein for human nature or being, and he uses Dasein and Existenz to indicate what the human nature lacked when it was assumed by God and brought into existence. This is true of the passages above.

[108] CD 1/2, p. 164 (KD, p. 180).

[109] Ibid., p. 162 (KD, pp. 177-78).

[110] CD 1/1, p. 410 (KD, p. 377).

[111] Karl Barth, Karl Barth's Table Talk, recorded and ed. John Godsey (Richmond: John Knox, 1962), p. 49.

[112] CD 1/1, pp. 408-15 (KD, pp. 374-81).

[113] Pittenger, p. 112. "Today 'person' tends to mean, both in popular usage and in theological discussion, the psychological centre of subjective experience; it has a primary reference to the conscious subject of these experiences, a subject which is distinct from yet in close relationship with other subjects. The 'person' of man--and by implication the person of God--is the organizing centre of the totality of experiences; it is the 'self.' But the emphasis seems to be placed upon the awareness of the 'self' and its capacity through that knowledge to direct the activities of the total organism. That is to say, 'person' has come to signify whatever it is that establishes self-consciousness and direction." See also p. 114. John Knox, The Death of Christ (Nashville: Abingdon, 1958), p. 70, presents a similar view. He argues that in order to be a man, Jesus must have had a human consciousness.

[114] Kehm, pp. 117-18, indicates that Barth's development of the concepts of anhypostasis and enhypostasis allows the human nature to be a self with its own personal center and subjectivity.

[115] Pannenberg, pp. 341-42, puts Barth's contrast with traditional views in this way: "In this way the enhypostasis becomes for Barth the designation of the miraculous invasion of the divine Lordship into our world,

while quite the contrary to this the New-Chalcedonian Christology invented it as an explanation for the mode of coexistence of divinity and humanity in Christ."

[116] Pittenger, p. 91, using E.L. Mascall as an example, reports that Alexandrians often argue against Nestorianism as though it were merely adoptionism. Such an argument, he thinks, is irrelevant, because Nestorians too affirm the need for grace.

[117] CD 2/1, p. 284 (KD, p. 319).

[118] Ibid., p. 286 (KD, p. 321).

[119] CD 4/2, p. 74 (KD, p. 80) and CD 1/2, p. 150 (KD, p. 164).

[120] An Antiochian theologian might be willing to use anhypostasis and enhypostasis to describe the relation of other creatures to God. For example, the words of the Bible and the creaturely media of the sacraments could be understood to be related to God in such a way that these two concepts might be used to describe the relation. Nevertheless, one would probably want to add that God's presence in Jesus is more determinative or more intense than it is in other creaturely media. Some means would have to be found to maintain the uniqueness of Jesus' relation to God.

[121] Pannenberg, pp. 341-42.

[122] For a study of the elements of occasionalism in Barth's theology, see Jerome Hamer, Karl Barth, trans. Dominic M. Maruca (Westminster, Maryland: Newman, 1962).

[123] For more details on the implications of these concepts for an Antiochican theology, see Groff.

[124] CD 4/2, p. 50 (KD, pp. 53-54).

[125] CD 1/2, p. 151 (KD, p. 165).

[126] Ibid., p. 138 (KD, p. 152).

[127] Ibid., p. 147 (KD, p. 161).

[128] CD 4/2, p. 61 (KD, p. 65).

[129] Ibid., pp. 61-62 (KD, pp. 65-66).

[130] Ibid., p. 62 (KD, pp. 66-67). See especially the footnote concerning recta ratio.

[131] Ibid., p. 51 (KD, p. 54). See also CD 1/2, p. 147 (KD, p. 161).

[132] CD 1/2, p. 155 (KD, p. 170).

[133] Ibid., p. 156 (KD, p. 170). "Our unholy human existence, assumed and adopted by the Word of God, is a hallowed and therefore a sinless human existence."

[134] Ibid., p. 158 (KD, p. 173).

[135] CD 4/1, pp. 181-83 (KD, pp. 197-99). Here Barth discusses the controversy in the seventeenth century between the Giessen and Tuebingen theologians and the later issues over kenosis in the nineteenth century. Barth opposes the views of the so-called modern "kenotics" and also those of the Giessen thinkers. He approves the Tuebingen concept of an abstention by Jesus Christ "in the exinanitio only from the visible use, a retractatio and occultatio of the revelation of His power, or positively, a majesty of the Son of God which is, in fact, exercised and operative and actual, but concealed." p. 181 (KD, p. 198).

[136] CD 4/2, p. 51 (KD, p. 54).

[137] Ibid., p. 51 (KD, p. 55).

[138] Ibid., pp. 51-52 (KD, p. 55).

[139] Ibid., pp. 51-60 (KD, pp. 54-64).

[140] Ibid., p. 54 (KD, p. 58).

[141] Theodore often used the analogy of husband and wife, emphasizing the scriptural affirmation that they become one flesh. See Norris, Manhood and Christ, p. 229.

[142] CD 4/2, p. 53 (KD, p. 57).

[143] Ibid., pp. 54-55 (KD, pp. 58-59).

[144] Ibid., pp. 105-12 (KD, pp. 116-24). The quoted phrase is found on the first of these pages. For the claim that Jesus Christ includes all history, see CD 4/3, pp. 191, 214 (KD, pp. 218, 244). In the latter of these references, Barth states, "The history of Jesus Christ embraces that of the world and all men."

For an attempt to differentiate Barth's unusual inter- pretation of the union of the two natures from the tradi- tional understanding, see Jenson, Alpha, pp. 126-30.

[145] CD 4/2, pp. 62-63 (KD, p. 67).

[146] Ibid., pp. 69-70 (KD, pp. 74-75).

[147] Ibid., p. 74 (KD, p. 80). This impartation is a "relationship of real giving and receiving, God and man in the fellowship of this history."

[148] Ibid., p. 74 (KD, p. 80).

[149] Ibid., pp. 77-83 (KD, pp. 83-91). Here Barth attacks the Lutheran notion of the divinization of the human nature.

[150] Ibid., p. 86 (KD, p. 94). "The actuality of the incarnate Son of God, the union of the two natures in Him,

is the direct confrontation of the totality of the divine
with the human in the one Jesus Christ."
[151] Ibid., p. 84 (KD, p. 92).
[152] Ibid., p. 88 (KD, pp. 96-97). See also p. 70
(KD, p. 76).
[153] Ibid., p. 93 (KD, p. 102).
[154] Ibid., p. 93 (KD, p. 103).
[155] Ibid., p. 94 (KD, p. 103).
[156] Ibid., p. 96 (KD, p. 106).
[157] Ibid., p. 97 (KD, p. 107).
[158] Ibid., pp. 98-99 (KD, pp. 108-10).
[159] Ibid., pp. 99-101 (KD, pp. 109-12).
[160] Ibid., pp. 113-14 (KD, pp. 125-26).
[161] Ibid., p. 114 (KD, p. 127).
[162] Ibid., p. 116 (KD, p. 129).
[163] Ibid.
[164] Ibid., p. 70 (KD, p. 75).
[165] Ibid., p. 109 (KD, p. 121).
[166] See Prenter, "Zweinaturlehre," pp. 10-30, and
Barr, p. 337.
[167] CD 4/1, pp. 222-24 (KD, pp. 243-45).
[168] Ibid., pp. 231-73 (KD, pp. 254-301). See also CD
2/1, pp. 393-406 (KD, pp. 442-57).
[169] CD 4/1, pp. 273-83 (KD, pp. 301-11).
[170] CD 4/2, pp. 156-66 (KD, pp. 175-85).
[171] Ibid., pp. 166-92 (KD, pp. 185-213).
[172] Ibid., pp. 192-264 (KD, pp. 214-93).
[173] Ibid., p. 252 (KD, pp. 279-80); also p. 516 (KD,
p. 584).
[174] CD 4/1, pp. 129-30 (KD, pp. 141-42). See also
pp. 157-210 (KD, pp. 171-231).
[175] CD 4/2, pp. 6, 19-21, 28-30, 71 (KD, pp. 4-5,
19-21, 29-32, 77).
[176] CD 4/3, p. 15 (KD, p. 14).
[177] For a more thorough defense of this interpretation, see Prenter, "Zweinaturlehre," especially pp. 1-10,
43-64; Barr, pp. 39-41, 337-41; and Klooster, pp. 94-95.
[178] The position we have sketched here is quite
similar to that of John Knox, Jesus, Lord and Christ: A
Trilogy Comprising "The Man Christ Jesus," "Christ the
Lord," "On the Meaning of Christ" (New York: Harper &
Row, 1958), pp. 225-35. Here Knox considers "The Event
and the Person." It seems apparent that Knox's view is

Antiochian, according to the definition we have proposed.

[179] Prenter, "Zweinaturlehre," pp. 10-30, argues that Barth understands the two natures as two persons, and that "Son of God" names the divine person, while "Son of Man" denotes the human person. Similarly, Kehm, pp. 251, 319, gives explanations of "Jesus" and "Jesus Christ" which seem Antiochian. He says, "'Jesus' denotes a particular man who lived and died in a particular, limited span of creaturely time." He adds, "To sum up, the name 'Jesus Christ,' as Barth uses it, designates the earthly-historical Jesus, not a 'state of affairs' in God."

[180] Barth sometimes uses "Holy Scripture" and "proclamation" to denote not simply the creaturely media but the event in which God speaks through them. See CD 1/1, p. 104 (KD, p. 95).

[181] CD 1/1, p. 371 (KD, p. 341). This is not at all an isolated case, but Barth's usual manner of speaking. See pp. 448, 457 (KD, pp. 411, 419).

[182] Ibid., p. 205 (KD, p. 187). This point is related both to Barth's emphasis upon the limitations of human knowledge and also Barth's understanding of the relation between philosophy and theology. We shall discuss this issue in more detail in the last chapter when we consider the question of whether Barth's entire theology, as well as his christology, should be considered Alexandrian. See below, especially pp. 183-86.

[183] Ibid., p. 206 (KD, p. 188). We have noted earlier that the "is" in such statements is interpreted as an "is" of becoming. Now we wish to point out that the two titles or names involved here are understood as denoting two separate, distinct persons.

[184] CD 4/2, p. 21 (KD, p. 21).

[185] CD 1/2, p. 37 (KD, p. 41). See also pp. 161-62 (KD, pp. 176-78).

[186] CD 4/1, p. 172 (KD, p. 187). See also p. 175 (KD, p. 191); CD 3/2, p. 483 (KD, p. 581); CD 2/2, p. 8 (KD, p. 7).

NOTES TO CHAPTER THREE

[1] CD 4/2, p. 107 (KD, p. 118). In this discussion of Jesus Christ as the act of God, Barth speaks of Jesus

Christ as the event (<u>Ereignis</u>) of revelation, the act
(<u>Tun</u>, <u>Tat</u>, <u>Akt</u>) in which God reveals himself, and the
history (<u>Geschichte</u>) in which God deals with man. See pp.
105-9 (KD, pp. 116-21). See also CD 1/2, pp. 167-88 (KD,
pp. 183-84); CD 4/1, p. 35 (KD, p 35); CD 4/3, pp. 7, 40
(KD, pp. 6, 42).
 [2] CD 1/1, p. 134 (KD, p. 122). For additional
statements of the identity of Jesus Christ with revelation, see pp. 131, 155 (KD, pp. 119, 141). Barth also
identifies Jesus Christ and revelation with the Word of
God. See pp. 131-33, 156, 163, 174 (KD, pp. 120-21, 142,
148, 159).
 [3] Further confirmation of this point will be found in
our discussion of the second moment in God's act, his
obedience as a man in Jesus Christ. At this juncture, see
CD 1/1, p. 361 (KD, p. 332) where Barth indicates that the
action of God in revelation is the divinity of Christ.
See also p. 465 (KD, p. 427) where Barth equates the
divinity of Christ with his revelation of God. For
example: "To confess him as the revelation of his Father,
is to confess him as being essentially equal in divinity
to this Father of his." For Barth's claim that our thinking must begin with the divinity of Christ, see p. 483
(KD, p. 443).
 [4] CD 1/1, p. 358 (KD, p. 329). "We come to the
doctrine of the Trinity by no other way than by that of an
analysis of the concept of revelation."
 [5] Ibid., pp. 339-40 (KD, pp. 311-12).
 [6] Ibid., pp. 458-60 (KD, pp. 420-22).
 [7] Ibid., p. 358 (KD, p. 329). See also pp. 436-40
(KD, pp. 400-404).
 [8] Ibid., pp. 442-43 (KD, pp. 405-6).
 [9] Ibid., pp. 362-69 (KD, pp. 332-39).
 [10] Ibid., pp. 417-18 (KD, pp. 383-84).
 [11] Ibid., p. 440 (KD, pp. 403-4).
 [12] Ibid., p. 474 (KD, p. 435).
 [13] Ibid., pp. 448-50 (KD, pp. 411-13).
 [14] Ibid., pp. 403, 412 (KD, pp. 370, 379).
 [15] Ibid., pp. 400-403 (KD, 367-70).
 [16] Ibid., p. 403 (KD, p. 370). See also p. 502 (KD,
p. 461).
 [17] Ibid., pp. 457-60 (KD, pp. 419-22).
 [18] CD 4/2, p. 61 (KD, p. 65).

[19] CD 1/1, p. 443 (KD, p. 406).
[20] Ibid., pp. 474-512 (KD, pp. 435-70). Barth's long discussion of "The Eternal Son" is a defense of the claim that Jesus Christ is the eternal act of God.
[21] Ibid., p. 474 (KD, p. 435).
[22] For support of this notion of the function of the trinity see Robert W. Jenson, God after God: The God of the Past and the God of the Future, Seen in the Work of Karl Barth (Indianapolis: Bobbs-Merrill, 1969), pp. 97-98.
[23] CD 2/1, p. 263 (KD, p. 294).
[24] CD 1/1, p. 401 (KD, p. 369).
[25] CD 2/1, p. 273 (KD, p. 306).
[26] Ibid., pp. 257-321 (KD, pp. 288-361). These pages, containing Barth's consideration of "The Being of God as the One Who Loves in Freedom," are particularly relevant for our discussion below.
[27] Ibid., p. 272 (KD, p. 306).
[28] CD 1/1, p. 407 (KD, p. 374). Barth uses Ordnung.
[29] Ibid., pp. 416-23 (KD, pp. 382-88).
[30] Ibid., p. 418 (KD, p. 384).
[31] Ibid., p. 421 (KD, p. 387).
[32] CD 2/1, pp. 262-63 (KD, pp. 293-94). "God is He who in this event is subject, predicate and object; the revealer, the act of revelation, the revealed; Father, Son and Holy Spirit." This quote indicates the double character of "act." Act indicates the "whole," the "event" which God is "in," and it also indicates the second "part" of this "whole."
[33] Ibid., pp. 261-63 (KD, pp. 292-94).
[34] Ibid., p. 260 (KD, pp. 291-92).
[35] Ibid., p. 271 (KD, p. 304). For a study of Barth's concept of God's decision as his being, see Eberhard Juengel, The Doctrine of the Trinity: God's Being is in Becoming (Grand Rapids: Eerdmans, 1976), pp. 68-83. See also p. 66.
[36] CD 2/2, pp. 94-127, especially p. 103 (KD, pp. 101-36, especially p. 110).
[37] CD 2/1, p. 275 (KD, p. 309). See also p. 279 (KD, p. 313). "But God loves because He loves; because this act is His being, His essence and His nature."
[38] Ibid., p. 275 (KD, pp. 308-9).
[39] Ibid., p. 301 (KD, p. 339).
[40] Ibid., p. 317 (KD, p. 356).

[41] Ibid., p. 317 (KD, p. 357). See also p. 305 (KD, p. 343). "And the freedom to exist which He exercises in His revelation is the same which He has in the depths of His eternal being, and which is proper to Him quite apart from His exercise of it ad extra."
[42] Ibid., p. 320 (KD, p. 360).
[43] CD 1/1, pp. 426, 481 (KD, pp. 391, 442).
[44] Ibid., p. 450 (KD, p. 413).
[45] CD 4/1, p. 175 (KD, p. 191). See also pp. 164-76 (KD, pp. 179-92).
[46] Ibid., p. 177 (KD, p. 193).
[47] Ibid., p. 177 (KD, pp. 193-94).
[48] Ibid., pp. 183-85 (KD, pp. 199-202).
[49] Ibid., p. 187 (KD, p. 204).
[50] Ibid., pp. 187-88 (KD, pp. 204-5).
[51] Ibid., p. 192 (KD, p. 210).
[52] Ibid., p. 193 (KD, p. 211).
[53] Ibid., p. 195 (KD, p. 213).
[54] Ibid.
[55] Ibid., pp. 202-3 (KD, pp. 221-22). Part of Barth's statement of the trinitarian implications of the obedience of Jesus should be reported here. "As we look at Jesus Christ we cannot avoid the astounding conclusion of a divine obedience. Therefore we have to draw the no less astounding deduction that in equal Godhead the one God is, in fact, the One and also Another, that He is indeed a First and a Second, One who rules and commands in majesty and One who obeys in humility."
[56] Ibid., p. 203 (KD, pp. 222-23).
[57] Ibid., p. 204 (KD, p. 223).
[58] Ibid., p. 204 (KD, pp. 223-24).
[59] Ibid., pp. 179-80 (KD, p. 196). See also p. 177 (KD, 193). "Who the one true God is, and what He is, i.e., what is His being as God, and therefore His deity, His 'divine nature,' which is also the divine nature of Jesus Christ if he is very God--all this we have to discover from the fact that as such He is very man and partaker of human nature, from His becoming man, from His incarnation and from what He has done and suffered in the flesh."
[60] CD 2/1, pp. 271-72 (KD, pp. 304-5). See also pp. 284-85 (KD, pp. 319-21). Here Barth states that God is "the person." "Man is not a person," but God is. "Not we but God is I." See also p. 285 (KD, p. 320).

[61] Ibid., p. 284 (KD, p. 319).
[62] CD 1/1, p. 400 (KD, p. 368).
[63] CD 2/1, p. 272 (KD, p. 306).
[64] There are serious theoretical difficulties created by this identification. Normally we assume that an actor is different from his act, at least in significant respects. Our manner of speaking implies a distinction between the two. For example, when we say "David ran," we assume that David is not completely identical with his running. William H. Poteat, "God and the 'Private-I,'" New Essays on Religious Language, ed. Dallas High (New York: Oxford University, 1969), p. 136, states that talking about God's acts is logically similar to speech about the acts of a human person. "In both cases an actor who is not assimilatable to his acts is the presupposition of the form of discourse."
Clearly Barth does not intend for God be be "swallowed up" in his act, as though he could not make a decision. Jenson, God after God, pp. 112, 125-27, gives a sympathetic defense of Barth's position. He states that in the case of humans, we posit an "I" to provide the continuity of a succession of events. The "I" bridges temporal discontinuities in "my" acts. "But precisely the absence of such discontinuities is what distinguishes God from us--and therefore the dichotomy between an event and its agent or sufferer does not apply to God" (p. 126). However, if we called God just "event," then it would seem that we had accepted the dichotomy and put God on one side. Therefore, we speak of God as "he," but this does not mean that God is essentially a substance, a "thing," which exists behind his acts.
[65] CD 2/1, p. 297 (KD, p. 334). "What we can describe as personality is indeed the whole divine Trinity as such, in the unity of the Father, Son and Holy Spirit in God Himself and in His work--not the individual aspects by themselves in which God is and which He has." See also CD 1/1, pp. 402-3 (KD, p. 370). Here Barth states that the essence which is one personality should be understood as one individual essence, one being. The Father, Son and Holy Spirit are not merely equal in essence, for this might be understood in a polytheistic sense. Their equality of essence is to be understood "in the sense of i d e n t i t y of essence." See also pp. 501-6 (KD, pp. 460-64).

[66] CD 2/1, p. 286 (KD, p. 321). The context clearly indicates that "The One" refers to God.

[67] CD 2/2, p. 108 (KD, pp. 115-16). This passage will be quoted in more detail below. See pp. 107-8.

[68] CD 1/1, pp. 426-31, 452-56 (KD, pp. 391-95, 415-19).

[69] CD 3/2, p. 59 (KD, p. 69). See also CD 4/2, p. 193 (KD, p. 214).

[70] CD 4/1, p. 127 (KD, pp. 138-39).

[71] CD 3/2, pp. 65-66 (KD, pp. 76-77). Immediately below the words quoted above, Barth states that the work of Jesus in history is a portion of the one divine act. It is not a separate, merely human work.

[72] CD 2/2, pp. 96-97 (KD, pp. 103-4). See also CD 1/1, p. 535 (KD, p. 490) where Barth states that Jesus Christ is "wholly and utterly God, the divine Subject."

[73] CD 2/2, p. 107 (KD, p. 114). See also CD 1/1, p. 177 (KD, p. 161). "Christ does not for the first time b e c o m e, but He already is" the Lord of lords.

[74] CD 1/1, pp. 485-86 (KD, pp. 445-46).

[75] CD 2/2, p. 104 (KD, pp. 111-12).

[76] Ibid., p. 108 (KD, pp. 115-16). For a similar understanding of Barth's development of this concept, see Jenson, Alpha and Omega, pp. 66-84, 165-67; and Hathaway, p. 112.

[77] See CD 4/2, pp. 75, 84 (KD, pp. 82, 92) for examples.

[78] Emil Brunner, The Mediator: A Study of the Central Doctrine of the Christian Faith, trans. Olive Wyon (Philadelphia: Westminster, 1947), especially pp. 265-68, 345. For a discussion of Brunner, see J.M. Creed, The Divinity of Jesus Christ (Cambridge: Cambridge University, 1938), pp. 134-36.

[79] Barth, Karl Barth's Table Talk, p. 49.

[80] CD 1/2, p. 164 (KD, p. 180). See our discussion above, pp. 56-58.

[81] CD 4/2, p. 49 (KD, p. 53). Here Barth uses the distinction between essence and existence to combat the argument that anhypostasis and enhypostasis threaten the humanity of Jesus. Following Hollaz, he states that the perfection of something is judged according to its essence, not its subsistence or existence.

[82] CD 1/2, p. 162 (KD, pp. 177-78).

[83] CD 1/2, p. 163 (KD, p. 178). Barth means that the existence of the human nature is directly identical with the existence of God. The human nature, having no existence of its own, "acquires" the existence of God. There is only one existence involved here, and therefore it is completely identical with itself. See our earlier discussion, pp. 55-64.

[84] CD 4/2, p. 49 (KD, p. 52). Barth seems to associate the concept of person not only with the concept of existence but also with the concept of independent existence. "By hypostasis, persona, was meant the independent existence (the propria subsistentia) of His humanity." I have transliterated hypostasis from the Greek.

[85] While Barth does not say explicitly in this context that the identity of Jesus Christ with God is direct rather than indirect, this is clearly his meaning. He affirms that "He who was born in time is the very same who in eternity is born of the Father." CD 1/2, p. 138 (KD, p. 152). The phrase "is the very same" indicates that the identity is direct.

[86] See below, pp. 115-20.

[87] CD 4/2, p. 50 (KD, p. 53).

[88] The German for "bearer" is Traeger. For example, see CD 4/2, p. 92 (KD, pp. 101-2).

[89] CD 4/2, p. 65 (KD, p. 70). "He, the divine Subject, carries and determines the divine essence, and not conversely. . . . The Godhead as such has no existence. It is not real. It has no being or activity. It cannot, therefore, unite with that which is existent and real and has being and activity (which is not the case, of course, with the human essence either). This is done by the divine Subject in and with His divine essence, by the One who exists and is actual, God the Father, Son and Holy Ghost."

[90] Ibid., p. 102 (KD, p. 113). See also pp. 65-66 (KD, pp. 70-71). On the second of these pages, Barth states: "Neither of the two natures counts as such, because neither exists and is actual as such." See also CD 1/2, p. 136 (KD, p. 150) where Barth says: "On the other hand, the flesh not only could not be flesh apart from the Word, but apart from the Word it would have no being at all, far less be able to speak, act, prevail, reveal or reconcile."

[91] CD 4/2, p. 114 (KD, p. 127).

[92] Ibid., p. 92 (KD, pp. 101-2).

[93] Ibid., p. 70 (KD, p. 76).

[94] Ibid., pp. 106-7 (KD, p. 118). This point will be strengthened in the fourth chapter when we show that the title "Son of Man" is used by Barth to denote the same subject that is denoted by "Son of God." See below, pp. 142-51.

[95] For an example of a statement in which Barth depicts the incarnation as involving three principal elements, see CD 4/2, p. 62 (KD, p. 67): "From the unity with His own existence into which the Son of God assumes human essence while maintaining His own divine essence, there follows, as we have said, the union of divine and human essence as it has taken place and been actualised in Him." See also pp. 114-15 (KD, pp. 127-28).

[96] CD 4/2, pp. 71-72 (KD, p. 77). In this section, Barth makes it clear that "Son of Man" names the single bearer of both natures who is also called "Son of God." For further confirmation of this point, see our discussion of the names and titles of Jesus Christ in the fourth chapter, especially pp. 142-51.

[97] Ibid., p. 51 (KD, p. 54).

[98] CD 1/2, p. 182 (KD, p. 199). The underlining has been added.

[99] CD 4/2, pp. 96-97 (KD, pp. 106-7).

[100] See above, pp. 69-72, 112-15.

[101] CD 4/2, pp. 56-58 (KD, pp. 60-62). In his discussion of Biedermann, Barth attacks the view that Jesus is a religious personality who is related to God in a special way.

[102] Ibid., p. 58 (KD, pp. 62-63).

[103] Ibid., pp. 55-57 (KD, pp. 59-62).

[104] Ibid., p. 60 (KD, p. 64).

[105] Ibid., p. 53 (KD, p. 57).

[106] Ibid., p. 89 (KD, p. 97).

[107] Barth, Karl Barth's Table Talk, p. 49. See above p. 110.

[108] Barth does not include the analogy of husband and wife among those which have value as illustrations, nor, to our knowledge, does he ever use it.

[109] CD 1/1, pp. 400-431 (KD, pp. 368-95).

[110] CD 4/1, pp. 209-10 (KD, pp. 229-30). The underlining has been added.

[111] Ibid., pp. 208-9 (KD, p. 228).
[112] CD 3/2, p. 332 (KD, pp. 399-400). The underlining has been added.
[113] CD 4/1, p. 253 (KD, p. 278).
[114] CD 4/2, p. 6 (KD, p. 5).
[115] Sellers, Two Ancient Christologies, pp. 24, 56, 94, 95, 252. According to Sellers, the Alexandrians believed that the actions of Christ involved both natures. He did not act exclusively through either nature, although certain aspects of his actions are more appropriate to the divine nature and others to the human nature.

NOTES TO CHAPTER FOUR

[1] CD 1/1, p. 458 (KD, p. 420).
[2] CD 1/2, p. 10 (KD, pp. 11-12).
[3] Ibid., p. 11 (KD, p. 13).
[4] CD 2/2, p. 54 (KD, p. 57).
[5] Arnold B. Come, An Introduction to Barth's "Dogmatics" for Preachers (Philadelphia: Westminster, 1963), p. 139. "It must also be remembered that by 'Jesus Christ' Barth does not mean some Absolute Idea that contains all concrete particular truths that are to be deduced by a rational dialectic (Hegel). 'Jesus Christ' is a history in which the living personal God moves from his freely made decision to share his eternal life with a creature, through the whole process of time that he gives that creature, to the fulfillment of his purpose. And the medium in which this history of God becomes visible is Jesus of Nazareth and his special history as witnessed to in the Bible by the Holy Spirit."
[6] CD 3/2, p. 58 (KD, p. 67).
[7] CD 4/2, p. 67 (KD, p. 72).
[8] Ibid., p. 67 (KD, pp. 72-73). Speaking of the Lutheran position, Barth says: "This meant in practice that statements may also be made of the humanity of Jesus Christ which in themselves denote and describe only the divine and not the human essence. It is in the fact that such statements can and may and must be made of the humanity of Jesus Christ that we see the concern of the older Lutheran theology with its particular doctrine of the communio naturarum."

[9] Ibid., pp. 68-69 (KD, pp. 73-74). Speaking of the Reformed, Barth says: "Thus they could not understand the propositiones personales in the sense that statements can and may and must be made about the humanity of Jesus Christ whose content corresponds only to the Logos existing in divine essence, and not to the human essence assumed by Him into unity with His existence." In their use of these propositions, the Reformed "tried to direct their true attention to the One who overcame in this overcoming, and to the act of His overcoming--to Jesus of Nazareth as the Christ, the eternal Son of God, and to the act of God which took place and is a fact in Him."

[10] Ibid. Their zeal "was a zeal for the sovereignty of the Subject acting in free grace in the incarnation, of the living God in the person and existence of His Son."

[11] Ibid., p. 69 (KD, p. 74).

[12] Ibid., p. 71 (KD, p. 77). The translation is mine. The published English translation does not reproduce the emphasis which is found in the original through spacing.

[13] We shall turn to this problem again later when we examine particular instances where Barth appears to use some of the names of Christ to denote a separate, human person. See below pp. 152-63.

[14] CD 4/2, p. 38 (KD, p. 40).

[15] Ibid. See also CD 1/1, pp. 188, 373 (KD, pp. 171, 343).

[16] CD 1/1, p. 462 (KD, p. 424).

[17] Ibid., p. 463 (KD, p. 424).

[18] Ibid., p. 460 (KD, p. 422).

[19] Ibid.

[20] Ibid., p. 461 (KD, p. 423).

[21] Ibid.

[22] Ibid., p. 464 (KD, pp. 425-26).

[23] Ibid., p. 463 (KD, p. 425).

[24] CD 3/2, pp. 448-49 (KD, pp. 537-38). Barth states that the deity of Jesus was unknown during his earthly life.

[25] CD 4/2, p. 134 (KD, p. 150).

[26] Ibid., pp. 73-76 (KD, pp. 79-83). On the first of these pages Barth states: "All that characterizes divine essence in distinction from human or any other . . . [and] all that characterizes human essence in distinction from

divine or any other . . . is unlimitedly and unreservedly proper to the one who as Son of God became also Son of Man." The translation is mine.

[27] Ibid., p. 76 (KD, p. 83).

[28] Ibid., pp. 104-5 (KD, p. 116).

[29] Since many of the passages in which Barth assigns divine predicates to Jesus Christ also identify him with the Son and Word of God, it is wise to quote some of them. For example, "In his Godhead, as the eternal Son of the Father, as the eternal Word, Jesus Christ never ceased to be transcendent, free, and sovereign." CD 4/1, p. 135 (KD, p. 147). "But again, He, Jesus Christ, as Son of Man is also the Son of God, and as such of one essence with the Father and the Holy Ghost, and therefore the Lord of all lords, the source of all good, the Almighty and All-merciful, the Word by which the world was created and is maintained, the Eternal before whom all His creatures can and must only disappear and perish like dust, and yet shall not simply perish and disappear but persist, the One who in great and little things alike is present to everything near or far in time or space and sustains and keeps and rules it, the gracious One, who knows the transgression and weakness of man, whose anger burns but as the fire of His love, who does not will the death of man but his life and salvation. He, the Son of God, is the One who was and is and will be, existing in the pre-temporality, the co-temporality and the post-temporality of God Himself." CD 4/2, pp. 74-75 (KD, p. 81). See also p. 73 (KD, pp. 79-80).

[30] For the claim that Jesus Christ elects, see CD 2/2, pp. 94-106 (KD, pp. 101-13). "Jesus Christ is the electing God," p. 103 (KD, p. 111). Barth explains that Jesus Christ "does not elect alone, but in company with the electing of the Father and the Holy Spirit. But He does elect," p. 105 (KD, p. 112).

For the belief that Jesus Christ is the creator, see CD 2/2, p. 94 (KD, p. 101). "It is by Him, Jesus Christ, and for Him and to Him, that the universe is created as a theatre for God's dealings with man and man's dealings with God." See also CD 4/2, p. 54 (KD, p. 57).

For the affirmation that Jesus Christ assumed flesh, see CD 1/2, p. 214 (KD, p. 233). "Just as, similarly, Jesus Christ cannot be understood from the standpoint of man's nature and kind, which He assumed and adopted, and which are only too familiar to us." See also p. 238 (KD, p. 259). When he assumed flesh he became man. "Jesus Christ is the Son of God who became man." CD 4/1, p. 204 (KD, p. 224). See also p. 192 (KD, p. 209).

Jesus Christ is the one who reveals himself as Lord. For example, in CD 4/2, p. 156 (KD, p. 174), Barth states, "the knowledge of Jesus Christ, and the presentation in the whole of the New Testament and therefore from the very outset in the Synoptics, rests on the self-declaration in which He revealed Himself to His disciples in the resurrection and ascension." Jesus Christ also speaks and is heard in the church, and this speaking can also be described by Barth as the speaking of God. CD 1/1, pp. 45-46 (KD, pp. 41-43).

With respect to reconciliation, Barth states that Jesus Christ "is the One who justifies, sanctifies, and calls." CD 4/1, p. 147 (KD, pp. 161-62). See also pp. 125, 197 (KD, pp. 137, 215-16).

[31] CD 4/2, p. 3 (KD, p. 1). See also CD 1/1, p. 474 (KD, p. 435), and CD 4/1, p. 163 (KD, p. 178).

[32] CD 1/1, p. 498 (KD, p. 457). See also p. 218 (KD, p. 199).

[33] CD 4/2, p. 44 (KD, p. 47).

[34] For example, see CD 4/2, p. 100 (KD, pp. 110-11). Here Barth uses several different forms of expression. He states that "the Word became flesh," became and is "also Jesus of Nazareth," and "became identical with this man." The "Creator condescended to be a creature." "As the Son of God" the Creator "goes into the far country." The Son of God "became this man."

If there is any doubt that God performs this act, Barth removes it. See CD 4/2, p. 109 (KD, p. 121). "But, at root, what is the life of Jesus Christ but the act in which God becomes very God and very man, positing Himself in this being?" He also states that God "goes into the far country." CD 4/1, p. 158 (KD, p. 173).

For the use of "Jesus Christ" to denote this one who goes into the far country and becomes man, see CD 4/1, p. 157 (KD, p. 171). "That Jesus Christ is very God is shown in His way into the far country in which He the Lord became a servant." For other statements of Jesus Christ's becoming a man, or humbling himself, or obeying the

Father, see CD 4/1, pp. 204-8 (KD, pp. 224-28) and also
pp. 133, 177, 294 (KD, pp. 146-47, 193, 324). For the
terminology of the obedience of the Son of God, see CD
4/1, p. 159 (KD, pp. 173-74).
    [35] CD 4/1, p. 22 (KD, p. 22). See also pp. 79, 126,
128-29, 157 (KD, pp. 83, 138, 140-41, 171); CD 1/1, p. 474
(KD, p. 435).
    [36] CD 1/1, p. 180 (KD, p. 163). See also p. 164 (KD,
p. 149).
    [37] Ibid., p. 474 (KD, p. 435).
    [38] Ibid., p. 157 (KD, p. 143).
    [39] CD 4/1, p. 206 (KD, p. 225).
    [40] CD 4/2, p. 95 (KD, p. 105). See also CD 1/2, p.
13 (KD, p. 15) where Barth states: "The Word or Son of God
became a man and was called Jesus of Nazareth."   In
addition, see CD 4/2, pp. 91, 101 (KD, pp. 100, 112).
    [41] CD 4/1, p. 163 (KD, p. 178). See also p. 13 (KD,
p. 13).
    [42] CD 4/2, pp. 97-98 (KD, pp. 107-8).
    [43] Ibid., p. 98 (KD, p. 108).
    [44] CD 1/1, pp. 368-72 (KD, pp. 338-42).
    [45] CD 4/2, p. 39 (KD, p. 41).
    [46] Ibid., p. 93 (KD, pp. 102-3).
    [47] Paul Ziff, Semantic Analysis (Ithaca: Cornell
University, 1960), pp. 94-102, discusses the connotation
of personal and proper names. For example, he states: "A
proper name connotes what is, as it were, noted with the
name by the hearer," p. 94.
    [48] CD 3/2, p. 58 (KD, p. 67). Here Barth states that
because "Jesus" means that Yahweh saves, it "tells a
story." See also p. 60 (KD, p. 70); CD 1/1, p. 364 (KD,
p. 335); CD 4/2, p. 501 (KD, p. 567); CD 4/4, pp. 92-93
(KD, pp. 101-2).
    [49] CD 3/2, pp. 60-61 (KD, pp. 70-71). Barth states
that "Messiah," "Son of Man," and "Savior" also "point in
the same direction." That is, they indicate that Yahweh
saves. See also CD 4/1, pp. 5-6 (KD, pp. 3-4) where Barth
considers "Emmanuel."
    [50] CD 1/1, p. 493 (KD, p. 453). See also pp. 494-501
(KD, pp. 453-60); CD 4/1, pp. 206-10 (KD, pp. 226-31). In
the last of these references, Barth explains that although
the metaphor of father-son conveys that God the Father is
of the same essence as God the Son, it does not indicate
clearly that they are one individual.

[51] CD 4/1, p. 169 (KD, p. 184). See also CD 1/1, p. 155 (KD, pp. 141-42).

[52] CD 2/1, p. 22 (KD, pp. 22-23). See also pp. 81, 84 (KD, pp. 88, 91-92).

[53] CD 2/2, p. 76 (KD, p. 81).

[54] Ibid., p. 309 (KD, pp. 339-40).

[55] CD 1/2, p. 56 (KD, p. 62).

[56] CD 4/2, p. 102 (KD, pp. 112-13). See also CD 1/2, p. 19 (KD, p. 21).

[57] CD 3/1, p. 54 (KD, p. 58). See also above, pp. 46-47.

[58] CD 4/2, pp. 132-33 (KD, p. 148).

[59] Ibid., p. 74 (KD, p. 80).

[60] Ibid., p. 73 (KD, pp. 79-80).

[61] Ibid., pp. 69-70 (KD, pp. 74-75). See also pp. 72-73, 116 (KD, pp. 78-79, 129).

[62] Ibid., p. 66 (KD, p. 71).

[63] CD 1/2, p. 155 (KD, p. 170). See also CD 4/2, pp. 44, 65, 70 (KD, pp. 46, 70-71, 76).

[64] CD 1/2, p. 151 (KD, p. 165). See also CD 4/2, p. 74 (KD, pp. 80-81).

[65] CD 4/2, p. 211 (KD, pp. 233-34).

[66] Ibid., p. 73 (KD, pp. 79-80).

[67] Ibid., p. 95 (KD, p. 105). The underlining has been added.

[68] Ibid., p. 32 (KD, p. 33). "As the Son of God He is the One who elects man and therefore His own humiliation. As the Son of Man He is the One who is elected by God and therefore to His own exaltation."

[69] CD 3/3, pp. 274-75 (KD, p. 311). "As the Son of God, He was the divine gift and answer, but as the Son of Man He was human asking."

[70] CD 4/2, pp. 115-16 (KD, pp. 128-29). Speaking of the common actualization of the two natures, Barth states that "what Jesus Christ does as the Son of God and in virtue of His divine essence, and what He does as the Son of Man and in exercise of His human essence" are in harmony with each other.

Barth also uses these phrases in another way, to avoid the implication that Christ sometimes acts exclusively through one of his natures. Since Christ is one person and all his actions involve both natures, it is proper to say that Christ performs "as the Son of God" even those actions which are more closely related to his human nature than his divine nature. For example, Barth states that "Jesus Christ is the Son of God, and as such He is . . . conceptus de Spiritu Sancto, natus ex Maria virgine, . . . crucified, risen and seated at the right hand of the Father, . . . [and] will come again to judge the quick and the dead." CD 4/1, p. 206 (KD, p. 225). See also CD 4/2, pp. 74, 97 (KD, pp. 81, 107). Conversely, Jesus Christ does not elect without his human nature, and therefore it is correct to say that he elects "as the Son of Man." Barth states: "But if He and the Father are one in this unity of the divine name and glory, a unity in which there can be no question of rivalry, then it is clear that the Son, too, is an active Subject of the aeterna Dei praedestinatio as Son of Man, that He is Himself the electing God." CD 2/2, p. 107 (KD, p. 115).

[71] CD 4/1, p. 131 (KD, p. 144). "In Him humanity is exalted humanity, just as Godhead is humiliated Godhead. And humanity is exalted in Him by the humiliation of Godhead."

[72] CD 4/2, p. 73 (KD, pp. 79-80). For Barth's wording on this point, see above p. 235, n. 26.

[73] CD 4/1, p. 131 (KD, p. 144).

[74] CD 4/2, p. 100 (KD, p. 111).

[75] Ibid., p. 19 (KD, p. 19).

[76] CD 4/1, pp. 134-35 (KD, p. 147). See also CD 4/2, p. 150 (KD, p. 168).

[77] CD 4/2, p. 153 (KD, p. 171).

[78] Ibid., p. 21 (KD, p. 21).

[79] Ibid., p. 94 (KD, p. 103).

[80] Ibid., p. 28 (KD, pp. 29-30).

[81] For the Antiochian view, see above, pp. 83-84.

[82] CD 4/1, p. 136 (KD, p. 149). See also CD 1/2, p. 16 (KD, p. 18); CD 4/3, p. 7 (KD, p. 5).

[83] CD 1/2, pp. 19-23 (KD, pp. 21-26). For example, speaking of the view of the synoptic gospels, which are characterized by the second type of statements, Barth says: "But that means that externally they must start from His humanity, from His life before the resurrection," p. 22 (KD, p. 24).

[84] CD 4/2, p. 73 (KD, pp. 79-80). For the quotation, see above, p. 235, n. 26.

[85] CD 1/1, p. 371 (KD, p. 341).

[86] Ibid., p. 373 (KD, p. 343).
[87] Ibid., p. 188 (KD, p. 171-72).
[88] CD 1/2, p. 136 (KD, p. 150).
[89] Ibid., pp. 165-66 (KD, p. 181).
[90] Ibid., p. 166 (KD, p. 182).
[91] Ibid., p. 17 (KD, p. 19).
[92] CD 1/1, p. 371 (KD, p. 341).
[93] CD 4/2, p. 99 (KD, p. 110).
[94] CD 2/2, p. 107 (KD, pp. 114-15).
[95] CD 4/1, p. 180 (KD, p. 197).
[96] Ibid., p. 181 (KD, p. 197).
[97] Ibid., p. 182 (KD, p. 199).
[98] CD 1/2, p. 162 (KD, p. 177).
[99] CD 2/2, p. 8 (KD, p. 7).
[100] Ibid.
[101] CD 3/2, p. 483 (KD, p. 580).
[102] CD 4/1, p. 175 (KD, p. 191). See also pp. 172, 183 (KD, pp. 187, 199); CD 2/1, pp. 56, 61 (KD, pp. 61, 67); CD 3/2, p. 613 (KD, p. 746); CD 4/2, p. 101 (KD, p. 112).
[103] In discussions of the unity of God with the man Jesus, the English translation of the Church Dogmatics sometimes translates Identitaet as "unity." For example, see CD 4/2, p. 101 (KD, p. 112). In addition, Barth seems to use Identitaet and Einheit interchangeably when speaking of the relation of God to Jesus. For his use of Einheit see CD 4/1, pp. 172, 175 (KD, pp. 187, 191). For Identitaet see CD 4/1, p. 171 (KD, p. 187).
[104] Karl Barth, "The Principles of Dogmatics According to Wilhelm Herrmann," in Theology and Church: Shorter Writings 1920-28, trans. Louise Pettibone Smith (London: SCM, 1962), p. 268.

NOTES TO CHAPTER FIVE

[1] For example, see CD 4/1, p. 45 (KD, p. 47). In this discussion Barth relates the claim that there is "only one revelation" to a rejection of natural theology.
[2] For example, McIntyre, p. 167, and Groff, pp. 173-74, argue that there is little justification for restricting revelation to Jesus. McIntyre states that the controversy ought "to be settled by simple appeal to fact.

If there are indeed some people who can honestly say that God reveals himself to them apart from Jesus Christ, and if we are to presume that they know what revelation means (say, from their awareness of revelation in Jesus Christ), then I wonder whether it is valuable or indeed proper to prosecute the controversy against them."

[3] Barth, Karl Barth's Table Talk, p. 49. Here Barth states that he thinks that Brunner's acceptance of a concept of a logos asarkos leads to his defense of natural theology.

[4] CD 1/1, p. 274 (KD, p. 252); CD 1/2, pp. 37, 43 (KD, pp. 41, 48); CD 2/1, pp. 82-83 (KD, pp. 90-91); CD 3/2, p. 343 (KD, p. 413); CD 3/3, p. 103 (KD, pp. 115-16). See also Balthasar, p. 147.

[5] See Kehm, p. 192, and Prenter, "Die Lehre vom Menschen bei Karl Barth," Theologische Zeitschrift 6 (1950):221. These two interpreters, who tend to see Barth as an Antiochian thinker, believe that Barth's analogia relationis is not an alternative to analogia entis but a new form of it.

[6] Hathaway, pp. 385-98, presents a capable defense of the view that Barth's analogia relationis is not simply another form of the analogia entis. He concedes that Barth can speak of nature over against grace and creature over against the creator, but he concludes that Barth does not grant to the creature or to nature the degree of independence necessary for one to speak about an analogy of being. See especially p. 390. For a similar view, see Hartwell, p. 56. For bibliographical data regarding the many discussions of this issue, see Hathaway pp. 388, 390, and Kehm, pp. 192-93.

[7] CD 1/1, pp. 367-68 (KD, pp. 337-38).

[8] CD 4/1, pp. 41-44, 83 (KD, pp. 43-46, 88). On the last of these pages, Barth states: "Everything depends on Him who is above, and therefore on what comes to man from Him and therefore from above. It does not depend at all on what man had or has or will have to contribute from below." See also CD 1/2, pp. 185-89, especially p. 186 pp. 202-6, especially p. 203). Here Barth rejects "all synergism." For a discussion of Barth's rejection of synergism, see Hartwell, pp. 52, 80, 112, and 127-28.

[9] See CD 1/1, pp. 460-65 (KD, pp. 422-26).

[10] CD 2/2, p. 108 (KD, p. 116).

[11] CD 4/2, p. 95 (KD, p. 105).
[12] Norris, Manhood and Christ, p. 200, states that Theodore conceives of the human nature as a subject or center of action. Further, Norris argues that, for Theodore, this subject of action is a person. Barth's subject of action, however, is not a complete, human individual.
[13] Pittenger, pp. 114, 219, argues that Alexandrian thought tends to make God the center of Jesus' activity, obliterating the purely human center of consciousness and activity. In so far as Alexandrian thought obscures the human center of consciousness and activity, it has a tendency toward Apollinarianism.
[14] See also Hathaway, p. 115, who questions whether Barth provides an adequate foundation for the statement that Jesus Christ is a man. In Hathaway's view, Barth's emphasis upon the claim that Jesus Christ is the humanity of all men undermines the affirmation that Jesus Christ is an individual human being.
[15] To suggest that Barth is Apollinarian is not the same as suggesting that he is a monophysite. Apollinarianism, in our understanding, is the belief that the human nature which God assumes in the incarnation is not complete. As is well known, Apollinarius denied that the human nature which God assumed in the incarnation had its own human soul. On the other hand, Cyril of Alexandria thought that the human nature involved in the incarnation had its own soul (Kelly, pp. 289-95, 317). In so far as Cyril and other Alexandrians obscure the completeness of the human nature they demonstrate a tendency toward Apollinarianism.
Monophysitism, in our view, is defined by the claim that the human nature and the divine nature become through their union one nature. Barth adamantly opposes monophysitism throughout his discussions of the union of the two natures. This point is apparent in Barth's emphasis upon the encounter of the divine and human natures and their different functions within the union. For confirmation of this emphasis, see our earlier discussion of Barth's formulation of the unity of the two natures in the second chapter, especially pp. 72-77. Barth shares with monophysitism the goal of maintaining the completeness and permanence of the union of the two natures, and his claim

that God is the bearer of the human nature in the incarnation, a claim which we believe tends toward Apollinarianism, helps Barth achieve that goal.

It might be argued that Apollinarius and Cyril of Alexandria were defenders of monophysitism since both spoke of the "one nature of the Incarnate Lord," a phrase which became a monophysite slogan (Hardy and Richardson, p. 352; Kelly, pp. 319, 330-34). However, both Apollinarius and Cyril lived before the Decree of Chalcedon in 451 A.D., and they did not have to declare whether they would accept its wording about the two natures remaining after the union. Orthodox theologians would likely claim that Cyril, if not Apollinarius, would have consented to Chalcedon. On the other hand, the famous monophysite theologian Serverus of Antioch rejected the formulation of Chalcedon and claimed that in the one person of Jesus Christ there is only one nature but two properties, a divine property and a human property. Severus, as Cyril, used the term "nature" in the sense of "person." A common explanation as to why Severus rejected Chalcedon is that the difference between Severus and Chalcedon is only verbal and that Severus refused to speak of two natures after the union because of his fear of Nestorianism. For confirmation of this point, see Harry Wolfson, The Philosophy of the Church Fathers (Cambridge: Harvard University, 1956), pp. 448-51. For a more thorough study of Severus and two other monophysite theologians, see Roberta C. Chesnut, Three Monophysite Christologies: Severus of Antioch, Philoxenus of Mabbug, and Jacob of Sarug (London: Oxford University, 1976). A brief examination of Chesnut's study of Severus suggests that there are some significant similarities between Severus and Barth. Severus stresses that the human component of the incarnation is inseparably united with the divine; that the human component has its own will but this will does not operate apart from, or in opposition to, the divine will to which it is subject; and that the two components join in one operation (Chesnut, pp. 10-12, 20, 25). A careful comparison of Barth and Severus would be worthwhile, but it is beyond our responsibilities here.

    [16] For example, see Barth's talk of the human nature as the "organ," the "clothing," and the "temple," of the eternal Son of God. CD 4/2, pp. 96-101 (KD, pp. 106-111).

[17] CD 1/2, pp. 158-59 (KD, p. 173). "The sinlessness of Jesus thus does not admit of a systematic connexion with the fact that here a true man had a serious struggle, but only of establishment and acknowledgment in its historical connexion with that fact. He who struggled here and won is He who was bound to win, He who when He entered the contest had already won. He really had no awareness of sin. That is the truth of the vere Deus."
[18] CD 3/2, p. 243 (KD, p. 291). While Barth describes "humanity as a being of man with others," he argues that "only the humanity of Jesus can be absolutely exhaustively and exclusively described as a being for man. There can be no question of a total being for others as the determination of any other men but Jesus. And to the humanity of other men there necessarily belongs reciprocity. . . . [but] reciprocity cannot arise in the humanity of Jesus with its irreversible 'for.'" For a discussion of the difficulties of Barth's position on this issue, see Ogletree, pp. 175-78.
[19] See CD 1/1, pp. 460-65 (KD, pp. 422-26).
[20] CD 3/2, pp. 157-62 (KD, pp. 188-93); CD 4/2, pp. 270-75, 516 (KD, pp. 299-305, 584). For discussions of this issue, see Hathaway, pp. 114-19, and Jenson, Alpha and Omega, pp. 130-40.
[21] For a list of pertinent questions as to whether Barth has provided sufficient distinctions in the one whole Jesus Christ, see Jenson, God after God, pp. 74-78.
[22] Barth states that the assumption of the human nature in the incarnation is the assumption of the human nature of all men. At the same time, it is the assumption of all men themselves. See CD 4/2, p. 59 (KD, pp. 63-64). "In His being as man God has implicitly assumed the human being of all men. In Him not only we all as homines, but our humanitas as such--for it is both His and ours--exist in and with God Himself."
[23] Jenson, God after God, p. 173, argues that Barth makes God a God of the past. See also his discussion of Barth's concept of Jesus as the eternity of God, pp. 70, 151-54.
[24] Jaroslov Pelikan, The Christian Tradition, vol. 1: The Emergence of the Catholic Tradition (100-600) (Chicago: University of Chicago, 1971), pp. 227-33. Pelikan states that the Antiochians and the Alexandrians

accepted the Nicean doctrine of the trinity and the Nicean orthodoxy of the Cappadocians, although both sides tried to "impugn the trinitarian orthodoxy of their opponents" (p. 228). However, the orthodox doctrine of the trinity did not lead directly to specific conclusions which could solve the christological controversies. Also, Pelikan continues, both Alexandrian and Antiochian theologians stressed the transcendence and impassibility of God; both groups agreed that the purpose of Christ's coming was salvation, and both affirmed that the humans who were saved would receive immortality and impassibility as a result of their salvation. However, according to Pelikan, none of these common conclusions enabled the two sides to avoid vehement disagreement regarding christology.

Harry Wolfson, in his The Philosophy of the Church Fathers, pp. 64, 77, states that there was no question of principle between Alexandrians and the Antiochians regarding the use of allegory in interpreting scripture, although the Antiochians did not use allegory as extensively as the Alexandrians. Some Antiochians got the impression that the Alexandrians intended to replace the literal meaning with an allegorical meaning, and they objected to discarding the literal meaning. However, according to Wolfson, that impression was mistaken, and the Alexandrians wished to preserve both the literal and the allegorical interpretations of scripture, except in certain cases where the literal meaning, in their view, made absolutely no sense and only the allegorical method could provide an intelligible interpretation.

The view that the Alexandrian and Antiochian theologians differ from each other primarily within the realm of christology rather than throughout their theologies appears to be in tension with much conventional wisdom. Since the time of Harnack, it has often been affirmed that the Antiochians were Aristotelian while the Alexandrians were Platonic. For examples of this way of distinguishing the two traditions, see Adolph von Harnack, History of Dogma, trans. James Millar and others, 7 vols. (London: Williams and Norgate, 1896-99), 3:283, 287; Kelly, p. 304; Sellers, Two Ancient Christologies, pp. 106, 109; and Charles E. Raven, Apollinarianism; An Essay on the Christology of the Early Church (Cambridge: Cambridge University, 1923), pp. 54-57. Although this way of contrasting Antiochian from Alexandrian thought may raise problems for those who stress similarities between the two schools of thought in matters other than christology, it does not automatically refute their views. In fact, Sellers, who characterizes Antiochian thought as Aristotelian and Alexandrian as Platonic, affirms that the two approaches are complementary and orthodox, even in the area of christology. See his Two Ancient Christologies, pp. 243-57. Further, the rationale for contrasting the two theologies in this way needs clarification and substantiation. Norris, Manhood and Christ, p. 252, states that the "identification of the Antiochene 'outlook' with Aristotelianism . . . [is] an identification which has in fact never been carefully examined." Norris, pp. 4-5 in the same work, also demonstrates that the Platonists of the second and following centuries adopted significant Aristotelian elements into their systems. For example, they valued Aristotle's syllogistic logic, and some defended Aristotle's doctrine of the categories, although Plotinus rejected it. In addition, "the Aristotelian conception of a transcendent supreme God, defined as self-thinking Intellect, who acts as the unmoved Source of cosmic motion" was combined with Plato's idea of a creator God.

[25] Although Barth's theology is often characterized as neo-orthodox, Barth himself rejects that label. He states that he finds it "comical." Karl Barth, Final Testimonies, ed. Eberhard Busch, trans, Geoffrey W. Bromiley (Grand Rapids: Eerdmans, 1977), p. 34.

[26] In our discussion of the relation of Barth's theology to Alexandrian theology we recognize the determinative roles played by Clement of Alexandria and Origen in shaping Alexandrian thought. While Cyril of Alexandria led Alexandrian forces in the christological controversies, his historical importance outside the christological sphere is overshadowed by the impact of Clement and Origen.

[27] For substantiation of these points, see Robert P. Casey, "Clement of Alexandria and the Beginnings of Christian Platonism," Harvard Theological Review 18 (January, 1925): 39-101. See especially pp. 74-78, 84-88, 90-91, 100-101. For example, on p. 74, Casey states that Clement's doctrine of God, which "is

intelligible and significant only from the premises of
Platonic immaterialism . . . is from the historical point
of view probably the most significant portion of his
theology."
[28] When Barth learned that almost all his German
theological teachers, including Harnack and Herrmann,
supported the war policy of Kaiser Wilhelm II, he
concluded that there must be serious defects not only in
their ethical views but also in the "exegetical and
dogmatic presuppositions" of those ethical views. See
Eberhard Busch, Karl Barth: His Life from Letters and
Autobiographical Texts, trans. John Bowden (Philadelphia:
Fortress, 1975), p. 81.
[29] For a brief but illuminating discussion of the
basic problems and tasks of Barth's theology, see Hans W.
Frei, "Revelation and Theological Method in the Theology
of Karl Barth," which was cited earlier. Compare also
Robert E. Cushman, "Barth's Attack Upon Cartesianism and
the Future of Theology," Journal of Religion 36 (October,
1956):207-23.
[30] Johannes Quasten, Patrology, vol. 2: The
Ante-Nicene Literature After Irenaeus (Westminster,
Maryland: Newman, 1953), p. 1.
[31] Clement of Alexandria's Stromata, for example,
was a rather rambling and unsystematic exposition of
various topics, including the value of philosophy, the
nature of faith, refutations of gnosticism, and
discussions of moral issues. Quasten, p. 12, states that
Clement "was not a systematic theologian and unable to
dominate great masses of material." For further
discussion of this point, see Casey, p. 46. Nevertheless,
Clement saw many of the logical implications of his
doctrine of God and accepted them, so that many of the
major tenets of his theology intimate a coherent, orderly
whole. For confirmation of this dimension of Clement's
theology, see Casey, pp. 51, 59, 78, and Quasten, pp.
20-23. On the other hand, Origen is a more formidable
systematic thinker than Clement, and his abilities are
reflected in his systematic work De Principiis. Quasten,
p. 57, states that De Principiis is "the first Christian
system of theology and the first manual of dogma." For a
discussion of the systematic character of this work, see
Quasten, pp. 57-61 and Casey, pp. 82-86, 99.

[32] For example, see Casey, pp. 47-49, 59. On the last page cited, Casey states, "Clement's philosophy is a natural and inevitable part of his religion, and he assumes that it is, or may become, so to many of his readers." For similar observations regarding Origen, see Richard A. Norris, Jr., God and the World in Early Christian Theology (New York: Seabury, 1965), pp. 132-33. On the other hand, Cyril of Alexandria was less adept and knowledgeable with regard to philosophical matters. For confirmation of this statement, see Wilken, p. 224. Wilken states that Cyril "did not find his spiritual home in Greek philosophy"; he was primarily a pastor, not a professor. William J. Malley, S.J., Hellenism and Christianity (Rome: Gregorian University, 1978), pp. 259-60, comes to the same conclusion regarding Cyril.

[33] Quasten, pp. 21-23, reports that Clement of Alexandria emphasized the importance of the Logos, who is the creator of the world and the revealer of God's truth in the Old Testament, in Greek philosophy, and in the incarnation. Norris, God and the World, pp. 154-55, indicates that Origen had a similar view of the Logos. For confirmation of the other points presented above, see Norris, God and the World, p 134; Casey, pp. 49, 53; and Quasten, pp. 13-14.

[34] Norris, God and the World, pp. 134-39; Quasten, pp. 41-42.

[35] For discussions of these two levels of Christian existence in Clement and Origen, see Charles Bigg, The Christian Platonists of Alexandria (New York: Macmillan, 1886), pp. 86-91; Norris, God and the World, pp. 135-39; Casey, pp. 70-74; and Wolfson, pp. 106-11. The two levels of Christian existence are related to two levels of truth which can be found in scripture. The first level is the historical and literal level, which can be understood by the common people. The second level is the spiritual level, which is often hidden to ordinary people but can be discerned by the intellectuals who understand the symbols and allegories.

[36] Norris, God and the World, pp. 130-31. For similar comments about Clement, see Casey, pp. 95-96.

[37] For Barth's discussion of the nature and task of dogmatics, see especially CD 1/2, pp. 797-884 (KD, pp. 890-990). For the elements of his position regarding

philosophy and theology which we shall stress in our discussion, see the following passages: CD 1/1, pp. 94, 294, 434, 145, 148, 188 (KD, pp. 86, 270, 398, 132, 135, 171) and 1/2, pp. 729, 731-35 (KD, pp. 817-18, 820-25).

[38] CD 1/1, p. 200 (KD, pp. 132-33). "The worldly form without the divine content is not the Word of God, and the divine content without the worldly form is also not the Word of God. We can neither remain rooted before the worldly form as such, nor fly beyond this and hope to enjoy ourselves still with the divine content only. The one would be realistic, the other would be idealistic theology, and both would be wrong theology. Both times, however, we in faith hear only the whole, the real Word of God. A removal of the distinction, nay opposition, between form and content we cannot achieve. The coincidence of both is God, but it is not discernible by us. What is discernible by us is always form without content or content without form. We may, of course, think realistically or idealistically, but we cannot think in a Christian sense. Obviously the thought of synthesis would least of all be Christian thought, because it would mean neither more nor less than that we wanted to achieve the miracle of God Himself. In faith and in the thought of faith it is not a case of thinking this synthesis. Faith means rather recognising that this synthesis cannot be achieved, committing it to God and seeking and finding it in God. By finding it in God we acknowledge that we cannot find it ourselves and so can neither achieve it in a definite attitude in life nor think it systematically. But by committing it to God and seeking it in Him, we do f i n d it, we hear the whole, the real word of God, i.e. now the divine c o n t e n t in its wordly form, now in the worldly f o r m the divine content. To hear in faith the whole, the real word of God does not mean discerning the unity of veiling and unveiling, of form and content, or accomplishing Christian thought by getting round faith. No, the thought of faith will always quite honestly be either a realistic or an idealistic thought, i.e. a thought in and of itself very unchristian."

[39] Balthasar, pp. 211-17, contrasts Barth with Thomistic theology.

[40] Rumscheidt, pp. 58, 24, 15, 111, notes that Harnack accused Barth of undermining the value of reason.

See also John E. Smith, "The Significance of Karl Barth's
Thought for the Relation Between Philosophy and Theology,"
Union Seminary Quarterly Review 28 (November, 1972):
15-30. Smith, a noted American philosopher, accuses Barth
of logical inconsistencies and then concludes that Barth
might reject such criticisms as "the illegitimate
intrusion of 'logic.'" See p. 22, n. 19.
    [41] John E. Smith, p. 29. See also the entire
article, pp. 15-30.
    [42] Wilhelm Pauck, Karl Barth: Prophet of a New
Christianity? (New York: Harper & Brothers, 1931), p. 219.
    [43] Robert W. Jenson, "Response," Union Seminary
Quarterly Review 28 (November, 1972): 31-34, argues
against John E. Smith's interpretation of Barth. In
Jenson's view, Barth is the "enemy of compartmentaliza-
tion." See pp. 32-34.
    [44] Charles Bigg's The Christian Platonists of Alex-
andria is a sustained defense of the view that the theologies of the Alexandrians were determined primarily by
their commitment to Platonism.
    [45] Bigg, pp. 136-49, explains and criticizes Origen's
hermeneutics. He states that Origen's attempts to find
hidden meanings in the text result in questionable
interpretations.
    [46] For a more detailed discussion of these points
than can be presented here, see Norris, Manhood and
Christ, pp. 10-20. For purposes of clarity, however, it
is appropriate for us to mention here some of the
theoretical difficulties which resulted from the
underlying dualism of Platonic thought and which were
apparent not only to the critics of Platonism but also
many Platonists as well. One set of problems had to do
with the realm of being. How many realities are "in" this
realm, and how are they related to each other? Are the
Demi-urg, the World-soul, and the eternal forms or ideas
the only realities here? Are the eternal forms the
thoughts of the Demi-urg, or do they exist independently
of the Demi-urg? Christian Platonists had additional
difficulties. They asked, for example, how the Logos
fitted into the picture and how the idea of the Good was
related to God.
    Another set of problems had to do with the relation of
the realm of being to the realm of becoming. Did material

things emanate out of being? Were material things created
by a divine being? Is the realm of becoming eternal, or
did it come to be in time? Does matter really exist? Is
it the source of evil, and if so, how could it have come
from being, which is good? The complexities of the
relation between being and becoming were glaringly clear
in regard to the concept of the soul. The Platonists
wanted to affirm the goodness of the soul, since the soul
was an intellectual substance naturally related to being,
and, at the same time, to explain the fact that the soul
is now living in a body, a state of existence which must
be somehow foreign or accidental. This dilemma was one
the Platonists did not fully solve. Using Plotinus as an
example, Norris explains that the Platonists were
"committed to the idea that the reasonable soul cannot
willingly or knowingly sin." If it did so, it would be
"false to its own nature." On the other hand, "if the
soul's descent is not voluntary, then the evils consequent
upon embodiment stand as a cosmic injustice." For these
quotes, see Norris, Manhood and Christ, p. 49. For a
readable discussion of the way Platonists attempted to
solve this paradox in their discussions of the nature of
the soul, the soul's parts, the concept of freedom, and
the union of body and soul, see Manhood and Christ, pp.
10-78.

[47] Norris, God and the World, p. 133. See also p.
137. For similar comments about Clement, see Casey, pp.
56, 60-61, 67, 68, 72, 76, 92-96. For example, Casey
states, p. 76, that for Clement "the final goal" of the
Christian's life is the contemplative, mystical knowledge
of God "in which comprehension is so perfect that the
distinction between subject and object becomes unreal."
Clement's acceptance of Plato's emphasis upon the
intellectual unity of the soul with reality, states Casey,
p. 96, makes Clement "the founder of Christian Platonism
and the father of Christian intellectual mysticism."

[48] Norris, God and the World, pp. 141-43, notes that
Origen thought that Plato's distinction between being and
becoming was found also in the Bible, for example in Paul.
In II Corinthians 4:18, Paul distinguishes the temporal
things that are seen from the eternal things that are
invisible. Origen applies this distinction not just to
cosmology but to practical living. The Christian must

live his life seeking eternal things, not temporal things.
For Clement on this topic, see Casey pp. 78, 88, 92-93.
On the last of the cited pages, Casey states that Clement
believed that the soul must be engaged in a persistent
effort "to abandon the sensible world for the world of
intellectual reality."

[49] Norris, God and the World, pp. 146-49. See also
Quasten, pp. 91-92.

[50] Norris, God and the World, pp. 149-52. Norris
admits that there is some controversy among Origen
interpreters regarding Origen's doctrine of the creation
of souls. Origen does say that human souls are created,
but he does not say that these souls are created in time.
He seems to mean that the souls are dependent upon God,
although they are eternal. Norris, p. 151, states that
Origen argues that the rational souls "must in some form
have existed eternally." Quasten, p. 42, states that
Origen's notion of the preexistence of human souls is one
of his most serious dogmatic errors.

[51] Quasten, pp. 65, 87; Casey, p. 100.

[52] Casey states that Clement's doctrine of God is
influenced by Platonic concepts. For Clement, according
to Casey, God is radically transcendent, beyond even the
Logos and the realm of human, immaterial spirits (p. 74);
God is reality (p. 58); God is goodness itself (p. 69);
God is the absolute, simple unity that we reach by
abstraction (pp. 87-88). Casey adds that the biblical
elements in Clement's doctrine of God seem inconsistent
with the Platonic elements, for the biblical "expressions
of God's personality" and also the Bible's "lively
anthropomorphism are strangely unsuited to express
Clement's conception of the divine nature" (p. 57). For a
similar view of Clement's concept of God, see Bigg, pp.
62-66. Bigg states that Clement apparently failed to see
the logical implications of his very abstract concept of
God. For Origen's emphasis upon God's radical
transcendence above becoming and also above being, see
Reinhold Seeberg, Textbook of the History of Doctrines,
trans. Charles E. Hay, 2 vols. (Grand Rapids: Baker,
1964), 1:148. For another discussion which emphasizes
similar points, see Joseph C. McLelland, God the Anon-
ymous: A Study in Alexandrian Philosophical Theology
(Cambridge: Philadelphia Patristic Foundation, 1976), pp.
11, 16, 20.

[53] Seeberg, 1:150. In regard to Clement, Casey, pp. 74-75, argues that God is in some sense beyond or above the Logos.
[54] Seeberg, 1:143.
[55] David L. Mueller, <u>Karl Barth</u> (Waco, Texas: Word, 1972), p. 153. See also Balthasar, pp. 179-81, 186, 210. See also Frei's discussion in <u>Faith and Ethics</u>, p. 40.
[56] An example of Barth's efforts to avoid subjecting his theology to any philosophical or even theological principle can be found in Barth's discussion of G.C. Berkouwer's study <u>The Triumph of Grace in the Theology of Karl Barth</u>, trans.   Harry R.   Boer (Grand Rapids: Eerdmans, 1956). Barth suggests that the triumph is the triumph of God's act in Christ, not the triumph of some principle, even if that principle is labeled grace.   CD 4/3, pp. 173-76 (KD, pp. 198-202).
[57] Natural theology is unnecessary, according to Barth, since it presupposes that God and nature are separate from each other. Since nature is not separated from God but included within God's act, engaging in natural theology involves speculating about what might have been if God had not acted in Christ.   Such speculations are not only beyond our knowledge and therefore fruitless, but they also tend to blind us to the happy fact that God has acted to reconcile and redeem us. See Balthasar, pp. 127-42. For example, Balthasar, p. 128, states that "any reflection on man apart from his grounding in the Word is purely abstract in Barth's view."
For additional support of the claim that God is not spatially removed from the realm of creation, see Barth's discussion of God's omnipresence in CD 2/1, pp. 461-90 (KD, pp. 518-51). For example, Barth states that God "stands in a very direct and very intimate relationship" to the universe; "He is present to it, yet He is not identical with it." For those words, see p. 462 (KD, p. 520).   See also Barth's discussion of "The Divine Accompanying," CD 3/3, pp. 90-154 (KD, pp. 102-75). For example, p. 92 (KD, p. 104), Barth states that "the activity of the creature . . . is therefore accompanied and surrounded by God's own activity."
[58] There are some similarities between Barth's views on this topic and the philosophy known as panentheism. In both cases, it can be argued, God's act "surrounds" and

"encloses" creation. However, Barth rejects panentheism as a system, and one of his major criticisms of it is that the defender of panentheism obscures God's freedom and transcendence by conceptualizing the relation between God and the world as a constant, continuous relation, as though God and the world constitute one whole, one unified structure. For Barth, panentheism seems to make God dependent on the world, rather than vice versa, as Barth emphasizes. See CD 2/1, pp. 312, 313-18, 562, (KD, pp. 351, 352-58, 633). For a discussion of Barth and Charles Hartshorne which is sympathetic to Barth, see Colin E. Gunton, Becoming and Being: The Doctrine of God in Charles Hartshorne and Karl Barth (Oxford: Oxford University, 1978). For a discussion of Barth and panentheism see especially pp. 198, 206.

[59] CD 1/1, pp. 272-74 (KD, pp. 251-53). In these pages, Barth refers to Brunner's discussion of the concept of the image of God in God and Man: Four Essays on the Nature of Personality, trans. with an Introduction by David Cairns (London: SCM, 1936), pp. 114-19. Although Brunner does not use the phrase "point of contact" on the pages Barth cites, he does state that the imago dei "is not destroyed" by sin and that its continued existence means that humans can hear the Word of God and answer it. For clear affirmations of this point, see both pp. 114-19 and also p. 155. In other works, Brunner does use the phrase "point of contact" to refer to a created human ability to understand God's Word. For example, see Man in Revolt: A Christian Anthropology, trans. Olive Wyon (Philadelphia: Westminster, 1947), p. 539. Here Brunner states that in spite of sin, humans remain responsible, free beings. There is a "structure of being of man" which is always presupposed by God's speaking to him. "This personal structure as actual being is that which is always proper to man, and this, in the general sense, is the 'point of contact.'" For more information, see Man in Revolt, pp. 536-41. Brunner gives these pages the sub-title "The Point of Contact."

[60] Barth's metaphor of the tangent touching the circle provides a basis for broadening the meaning of the phrase "point of contact," since it suggests a point where God and the world meet. See Barth's famous work The Epistle to the Romans, trans. E. C. Hoskyns (London:

Oxford University, 1933), p. 30. This metaphor occurs in Barth's discussion of Romans 1:4.

[61] CD 1/1, p. 273 (KD, p. 251). "The reconciliation of man with God in Christ includes in itself or else begins with the f r e s h establishment of the l o s t 'point of contact.' This point of contact is, therefore, not real outside faith but only in faith. In faith a man is created b y the Word of God f o r the Word of God, existing i n the Word of God, not in himself, not in virtue of his humanity and personality, nor from the standpoint of creation, for what is possible from the standpoint of creation from man to God has actually been lost through the Fall."

[62] For a statement that the world is reconciled with God, see CD 4/2, p. 132 (KD, p. 148). "The humiliation of God and the exaltation of man as they took place in Him are the completed fulfillment of the covenant, the completed reconciliation of the world with God."

[63] For Barth's doctrines of justification and sanctification see CD 4/1, pp. 514-642 (KD, pp. 573-718) and 4/2, pp. 499-613 (KD, pp. 565-694). Mueller, p. 136, states that Barth's treatment of justification and sanctification avoids "illegitimate individualism and subjectivism." Additional defense of this interpretation of Barth is provided by Barth's affirmation of the resurrection of the body and the resurrection of the flesh. For example, see Barth's discussion of hope in CD 4/3, pp. 924-26 (KD, pp. 1061-63).

[64] CD 2/1, pp. 270-72 (KD, pp. 303-5). See also our earlier discussion in the section entitled "Jesus Christ as the Person God" in the third chapter pp. 101-4.

[65] See our earlier discussion in the section entitled "The Essential Divinity of Jesus Christ" in the third chapter, pp. 88-101.

[66] CD 1/1, pp. 460-65 (KD, pp. 422-26). CD 1/2, p. 158 (KD, p. 173).

[67] An investigation to determine whether Barth's development of the doctrinal implications of an Alexandrian christology throughout his entire Church Dogmatics provides the only viable "thinking out" of an Alexandrian foundation, or whether there might be other, non-Barthian theologies consistently developed from an Alexandrian christology would be an important study, but one too involved for us to begin here.

[68] For an analysis of the debate between Harnack and Barth which is sympathetic to Barth, see H. Martin Rumscheidt's Revelation and Theology, which was cited earlier. For Harnack's criticisms of Barth, see especially pp. 29-31, 35-39, 52-59, 64-69. For Barth's responses, see especially pp. 31-35, 40-52, 59-64. Other sympathetic appraisals of Barth's hermeneutics are offered by James Wharton, "Karl Barth as Exegete and His Influence on Biblical Interpretation, "Union Seminary Quarterly Review 28 (November, 1972): 5-13, and James D. Smart, The Divided Mind of Modern Theology (Philadelphia: Westminster, 1967). Smart is basically supportive of Barth's hermeneutics, but he offers a subtle criticism. He states, on p. 172, "Barth has always recognized the necessity and importance of historical interpretation as well as theological, but he has insisted that it is only preparatory to the theological and can neither help nor hinder the theological. He seems never to have recognized that the facing of the historical questions is theologically necessary and has important theological consequences." A less sympathetic criticism is offered by John Cobb in the previously mentioned work Living Options in Protestant Theology, pp. 192-97. For example, Cobb argues that Barth is not being faithful to scripture but is imposing his own views on scripture when he maintains that scripture is the exclusive witness to revelation. See especially p. 196.

[69] See Rumscheidt, pp. 36, 39, 52, and 64. See also Pauck, p. 54.

[70] Rumscheidt, pp. 121, 124, 125-26, and Mueller, p. 145.

[71] That Barth did not intentionally impose his Platonic presuppositions or any other kind of presuppositions upon the Bible seems clear from his argument with Bultmann over hermeneutics. In his essay "Rudolph Bultmann: An Attempt to Understand Him," Barth affirms that one should be continually open to the scriptural text, that one should let the text speak, and that one should allow the text to challenge one's presuppositions. In Barth's view, Bultmann's method leads one to impose his or her own presuppositions upon the text. For Barth's essay on Bultmann, see Hans Werner Bartsch, ed., Kerygma and Myth: A Theological Debate,

trans.   Reginald   Fuller,   2   vols.   (London: SPCK,
1953-62), 2:83-132.

[72] CD 1/2, pp. 183-84 (KD, pp. 200-201).   These pages
contain Barth's account of the debate with Brunner on this
topic.

[73] Brunner makes this point in his work The Mediator,
pp. 324-26.

[74] Our point here should not be taken to imply that
Barth ignores the historical elements in the Bible, for
those   elements   are   crucial   for   his   theology.
Christological claims, for example, are also historical
claims; they affirm that God became man at a particular
place and time in history.

[75] Cobb, p. 193, states that Barth's "interpretations
of many passages differ markedly from those which are
generally taken as standard."

[76] See above, p. 177.

Note on Bibliographical Data

Bibliographical information for each work consulted in this book is available in the section of notes following the text. Ready access to that information is provided by the Index of Names, where the numbers of the pages which contain bibliographical data are underlined. One may obtain bibliographical data for a particular book or article by locating the author's name in the Index of Names and turning to the underlined page(s). For example, bibliographical information concerning the work of Han Urs von Balthasar can be found on page 201.

Index of Names

The pages with underlined numbers contain bibliographical information. For an explanation, see the Note on Bibliographical Data, page 259.

Index of Topics

WILFRIED HÄRLE

Sein und Gnade

Die Ontologie in Karl Barths kirchlicher Dogmatik

Oktav. X, 428 Seiten. 1975. Ganzleinen DM 114,−
ISBN 3 11 005706 9 (Theologische Bibliothek Töpelmann, Band 27)

HERBERT NEIE

The Doctrine of the Atonement
in the Theology of Wolfhart Pannenberg

Octavo. X, 237 pages. 1978. Cloth DM 76,−
ISBN 3 11 007506 7 (Theologische Bibliothek Töpelmann, Volume 36)

JOHN P. CLAYTON

The Concept of Correlation

Paul Tillich and the Possibility
of a mediating Theology

Octavo. XII, 329 pages. 1980. Cloth DM 84,−
ISBN 3 11 007914 3 (Theologische Bibliothek Töpelmann, Volume 37)

MICHAEL PALMER

Paul Tillich's Philosophy of Art

Octavo. XXII, 217 Seiten. 1983. Cloth DM 84,−
ISBN 3 11 009681 1 (Theologische Bibliothek Töpelmann, Volume 41)

Prices are Subject to change

Walter de Gruyter · W DE G · Berlin · New York